Collins Illustrated Guide to

MALAYSIA

Wendy Moore
Photography by R. Ian Lloyd

COLLINS
8 Grafton Street, London W1
1989

William Collins Sons & Co. Ltd
London • Glasgow • Sydney • Auckland
Toronto • Johannesburg

British Library Cataloguing in Publication Data
Collins Illustrated Guide to Malaysia
1. Malaysia — Visitors' guides
I. Series
915.95'0453

ISBN 0-00-215221-5
First Published in Great Britain 1989

Editors: Sallie Coolidge, Ralph Kiggell and Robyn Flemming
Picture Editor: Carolyn Watts

Map artwork: Bai Yiliang
Design: Unity Design Studio

Printed in Hong Kong

Contents

(following page) The mosque at Kuching, Sarawak

Special Topics

Maps

Introduction

Malaysia, long known to the ancient mariners as 'The Land Where the Winds Meet', has lured travellers since the dawn of time. Seafaring Malays settled the seaboard and traded with the early Indian, Arab and Chinese traders who sailed to her shores with the monsoon winds in search of gold, spices and jungle exotica. In the twilight world of the great rain forests, nomadic tribes hunted with the blowpipe and collected heads as trophies. Legendary kingdoms arose, and Malacca — the most powerful — was lauded as 'the greatest emporium the world has seen'. Lured by their lust for spices, the Portuguese were the first to conquer this ancient land, followed by the Dutch, and then the English. After four centuries of rule under a foreign yoke, the nation achieved Independence in 1957.

Malaysia today is a land of astonishing variety, for each historical era has left its imprint. With its pot-pourri of Malays, Chinese, Indians and countless native tribes, the country is an anthropologist's delight. Its landscape is as varied as the population, a kaleidoscope of ever-changing images. From the deep-green of a Sarawak jungle to the lime-green of a Kedah rice field; from sleepy East Coast fishing villages where time appears to have stood still, to ultra-modern Kuala Lumpur, the hub of the nation; and from the peace of an idyllic deserted island to the bustle of a crowded smoke-filled temple in old Malacca — Malaysia has it all.

Until comparatively recently, the country was little known to the outside world and virtually untouched by tourism. Patrick Balfour, a traveller to Malaysia — then Malaya — during the 1930s, wrote of his love of the land and its people in his book *Grand Tour*. 'My feelings warmed to the attractive people around me . . . . They were human and carefree, gay and good looking, untroubled in this luscious, lethargic country . . . . The freshness of the landscape was a joy . . . . Marsh and jungle, rice-fields, rubber trees, undulating forest and distant hills were an endless panorama of delicious green with the plumes of the palm trees dipped in silver.'

If Patrick Balfour were to make his 'Grand Tour' today, he would find that his empty Penang beaches now lie in the shadow of high-rise luxury hotels, expressways carve through the jungled interior, the rest houses no longer have thatched roofs, and, unfortunately, the common traveller isn't such a novelty as in the 1930s when Balfour was invited to breakfast by the Sultan of Kelantan. But in the fishing villages of the East Coast, along the narrow lanes of Malacca's Chinatown, in the traditional Malay villages, and deep in the primeval jungle, Balfour would still feel quite at home.

History

Early Origins Malaysia's history, like the dense jungle that still covers much of the country, remains shrouded in mystery. However, man is known to have been around these parts practically since the dawn of time. Stone-age implements discovered recently in Perak in peninsular Malaysia are evidence that early man roamed this region 35,000 years ago. Before this discovery, the earliest human evidence was from Sarawak's Niah Caves, prompting scholars to surmise that prehistoric man came to peninsular Malaysia some time later. While this new evidence changes this view of history, scholars seem to agree that the earliest Negritos and, later, the descendants of the Malays, came from somewhere near Taiwan and gradually filtered down through maritime Southeast Asia.

For the *orang asli*, literally 'original people', the jungle was a sea of resources, but the mountainous terrain and the dense rain forest made communication difficult. When development came it was from the sea, which forms three-quarters of Malaysia's borders.

Malay Emergence The seafaring ancestors of the Malays settled the coastal plains and ventured upriver. These skilful sailors and navigators, unbeknown to most, were the world's earliest and furthest sea rovers and their settlements spanned two-thirds of the globe, from Madagascar to Easter Island. Throughout this huge waterbound region, the local words for 'sail', 'outrigger' and 'steering oar' are almost identical — linguistic proof of the reach of these early seafarers.

Located at the crossroads of two major sea routes, Malaysia was in a strategic position for trade, being also linked to the great markets of India and China by the annual monsoon winds.

Early Hindu Kingdoms Blown across the seas on the southwest monsoon, the first Indians arrived at Kedah in the north in around the first century BC in search of the famed Suvarnadvipa, or 'Land of Gold', immortalized in their ancient literature. They bartered their cottons, ironware, beads and musical instruments for the gold, aromatic woods and other jungle exotica of the Malays. The Malay courts embraced Hinduism and Buddhism, and remnants of this era still linger today in the *bersanding* ceremony of the Malay wedding and in the investiture of Malay kings. By the third century AD, Chinese merchants' reports told of legendary kingdoms where wealthy courtly societies were led by an elite of Hindu brahmins. The legendary Langkasuka, founded in the second century AD and famed for its camphor wood, was situated somewhere in the far northeast. According to a Chinese history of AD 502, it took 30 days to cross this great Malay state from east to west. Within the walled capital, the king and his nobles wore gold girdles and travelled atop elephants, seated under white howdahs and escorted by a huge entourage. Unlike Kampuchea's Angkor and Java's Borobodur, little tangible

evidence remains of this ancient kingdom, but Chinese, Arabic and Indian literature abounds with references to such mysterious realms, whose locations are still hotly disputed by scholars. Srivijaya, the first great maritime kingdom of the Malay world, which then included today's Malaysia, Indonesia, the Philippines and southern Thailand, was the first of the Malacca Straits kingdoms. When Srivijaya declined, the seat of power moved to Melayu, on the Jambi River in Sumatra, and in 1000 an Arab text referred to the Malacca Straits as 'the sea of Melayu', the first reference to the roots of Malaysia's name and the origins of the rulers of the Malacca — the greatest Malay kingdom of all.

Malacca According to the *Sejarah Melayu*, the Malaccan court history of the 15th and 16th centuries, the genealogy of Parameswara, the founder of Malacca, can be traced back to Alexander the Great — known to the Malays as Iskandar Zulkarnain — whose descendants miraculously appeared on a sacred hill overlooking Palembang in Sumatra. Melayu had been conquered by the Javanese, and Parameswara fled north before eventually arriving at Malacca. Under a rule of such impeccable pedigree, Malacca's rise to fame was swift. The Sumatran prince's loyal navy of *orang laut*, the 'sea people', controlled the Malacca Straits, ensuring pirate-free waters, a must for a successful entrepôt. Shortly after the port's founding, China's Ming emperor sent an envoy and proclaimed Parameswara as king, giving Malacca added prestige.

The Coming of Islam Influential Indian Muslim traders first brought Islam to Malacca; when the rulers converted to this new faith, Malacca was thrust into international prominence. At this time, Egypt controlled the Spice Route to Renaissance Europe and allowed only Muslim shipping. From Malacca, Islam spread to other parts of the Malay peninsula and throughout the Indonesian archipelago. During the 15th century, Malacca's reputation surpassed that of all the other kingdoms of the Malay world and her territories increased with each successive sultan. To be called Melayu (Malay) in those days was to be closely associated with the ruler and his descendants; even today most of the Malay states of the peninsula can trace their genesis back to the Malaccan Sultanate.

Enter the Europeans Meanwhile in Europe, merchants looked greedily to the East and its coveted spice trade, which was centred around Malacca and under Muslim control. When Vasco da Gama rounded the Cape of Good Hope, the Portuguese hoped to divert the trade to this new route and away from Islamic dominance. Malacca's death knell sounded in 1511 when, after a month's siege, the city fell to the Portuguese. The Malay kingdom of Malacca, which had dominated both sides of the Straits of Malacca for a hundred years, marked the classical age of Malay culture. With the arrival of the Portuguese the era of colonial intervention began, ending only when Malaysia attained Independence in 1957.

In true crusading spirit the Portuguese cared only for their subjects' souls if they converted to Catholicism. They declared that anyone was free to enter Malacca provided that they defected to the faith; those who refused were shipped off as slaves to Goa and Macau. As a result, the wealthy Muslim Indian and Arab traders overlooked Malacca in favour of Islamic Sumatra and the port never again attained the prominence it enjoyed under Malay rule. From Johor, in the south, the ousted sultanate continued to harass the Portuguese, but they were also having troubles with their local rivals, the Bugis, Achinese and Minangkabau. When the Dutch made their first overtures, Johor welcomed them as possible allies against both Portugal and their local enemies. The Portuguese were by this time in trouble: their tiny homeland did not have the manpower or treasury to ensure the survival of its far-flung empire. Malacca had become so corrupt that it was named 'The Babylon of the East'. It took the Dutch, together with the Johoreans, six months to wrest Malacca from the Portuguese, but the Malays soon discovered that they had merely exchanged one master for another. They were no closer to reclaiming their old kingdom and, as a result, the present-day states of the peninsula gradually emerged as sovereign units in their own right.

Up in the north, the Thais were demanding tribute from the northern states of Kelantan, Kedah, Terengganu and even Pahang. One enormous disadvantage of Thai overlordship was the annual summons to court, when the Malay ruler was to prostrate himself before the king. Most sultans feigned illness so as to avoid the humiliation. Kedah's Sultan Muhammad actively encouraged independence from the Thais and denied the Dutch commerce, but Perak's Sultan Iskandar formed an alliance with the Dutch, who had a monopoly over the tin trade; in so doing, he brought unprecedented peace to his kingdom in the era known as Perak's 'Golden Age'.

British Intervention English adventurers had gradually been filtering into the trade picture. Having gained control of the Indian cloth-producing and opium-growing areas and squeezed out the Indian traders, they were now looking for a port to protect their valuable tea trade with China. In 1786 Francis Light, an English adventurer and trader with the backing of the East India Company, persuaded the Sultan of Kedah to allow him to establish a settlement on Pulau Pinang (Penang). The English were meant to provide the sultan with armed protection against the Thais, but the support never materialized. Disenchantment soon set in as the various Malay rulers, who had initially thought that the British might aid them against their respective enemies, realized that their wishes were fruitless. In 1819 when Raffles planted the British flag on the island of Singapore, thereby establishing two British ports in the region, there was no need for English traders and Chinese junks to frequent the other Malay ports which thereafter fell into decline.

Another devastating blow struck the Malay world in 1824 when the Anglo-Dutch Treaty partitioned Dutch Indonesia from English Malaya, severing the cultural unity that had existed since time immemorial. Traditionally part of the Kingdom of Johor, the Riau archipelago fell to the Dutch, and access to East Coast Sumatra — the legendary homeland of the Malaccan sultans and birthplace of the Malay language — was denied to the Malays living in the British-controlled peninsula. Two years later Singapore, Malacca and Penang were officially brought under the banner of the Straits Settlements and British influence and power spread over the Malay peninsula. The process of political integration of the Malay states had begun. Munshi Abdullah, Raffles' Malay scribe, wrote of the transformation: 'I am astonished to see how markedly the world is changing. A new world is created, the old world is destroyed. The very jungle becomes a settled district and elsewhere a settlement reverts to jungle . . . . '

Borneo was also reverberating to change. It was not included in the Anglo-Dutch Treaty and was thus easy pickings for exploiters and adventurers. James Brooke, an Englishman looking for adventure, sailed into Borneo at the height of a rebellion. As a reward for helping the Raja of Brunei to suppress the uprising, he attained land grants in today's Sarawak and established a dynasty of 'white rajas' which ruled Sarawak for over a hundred years.

North Borneo, now Sabah, was run by the British North Borneo Company who met with recurring resistance. The Mat Salleh Rebellion of 1895–1905 broke out partly as a result of a controversial rice tax which the colonials had imposed in an attempt to boost the state coffers which had dwindled under successive poor management.

Meanwhile on the peninsula, the English were pushing into the interior in their quest for tin, and Chinese immigrants poured into the country lured by the promise of riches and to escape from the grinding poverty of their homeland. Canned food had caught on in America and tin plate was in demand in England, but Selangor and Perak, the great tin states, were plagued by unrest as Chinese miners from rival secret societies continually warred with one another. Eager to end these problems and to ensure a steady flow of tin ore, the English persuaded the Malay chiefs to accept British Residents, who would keep the peace but not interfere with Malay law and religion. Perak's Resident, J.W.W. Birch, favoured a heavy-handed approach, and his habit of giving the Malay chiefs 'a good dressing down' in public did little to further the English cause. In 1875, when Birch was posting notices of a controversial new enactment whereby the British had control of judicial matters, he was murdered. This exposure of the fiction of Malay rule by British advice was the final insult, and as an outburst against British authority it was the first stirrings of an incipient nationalism.

The tide was beginning to turn and rumblings of discontent became louder when, after the creation of the Federated Malay States in 1896, the sultan's power diminished further and Malays began to feel like strangers in their own

land. Another slap in the face occurred when, virtually unbeknown to the northern states, England conceded a treaty with Siam which put Kedah, Kelantan and Terengganu under British rule. The indignant Sultan of Kedah announced that his country had been 'bought and sold like a buffalo', and Terengganu's Sultan Zainal Abidin accused the Siamese of bargaining with stolen property. Although Johor's late Sultan Abu Bakar had wisely introduced a constitution prohibiting his state's alignment with European powers, his son Ibrahim, at ease in English society, was soon convinced of the British right to rule and by 1919 the Union Jack fluttered from every flag-pole on the Malay peninsula, in Singapore, and even in far off Sarawak, Brunei and Sabah. Conquest was complete. As in India, the British pursued their 'divide and rule' policy and the racial gaps widened.

Japanese Occupation The situation changed overnight in 1941 when the Japanese invaded Malaya and Borneo, culminating in the humiliating British surrender of Singapore and the shattering of Western colonial supremacy. The Japanese tried to win over the population with their slogan 'Asia for Asians', but were feared for their brutality. The picture changed once again when the war ended and the British returned. It was a tenuous world they inherited.

The Road to Independence The troubles began immediately when the British attempted to form the Malayan Union, a plan which transferred the sultan's sovereignty to the British Crown and which would give all citizens, regardless of race, equal rights. The British were astonished when the normally apathetic Malays objected strongly and formed UMNO, the United Malays National Organization, in opposition. Forced to rethink the situation, the British tossed out the Malayan Union and in 1948 came up with the Federation of Malaya, which gave the sultans power over their states and conserved special privileges for the Malays. A victory for the Malays, the Federation was seen by some Chinese as a British betrayal and they put their hopes for a just society in the Malayan Communist Party. During the Occupation, guerilla groups of British officers, Chinese and Malays had lived in the jungle where they organized resistance in an attempt to harass the Japanese. Chinese communist guerillas, known as the MPAJA (Malayan People's Anti-Japanese Army), had sought a Malaysian republic and after the war the communists infiltrated trade unions and organized strikes to disrupt the economy. The infamous Chin Peng reorganized the party, moved its operations underground, and led the workers on the road to violent action. After a spate of murders directed against European planters and miners, the government proclaimed a State of Emergency in 1948. Sir Henry Gurney, the British High Commissioner, was shot and his predecessor, General Gerald Templer, was flown in. Templer directed the relocation of Chinese squatters from the 'hot' communist areas and resettled them in 'new villages', where they were constantly under surveillance and subjected to curfews and food restrictions. The sympathizers found it difficult to maintain contact with the insurgents, who were forced deeper and deeper into the jungle. Finally, when the Malayan Chinese Association (MCA) formed an alliance with the Malay UMNO, communist hopes for control quickly faded. In 1948 the British had committed themselves to preparing the way for Independence; now that the problem of political co-operation between the main ethnic groups had been overcome the machinery was set in motion. In 1955, at Malaya's first national election, the Alliance won 80 percent of the vote.

Post-Independence In 1957 the British relinquished their sovereignty and Independence was granted. Independence ushered in a new era of vitality, challenge and excitement about the future. The Malayan Constitution gave certain powers and rights to the states under the traditional sultans, but the central federal government held supreme power. In 1961, Tunku Abdul Rahman, the first Prime Minister, proposed the idea of Malaysia — to include Malaya, Singapore, North Borneo, Sarawak and Brunei. Only Brunei declined, for the sultan was not about to share his substantial oil revenues. When the Federation of Malaysia was announced in 1963, the Philippines and Indonesia immediately severed diplomatic relations, alleging that some of the territories were theirs. Indonesia launched *konfrantasi* (confrontation); fishing boats were sunk off Sarawak and planes droned over Sabah, but when Sukarno was ousted in 1966 the government made peace with Malaysia, and the Philippines also dropped active pursuit of its claims over Sabah. In 1965 Singapore dropped out of the Federation to become a separate nation.

In general elections held since Independence, the Alliance (now known as the Barisan National) has easily retained its majority in Parliament. However, in 1969, the coalition lost its overall two-thirds majority. Communal tensions broke out, resulting in the establishment of an emergency government, but parliamentary rule was restored in 1971. Since then, the broad aim of the administration has been the fulfilment of the New Economic Policy, which is designed to eradicate poverty and to eliminate the identification of occupation with race, a legacy of the British 'divide and rule' policy. Economic prosperity achieved in the 1970s enabled the governments of Tun Abdul Razak and his successor, Tun Hussein Onn, to make considerable progress towards these ends. In 1967 Malaysia helped to found ASEAN and in 1974 it recognized communist China. In 1974 the nation identified itself with the non-aligned countries of the Third World.

The 1980s have brought new political directions and economic challenges. The administration of Dato' Seri Dr Mahathir Mohamad (1981) saw the search for new sources of support and development (the Look East Policy) and the initiation of a bold policy of heavy industrialization (the national car, a steel industry and oil refineries).

Malaysian businesses now compete on the world market, steel and glass office towers loom over the city, and new expressways carve the mountainous interior that only five years ago was virgin jungle. Malaysia is now rapidly throwing off the cloak of a Third World nation and is firmly on the path to national prosperity.

Geography — A Verdant Land

'Trees, nothing but trees. A monotonous country. One enters it . . . . and finds the enchanted forest' (Henri Fauconnier, *The Soul of Malaya*). Even though Fauconnier wrote in the 1920s, and despite large-scale logging and clearing for plantations, much of Malaysia — at least 70 percent — is still forested. The Federation of Malaysia, comprising peninsular Malaysia and Sabah, and Sarawak in Borneo, lies between latitudes 1° and 7° north and covers a total land area of around 330,433 square kilometres (127,580 square miles). During the last Ice Age, when the waters of the world contracted, peninsular Malaysia and Borneo were joined in a vast expanse of tropical rain forest known as Sundaland. Across the land bridge trooped a great multitude of birds and beasts, but when the ice melted, Borneo returned to its former isolation, separated from the peninsula by 530 kilometres (330 miles) of the South China Sea.

From the border of Thailand, in the north of peninsular Malaysia, a mountainous spine runs south through much of the country. Because of this mountainous, heavily-jungled interior, the east coast was until comparatively recently cut off from the west and the only means of access was by sea or river travel. Until as recently as 100 years ago, rivers were the main arteries for trade and travel. Their historical importance is indicated by the fact that nearly all the states of the peninsula take their name from the principal river in each. The longest of these rivers is the Sungai Pahang, which flows for 475 kilometres (295 miles).

In the East Malaysian states of Sabah and Sarawak are both longer rivers and higher mountains than on the peninsula. Both Sarawak's Rejang River and Sabah's Kinabatangan flow for 563 kilometres (350 miles). Much of the interior of East Malaysia is mountainous, and crowning the Crocker Range of Sabah is Mount Kinabalu which, at 4,101 metres (13,454 feet), is the highest mountain in Malaysia and the loftiest peak between New Guinea and the Himalayas.

Unless travellers cross the country from east to west, they may be unaware of the extent of Malaysia's forests, for much of the coastal plains and rolling hills of the west coast are covered with the rubber trees and oil-palms of the great estates. Although Malaysia is today the world's largest producer of rubber, 100 years ago there was scarcely a tree to be seen. H.N. Ridley, later nicknamed 'Rubber Ridley', the Director of Singapore's Botanical Gardens, had been experimenting with Amazonian rubber seeds and persuaded some planters to try them out. His zeal paid off, rubber caught on, and 20 years

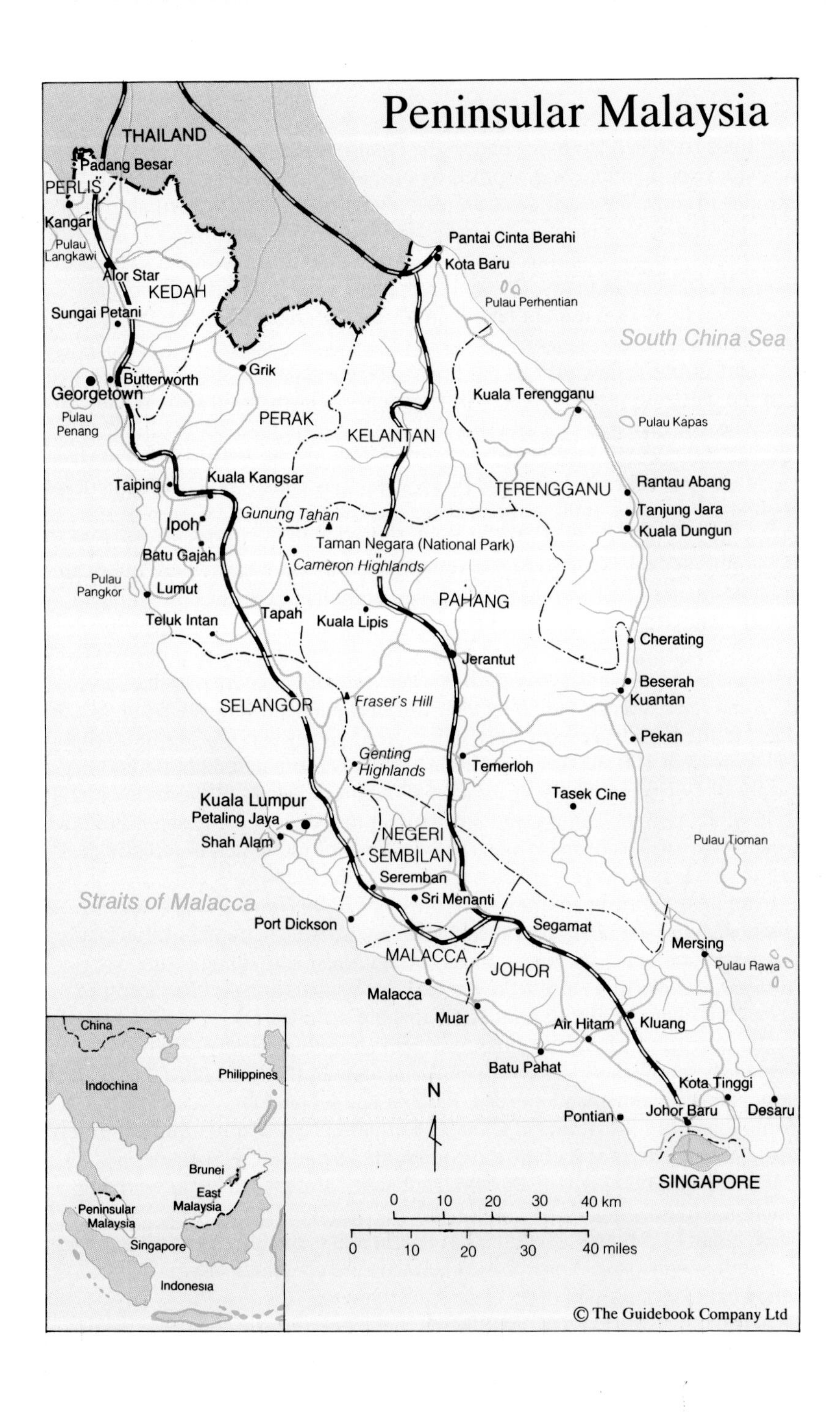
Peninsular Malaysia
THAILAND
Padang Besar
PERLIS
Kangar
Pulau Langkawi
Alor Star
KEDAH
Sungai Petani
Butterworth
Georgetown
Pulau Penang
Grik
PERAK
KELANTAN
Pantai Cinta Berahi
Kota Baru
Pulau Perhentian
South China Sea
Kuala Terengganu
Pulau Kapas
TERENGGANU
Rantau Abang
Tanjung Jara
Kuala Dungun
Taiping
Kuala Kangsar
Gunung Tahan
Ipoh
Taman Negara (National Park)
Batu Gajah
Cameron Highlands
Pulau Pangkor
Lumut
Tapah
Kuala Lipis
PAHANG
Teluk Intan
Cherating
Jerantut
Beserah
Kuantan
SELANGOR
Fraser's Hill
Pekan
Genting Highlands
Temerloh
Tasek Cine
Kuala Lumpur
Petaling Jaya
Shah Alam
NEGERI SEMBILAN
Pulau Tioman
Seremban
Straits of Malacca
Sri Menanti
Port Dickson
Segamat
Mersing
MALACCA
JOHOR
Pulau Rawa
Malacca
Muar
Air Hitam
Kluang
Batu Pahat
Kota Tinggi
Pontian
Johor Baru
Desaru
SINGAPORE
N
0 10 20 30 40 km
0 10 20 30 40 miles
China
Indochina
Philippines
Brunei
East Malaysia
Peninsular Malaysia
Singapore
Indonesia
© The Guidebook Company Ltd

later trees stretched from one end of the country to the other. In 1980, rubber, the chief export earner, was toppled by oil-palm, the new boom crop. Introduced from West Africa as an ornamental palm in 1875, oil-palm was only developed on a large scale in the 1960s. Although renowned as an agricultural nation, Malaysia is now shedding that image with the success of its new petroleum industry. When Terengganu's offshore oil fields began production in 1978 it did not take long for oil earnings to outstrip the agricultural sector.

Apart from the new oil and gas towns, the east coast is still less developed than the west and in many places time appears to have stood still. White sandy beaches fringed by casuarina trees and interspersed with fishing villages and coconut groves are the norm. Off shore are jewel-like islands encircled by coral reefs, crowned by mountainous peaks and covered in dense tropical rain forests. Behind the beaches are swamp forests of deep peat, where rattans and stemless plants abound. Where the swamps end the dry lowland forest begins. This is the triple-canopied rain forest where trees can reach 45 metres (150 feet) in height. Their smooth bare trunks only branch out 30 metres (100 feet) up, and their massive crowns cut out most of the light. The unlogged virgin forest is therefore relatively easy to move around in for there is little undergrowth. But where the jungle is open to the light, ferns and rattans make the going very difficult indeed. Malaysia's jungles, the oldest in the world, are extremely rich in tree species and it is not unusual to find more than 100 species on a single acre. It is estimated that of 8,000 species of flowering plants, at least 2,500 are trees. Many of these flowers occur high up in the canopy and are difficult to see from the ground. From a distance the crowns of many trees show a flush of red which is actually the tips of new leaves, as few species are actually deciduous.

Unique to Sarawak are the heath forests of Bako National Park, and on Sabah's Mount Kinabalu four distinctive regions are encountered: lowland rain forest, montane oak forest, mossy cloud forest and alpine scrub. The *Rafflesia*, the world's largest flower, and the *Nepenthes raja*, the largest of the pitcher plants, are both found on Kinabalu's slopes.

The jungles of Malaysia abound with an enormous variety of wildlife. King of the jungle and Malaysia's national animal, the Malayan Tiger is still fairly plentiful, but is seldom seen. Panther and leopard are occasionally encountered, but the beautiful Clouded Leopard is extremely timid and rarely seen. Other carnivores include the commonly encountered civets or *musang*, which lurk around *kampung* or cultivated areas, and the Malayan wild dog, which is seldom sighted. The largest of the omnivores is the Honey Bear, which attains 1.5 metres (five feet) in height and is distinguished by a black coat with a white star. Apparently when they are contented they purr somewhat like the sound of an electric refrigerator. Elephants, the largest of the herbivores, still roam in small herds in the deep jungle and occasionally venture into newly-cleared areas where they trample orchards and create havoc. Malaysia is home to the largest member of the wild ox family in the world, the *seladang*, which can weigh up to 1,500 kilograms (3,306 pounds). It is most vicious if injured or cornered. Other rare animals include the tapir and the rhinoceros, which is now in danger of extinction. Smaller jungle animals include the deer family, which range from the *rusa* (sambur deer) to miniature mouse-deer known as *pelanduk* and *kancil*. These tiny deer are the heroes of Malay folk tales which relate how the quick-witted mouse-deer outsmarts dim-witted elephants and tigers. The monkey family covers a huge range, from the *beruk* (pig-tailed monkey), which is trained to harvest coconuts, to the gibbons, which are heard booming through the jungle long before they are seen. Sabah and Sarawak are home to the orang-utan, which is elsewhere found only in zoos and is considered an endangered species.

Malaysian birds are so diverse that they would need a volume to do them justice. In the peninsula alone, 620 species have been recorded. Many are extraordinarily beautiful with their bright plumage flashing in the sun. Peafowls, argus pheasant, golden oriole, kingfishers and the exotic hornbill are just a few of the diverse species. *Merbuk* (a dove) and mynahs are coveted for their song, and special contests are conducted nationwide to judge the caged songbirds' ability.

From the fast-flowing jungle streams to the slow, meandering coastal rivers come an abundance of fish. Largest of all is the catfish, which can reach 1.8 metres (six feet) in length and weigh over 45 kilograms (100 pounds). Other famed varieties include the *kalesa, toman* and *kalui*, all of which can attain one metre (3.2 feet) in length. The archer fish is the most unusual for it shoots down its prey by spitting drops of water at it.

Malaysia has over 100 species of reptiles but only five are considered dangerous to man. The most threatening is the king cobra, which can grow to six metres (18 feet) and is known to threaten, whether provoked or not. Other dangerous snakes include coral snakes, kraits and vipers, but seldom do they attack humans. Pythons can reach astonishing lengths but are slow-moving and non-poisonous. Crocodiles are either the fish-eating garial, which is harmless, or the estuarine type which can grow to a large size and occasionally in remote Sarawak villages attacks man. *Biawak*, large monitor lizards, can often be seen lumbering along plantation roads, but the most familiar lizard is the household *cicak*, or gecko, which performs a most useful service by ridding even hotel rooms of flies and insects. The best-known of the turtles is the giant leatherback, which lays its eggs on the beaches of Terengganu from May to September.

Malaysia, like many other tropical countries, has its share of insects. Amongst the most beautiful are the butterflies, including the famed Raja Brooke's Birdwing, but even more numerous are the moths, the largest and best known being the Atlas Moth. In the rain forest the din of insect life must

be heard to be believed. Other less savoury creatures, such as the predatory leech, are something venturers into the jungle must come to terms with if they are to enjoy the diverse flora and fauna of the tropical rain forest.

People

With its highly diverse mix of peoples, Malaysia is often billed as a 'mini Asia'. Broadly speaking, the population falls into two main categories: those with cultural affinities indigenous to the region and to one another, who are classified as *bumiputra*; and those whose cultural affinities lie outside the region. Amongst Malaysia's 16.5 million people, *bumiputra* account for 59 percent. They comprise the aboriginal groups of *orang asli*, the Malays, and the Malay-related peoples which include the Bajau of Sabah, the Bugis, Minangkabau, Javanese and Boyanese. These peoples of Malay descent share a common culture and above all the bond of Islam. In Sarawak and Sabah, a diverse spectrum of the population also fall into the *bumiputra* category. These are the Iban, the Bidayuh, the Melanau, Kenyah, Kayan and others. In Sabah, the Kadazan (Dusun) form the largest single ethnic group, with the Murut, Kelabit and Kedayan forming significant minorities. These groups filtered into Borneo through centuries of immigration and though they follow the same shifting mode of agriculture they still maintain quite distinct identities. Some are Muslim, some Christian, and others keep to their traditional animist beliefs.

Amongst the non-*bumiputra*, the biggest group is the Chinese (32 percent), followed by the Indians (8.6 percent). There are also much smaller communities of Arabs, Eurasians, Europeans and Sinhalese. Although Chinese and Indian contacts with Malaysia go back to the dawn of history, there was no significant permanent settlement until the 19th century. The exception to this is the *baba*, or Straits Chinese community of Malacca, who can trace their ancestry back to the 16th century. Under British rule, massive immigrations of Chinese came to Malaysia to work the tin mines and the Indians came as coolie labour for the rubber plantations. The Chinese are largely from South China, with Hokkien and Cantonese forming the largest dialect groups. Amongst the Indians, the majority are Tamils from South India. Although Malaysia's population is scattered, the Chinese still favour the urban areas and the Malays still predominate in the villages of the countryside. On the east coast of the peninsula, which escaped much of the colonial immigrations, the population is still largely Malay.

Lifestyle

Malaysian lifestyles run the gamut of civilization. Deep in the mountainous back country of Sarawak the nomadic Penan still depend on the jungle for their livelihood. The Iban and other tribal peoples still carry on their traditional slash-and-burn shifting cultivation. Malay fishermen of the peninsula's East Coast still put to sea in boats, whose only change has been the switch from sail to outboard motor. Kedah's rice growers may have seed which produces a higher yield, but their lives still sway to the rhythms of planting and harvesting. Along the shaded avenues of the rubber and oil-palm plantations, motor bikes drone as tappers and cultivators arrive for work, but it is still a gentle sound compared to the big towns and cities where the sounds are more clamorous. As rush hour approaches, Kuala Lumpur's arteries are clogged with commuting traffic in the familiar pattern of nine-to-five life worldwide. But KL is the exception to the rule, for even in some of Malaysia's busiest towns there is a certain casualness and ease which pervades national life. Perhaps it is the everpresent jungle and the tropical heat and humidity that slow one down, but perhaps even more than this is the idea of an unhurried life that the Malays have so indelibly stamped on their land. Somehow even modern-day life has not changed the Malays' basic attitude to life, which is summed up in their everyday word *senang*, which means 'comfort, ease, peace of mind and freedom from worry'. *Senang* undoubtedly denotes the most desirable things in life. To be a proud father and loving husband is *senang*. To live close to the mosque is *senang*. To have an assured income is *senang*. And most of all, to live a happy life at home in the ancestral *kampung* is most *senang*.

While travelling through Malaysia, some of this easy-going feeling invariably rubs off on even the most hyperactive tourist, and the longer one stays the more seductive this *senang* tropical lifestyle becomes. The Malays, having lived for centuries in this equatorial country, have learnt the fine art of sparing oneself, which other races often do not learn until it is too late. 'So short the life, so long the art to learn.'

Islam and Other Beliefs

Possibly nowhere in the world is the calendar as full with religious holidays as in Malaysia, for this diverse population gives rise to a multi-devotional nation, and all of the world's major religions are represented here. Although Islam is the national religion, the Constitution provides freedom of religion for all. Traditions have crossed religious barriers. *Angpau*, the little cash-filled envelopes popularized by the Chinese for the New Year, have now found their way into Muslim Hari Raya celebrations. Four times a year — at Chinese New Year, Hari Raya, Christmas and the Indian festival of

Deepavali — Malaysians throw 'open house', a time when friends of other faiths can visit and enjoy the food and merrymaking.

Malaysia's relaxed attitude to religion is evident in the older towns where mosques and Chinese and Indian temples are located in the same street, almost next door to each other. But it is still apparent, wherever you are, that Islam is the national faith of the country. Five times a day, from just before dawn until after dark, from the tops of minarets or from the village *surau* (prayer house), the muezzin calls the faithful to prayer. For its followers, Islam is a way of life which if followed will lead to peace, for Islam means 'the way to achieve peace', and the *rukun*, or rules of the faith, encompass a man's lifetime. Muslims must obey the five principles of Islam (*Rukun Islam*): the Declaration of Faith — that there is no god except Allah and that Muhammad is the messenger of Allah; the performance of the five daily prayers; the payment of *zakat*, a charitable tax for the poor, once a year; to fast in the month of Ramadan; and, if possible, to make at least one pilgrimage to Mecca for the performance of Hajj.

From birth, when the declaration of faith is whispered in the baby's ear, through the early *Koran* studies, marriage and until death, Islam pervades all. What befalls one in life, whether good or bad, must be accepted as one's *takdir*, or destiny, and however hard the going gets one does not lose hope, for suicide is one of the greatest sins in Islam.

The Malays have incorporated a little of each religion embraced in the past, particularly in the more remote villages. In universal animist belief, every living thing contains a soul, or *semangat*. Certain jungle trees that loom above the *kampung* are never cut down for fear that someone will fall sick, and a stretch of young forest where a *pontianak*, the ghost of a woman who died in childbirth, still haunts is never visited after dark. Many Malaysians, regardless of race, still visit the *bomoh*, the traditional medicine man, and some highly revered ones are summoned to royal events to prevent rain from ruining some auspicious ceremony.

Gongs beat frantically as a medium goes into a trance to rid a new house of its evil spirits. An old Chinese woman offers her smoking joss-sticks to the Goddess of Mercy at a centuries-old temple, and dressed in a red silk sari, a shy Hindu bride sits on the *manavarai*, the marriage dais, and the priest begins his age-old ceremony by lighting a small fire and calling upon God to witness the event. From a speeding bus there is a glimpse of an old wooden mosque set amongst the coconut trees where men and boys, dressed in traditional Malay dress, gather together to kneel in prayer to praise Allah, the one God.

For the visitor to Malaysia, this multi-devotional aspect creates the opportunity for many different and memorable experiences.

The Sultanates

Before the coming of Islam in the 13th century, the territorial chiefs and rulers of Malaysia were known as maharajas or rajas in the Hindu tradition. Although Malacca's founder, Parameswara, converted to Islam in 1410, it was not until some 40 years later that it became firmly established as the state religion under Sultan Muzaffar Shah. Sultans were known as 'The Shadow of God upon the Earth' and their power was absolute; they could do no wrong as they were punishable only by God. Dircctly under the sultan was the Bendahara (Chief Minister), the Temenggung (Chief of Police), the Laksamana (Admiral of the Fleet), and beneath these were scores of various titled nobles.

Sultan Muzaffar Shah was succeeded by his son, Sultan Mansur Shah, whose reign from 1459 to 1477 marked the high point of Malay power and culture. The *istana*, or palace, was the centre of Malay life and according to the *Sejarah Melayu*, the court history of the Malaccan Sultanate, Sultan Mansur Shah's palatial home was the finest royal palace in the world. Huge wooden carved pillars held up the seven-tiered roof made of copper and zinc tiles and the whole was surmounted by gilded spires that shone like 'fire in the sunlight'.

After the Portuguese conquest of Malacca in 1511, Sultan Mahmud removed his court to Bentan, an island off Singapore. His son, Sultan Alauddin Riayat Syah, succeeded him and moved to Johor, establishing the Kingdom of Johor. Further north in Perak, a region coveted for its tin deposits, Sultan Muzaffar Syah, another son of Sultan Mahmud, established the Kingdom of Perak.

During the British colonial period, restrictions were placed on the power of the sultans. This met with increasing opposition from the Malays, and on the granting of Independence on 30 August 1957 the sovereign rights of the rulers were guaranteed in the Constitution. Malaysia became a constitutional monarchy. The head of state, known as the Yang di-Pertuan Agung, is one of the Malay sultans who is elected for a term of five years by his brother rulers in a unique system of rotating royalty. Although His Majesty is the Supreme Head of the Federation, and as such has precedence over all other persons, on government affairs he acts on the advice of Parliament and the Cabinet. Malaysia's government consists of a Senate and a House of Representatives. Elections are held every five years and the Cabinet is headed by the Prime Minister. Within each state the traditional ruler is the sovereign monarch, but generally these rulers cannot act contrary to the advice of the State Executive Council.

The present Yang di-Pertuan Agung is Sultan Mahmood Iskandar of Johor, who was installed as Supreme Ruler in 1984 and is the eighth monarch since Independence. His Majesty is a well-loved monarch who

Tukang Jahit
TAILOR
BAR
ANCHOR DRAFT
KOK HONG
TRADING CO.
TEIK HOOI
ENTERESS
BOSCH
ECHO
時
商
HOTEL
TYE ANN
大安
ENAR BENAR
BERKUASA!
Bateri National
SIRIM
FRAME-
MAKER

mixes easily with his subjects. He is a capable administrator, a successful businessman and a very keen sportsman.

In the period of the Malaccan Sultanate, royal power was such that no commoner could wear yellow clothes, use white umbrellas or wear gold anklets, for these were the prerogative of royalty. Times have changed, but every five years, when the royal enthronement ceremony is enacted, priceless heirlooms and sacred regalia are brought out of storage and the pomp and pageantry of the sultanates are revived.

Art and Culture

With its diverse population, Malaysia has a staggering variety of cultural expressions. Chinese opera, or *wayang*, a remnant of the imperial courts, is performed on auspicious festival days, and in Kuala Lumpur young Indian girls still train in classical dance techniques that have remained unchanged for thousands of years. But both these cultures, Chinese and Indian, have been imported from their motherlands and as such are not native to Malaysia. The art and culture of the Malays and the other indigenous peoples may have been influenced over the centuries by outside ideas, but they remain the original cultures of the land.

Artistic expressions of 40,000 years ago have been found painted on the walls of the Niah Caves in Sarawak and stone-age workshops have been unearthed on the peninsula, but little is known of this early culture. Some *orang asli* of the peninsula and the early peoples of Sabah and Sarawak carved religious statues, mainly for ceremonies held to rid people of illness, but these were never kept, for once the evil spirit had entered the wooden deity it was left deep in the jungle. Stone dolmens have been found in Malacca, Sabah and Sarawak, but their origins are shrouded in mystery. The foundations of Indian temples from 1,000 years ago, containing Hindu and Buddhist relics, have been discovered in Kedah's Bujang valley, but scarce evidence remains of the legendary Malay kingdoms, written of in old Chinese and Arabic texts. Sanskrit words survive in the Malay language from the Hinduized courts, and cultural remnants linger in the *bersanding*, the Malay wedding ceremony, where the bejewelled bride and groom, dressed in heavy brocades, sit in state and feed each other yellow rice with hennaed fingertips. The enthronement ceremony of Malaysia's king is still heavily Hindu, as is the *wayang kulit*, the puppet-shadow plays of Kelantan.

Islam arrived in the 14th century and profoundly influenced the Malay way of life. Malay art and culture reached its pinnacle during the heyday of the Malaccan Sultanate in the 15th century. Middle-eastern tales and legends, translated into Malay, were told to spellbound court audiences. The finest literary work in the Malay language is a 15th-century history, the *Sejarah Melayu* or *Malay Annals*, written by an unknown author, of the vivid

Malaccan court life. Traditional Malay dances such as *tarian mak inang*, 'The Lady-in-waiting Dance', and the *tarian lillin*, 'Candle Dance', were popular court entertainments of that time and are still performed at cultural events. Top-spinning, kite-flying, *sepak takraw* (Malay football) and *silat* (the Malay art of self-defence) all originated from the Malaccan Sultanate.

Royalty provided the patronage for the artists and craftsmen of the realm. Silk-weavers wove the cloths shot with gold and silver — the traditional court attire; wood-carvers embellished the beams and panels of huge timber palaces; silver- and goldsmiths created lavish jewellery and ceremonial regalia; and the *pandai besi* (ironsmiths) forged weapons, notably the *kris*, the wavy-bladed dagger and most well-known Malay cultural symbol.

From the royal courts of Kelantan came the *makyung*, a combination of ballet, opera, romantic drama and comedy. The *makyung*, or main actress, develops the story which is usually about princes and princesses of old, adapted from centuries-old oral tales and backed by an orchestra of gongs, drums and violins (*rebab*). Another dance drama exclusive to Kelantan is the *Mendora*, where males play the part of women. Grotesque masks are used and with slow rhythmic movements the performers act out adventures from ancient folklore to the accompaniment of drums, gongs and the *serunai* (Malay oboe). *Rebana kercing* is a performance of dance and chanting to the rhythmic tapping of a tambourine. *Ronggeng*, a popular Malay dance, is performed outdoors at wedding ceremonies, but *ghazal*, a kind of musical salon, is performed inside. The *ghazal*, where folk songs and *pantun* (rhyming poetry) are accompanied by tabla drums, harmonium and a stringed instrument known as a *gambus*, probably developed in the 18th- and 19th-century courts of the Johor Sultanate. *Berdikir barat*, a team session of wit and repartee set to music, is a comparatively new entertainment, having been developed since the Second World War.

Most of these traditional performing arts are staged nowadays only for ceremonial events and cultural presentations. Some are still performed regularly in the more remote villages, but today's Malaysian, like his counterparts the world over, tends to seek his entertainment from television, the cinema and videos. Malays are a creative, talented and artistic race and although many of today's artists and musicians look to the West for trends and technical expertise, much of the inspiration is still home grown.

Malaysian Food

Malaysia comprises such a variety of races, landscapes and cultures that a common tradition of cooking and eating would seem unlikely. However, there is a certain unity among the diverse recipes of the region and both Chinese and Indian food have been influenced by Malay cuisine. Rice is the staple food of most Malaysians, though noodles cooked in a variety of ways are also popular. Malaysians prefer their food hot and spicy and many of the popular spices are those that first brought the Europeans to the East Indies. Chillies, ginger, tumeric, coriander, galingale, lemon grass, cloves and cinnamon are pounded in stone pestles to provide the base for countless dishes in the Malay cuisine.

Seafood is abundant in the seas that surround most of the nation, and growing close to the coast is the coconut which provides the *santan*, coconut milk, which forms the basis of most soups, curries and desserts. Traditionally, practically everything the Malay housewife needed for cooking was readily at hand in the *kampung* compound. Coconuts dropped conveniently to the ground, herbs, sweet potatoes, yams and other vegetables were cultivated, rice was harvested from the paddy-fields, the rivers were abundant with fish, fruit trees surrounded the house, chickens provided eggs and meat, and at feast times a cow or goat was killed. In the *kampung*, much of this traditional life still goes on. In the towns and cities, blenders may have replaced the mortar and pestle, but Malaysians still prefer to cook from the basics, and tinned and fast food have yet to catch on in a big way.

Diners can take their pick from lavish buffets in five-star hotels, airconditioned restaurants or the many open-air eating stalls that are the favourite haunts of most Malaysians. It is not unusual to see Mercedes and BMWs parked outside the humble roadside *warung*, for this is where the best food is to be found.

Below is a selection of the more common dishes in Malaysian cuisine.

Malay specialities include *nasi lemak*, a breakfast dish of rice cooked in coconut milk with prawn sambal, cucumber, *ikan bilis* (dried anchovies) and roasted peanuts. *Nasi padang* is the midday meal, which consists of rice and a selection of curried meat, fish and vegetables. Favourite noodle dishes include *laksa*, a spicy coconut milk and fish soup; and *mee goreng*, stir-fried noodles with meat and vegetables. *Satay*, Malaysia's best-known dish, is marinated skewered meats (chicken, beef or mutton) eaten with peanut chilli sauce and *ketupat* (rice wrapped in coconut leaves). *Rendang* is a spicy dry curry made at festive times. Cold treats include *air batu campur*, popularly known as ABC, a mound of shaved ice with syrup, corn and other toppings, and *cendol*, made with coconut milk. *Gula melaka* is a delicious sago pudding topped with coconut milk and palm-sugar syrup.

Chinese popular dishes include Hainanese chicken rice (rice with roasted chicken), *ngah po fan* (rice cooked in a claypot with chicken, sausage and salted fish) and *wan tan mee* (soya noodles with prawn dumplings, roast pork and vegetables). Steamboat is a feast of skewered seafood cooked in a hotpot at the table. A favourite Chinese dessert is *bubur cha cha*, a coconut-milk pudding with diced yam, sweet potato, sago and jelly.

Indian specialities include the rich *nasi biriyani*, rice steamed in milk and meat stock and usually eaten with mutton curry. *Roti canai*, a thin pancake

eaten with curry, is a breakfast speciality, and *murtabak,* an oversized crepe filled with meat, eggs and onions, makes an excellent supper.

Conduct

Hospitality comes naturally to Malaysians, who will often throw open their house and offer a meal and a bed to a traveller they have only just met. It can often be a lonely experience to travel solo, but not in Malaysia. There is always someone ready to give directions, to buy you a cup of coffee, or even to offer an invitation to a sister's wedding. If you are invited into a Malaysian home there are certain matters of etiquette which it is wise to be aware of beforehand. All Malays, Chinese and Indians remove their shoes at the door; this is always done whether it is a mosque, an Indian temple or a private home. Usually on entering a Malay home the family will be introduced. The correct conduct is to shake hands with the menfolk, but Muslim women can only shake hands with each other or with close relatives. Some of the more cosmopolitan women will extend their hand, in which case the right thing to do is accept and reciprocate. It is considered polite to accept the food and drink the hostess offers. Even during Hari Raya (the Muslim celebration after Ramadan), when often a dozen houses are visited in one day, it is impolite if you leave without taking a sip and a nibble. If you invite a Malay friend to have a meal with you it is worth remembering that all Malays are Muslims and so observe certain dietary rules. The safest course of action is to choose a Malay or North Indian Muslim restaurant which serves *halal* food.

Politeness, as in many Asian countries, is considered the most important character trait, especially among tourists. Although it is sometimes difficult to remain calm under trying circumstances, if you can manage to do so your esteem in the eyes of others will soar. To argue or use loud voices in public, particularly between husband and wife, is considered very low class. Tourists should avoid wearing provocative or revealing clothing, not only because it may offend Malaysian sensibilities, but also because it attracts the wrong kind of attention.

Malaysia is a relaxed and friendly country and even if you unintentionally give offence you will be laughingly forgiven, for you are an honoured guest in their land.

General Information for Travellers

Getting There

By Air Apart from Malaysia Airlines, the national carrier, 27 international airlines have regular direct services with Kuala Lumpur. Malaysia Airlines has flights from the United States (Los Angeles), Europe (London, Amsterdam, Paris, Frankfurt), the Middle East, India, Australia, Korea and Japan. Kuala Lumpur is also easily reached from Hong Kong, Taipei, Bangkok, Jakarta, Denpasar and Manila. Shuttle flights connect Singapore with Kuala Lumpur a dozen times a day. Penang in the north has an international airport which is serviced by Malaysia Airlines, Thai Airways International, Cathay Pacific and Singapore Airlines. Visitors to East Malaysia can fly direct to Kota Kinabalu in Sabah by Malaysia Airlines and Cathay Pacific, and to Kuching in Sarawak by Malaysia Airlines. Domestic flights connect all the major towns and reach out even to grassy village airstrips in the heart of Sarawak which are only accessible by air.

By Rail Affectionately known as 'The Asian Express', this comfortable train service links Bangkok, Malaysia and Singapore. Although the Thai Railway and Malayan Railways control their respective sections, it is possible to book all the way through from either end. From Bangkok to Penang is an overnight trip. The full journey from Bangkok to Singapore (or vice versa) is two days and two nights.

By Road Express buses connect with Singapore and most of Malaysia's major towns. Local Singapore buses cross to Johor Baru, the border town across the causeway, and from here buses connect to all over Malaysia. Economical 'share taxis', where passengers share the expense, can be picked up in Johor Baru, at the Thai border in the north, and in all Malaysian towns. Over 25,000 kilometres (15,534 miles) of good paved roads criss-cross the country and moderately priced hire cars can provide a more in-depth look at Malaysia off the beaten track.

Visas

Commonwealth citizens (except those from India), British Protected Persons, and citizens of the Republic of Ireland, Switzerland, the Netherlands, San Marino and Liechtenstein do not need a visa to enter Malaysia. Citizens of the United States, West Germany, Italy, Norway, Sweden, Denmark, Belgium, Japan, Korea, Austria, Finland, Luxemburg, Iceland and Tunisia do not require a visa for a visit not exceeding three months. On entry, visitors from all the above-mentioned countries can obtain a one-month visit pass. This is renewable and no fee is charged for up to three months. A 14-day

visa-free visit is available to citizens of the Soviet Union and other Eastern European communist countries. All these conditions apply only for social visits; separate arrangements must be made for business and employment purposes.

Customs

At Kuala Lumpur's Subang Airport there are ten customs lanes in the arrival hall, including a green lane for visitors who do not have dutiable items. Duty-free items are the usual one litre of liquor, one carton of cigarettes, and personal effects of reasonable quantity. Prohibited items include narcotics and pornography, and firearms are subject to licensing. Although Malaysian customs procedures look casual, their anti-drug laws carry the death penalty. The export of Malaysian antiques is only allowed with a licence from the Director General of Museums, Malaysia. The importation of travellers cheques and letters of credit is unlimited and visitors are allowed to bring in or take out any amount of Malaysian currency.

Health

Malaysia's health standards are ranked among the highest in Asia. No cholera or smallpox vaccination is required for travellers entering the country. Yellow Fever vaccination is required for arrivals from infected areas and from Yellow Fever endemic zones, except for children under one year. Tap water is generally quite safe to drink but most people boil their drinking water first out of habit. All hotels, even the most economical, provide boiled drinking water. For those with delicate stomachs it is best to eat hot, freshly-cooked meals. The humble roadside stall, known as *warung*, where you can watch the cook at work, often serve the best food. As this is a tropical country and hence very hot and humid, travellers should not overdo it for the first couple of days until they have adjusted to the climate. Those with pale skin are advised to wear a hat and sunblock lotion when exposed to the sun. There are modern hospitals and clinics throughout Malaysia and all doctors speak English. It is very inexpensive to visit a private doctor and they can dispense medicine on the spot. The approximate charge is M$20 including medicine.

Money

The Malaysian *ringgit* (dollar) is issued in notes of denominations of $1,000, $500, $100, $50, $20, $10, $5 and $1. There are coins of $1 and 50, 20, 10, 5 and 1 *sen* (cents). Credit cards are popular and American Express, Diners Club, MasterCard and Carte Blanche are well established in the urban centres. Other currencies and travellers cheques can be exchanged at most banks, and money changers operate in the airports and large urban centres. Banks throughout the country operate Monday to Friday from 10 am to 3 pm and on Saturdays from 9.30 to 11.30 am, with the exception of the states of Kedah, Perlis, Kelantan and Terengganu, where banks are closed on Fridays instead of Sundays and open half-day on Thursdays. If possible, avoid changing money at the luxury hotels as their rates are not as good as banks and they charge a nominal fee; the same applies to department stores. If travelling around the rural areas, it is best to change your money beforehand in one of the main centres as this saves time in the long run. A service charge of 10 percent is added automatically to restaurant and hotel bills, plus a 5 percent government tax, so tipping is unnecessary unless service is exceptionally good. Small change is generally left for waiters.

Transportation

Only a little more than 100 years ago the few travellers who ventured around Malaysia did so mainly by the waterways; when they were forced on to *terra firma* they usually rode atop elephants through the virgin jungles. In some places in upriver Sarawak and Sabah, the only transportation today is still the longboat, but even in the remotest villages the ubiquitous snarl of the outboard motor brings even the most stolid romantic back to the here and now.

The national flag carrier, Malaysia Airlines, services the entire country, from Kota Baru in the north to Johor Baru in the south, and Alor Star, Penang, Ipoh, Kuala Terengganu and Kuantan in between. Sarawak and Sabah have a limited road network so it makes more sense to fly if you are pressed for time. For some destinations there is no choice but to fly, unless you plan to make a lengthy overland safari. Many of Sarawak's riverine towns are very accessible nowadays as powerful express boats link most major upriver destinations. It is now possible to ply between peninsular Malaysia and East Malaysia (Sabah and Sarawak) by ship. Feri Malaysia operates a cruise ship which runs between Singapore, Kuantan, Kuching and Kota Kinabalu once a week in either direction. The idyllic tropical island of Pulau Tioman off the east coast and Pulau Langkawi on the west coast can also be reached by ferry or hovercraft. Penang is now connected to the mainland by the elegant new Penang Bridge, but nostalgia buffs will probably opt to make the crossing on the Butterworth ferry.

The main railway line, running from the Thai border in the north to Singapore in the south, branches at Gemas and runs up through the remote northeast to Kota Baru. In Malaysia the trains run on time, the fans or airconditioning work, there are buffet-cars, and the scenery is often more untouched than along the roadside. KTM (*Keretapi Tanah Melayu*) offers a special Rail Pass for unlimited travel in any class and to any destination for from ten to 30 days at a moderate cost.

Long-distance airconditioned buses ply the nation's roads, and all large towns have a bus depot where tickets can be purchased and schedules perused. Bus travel is cheaper than rail but not as relaxing.

One preferred mode of transport is the share taxi, a system whereby the passengers split the fare. At taxi stands the drivers will usually try to talk tourists into chartering a taxi for themselves, but this can be costly. If you say you want to share, it is readily understood. Sometimes you may have to wait a short while until the taxi is full (four passengers). Share taxis are often airconditioned, are faster than buses and reasonably priced.

In the older towns of Georgetown (Penang), Malacca, Kota Baru and in the smaller towns, three-wheeled trishaws still ply the streets and are an excellent way to sightsee. Many of the drivers are knowledgeable about local history and are self-taught tour guides. It is best to agree on a price before starting.

City taxis are plentiful and cheap; if there is no meter, agree on the price beforehand. A great way to see the countryside and to get around easily is to hire a car. Malaysia's roads are good and very extensive. International Driving Permits are required or national driving licences are acceptable if endorsed by the Registrar of Motor Vehicles. (Most car hire firms do not specify this latter condition.) Car hire fees are moderate and many international and local companies operate from the major hotels. Driving is on the left-hand side of the road.

Communications

Postal services in Malaysia are efficient and all postal workers speak English, making it easy to arrange registered mail, telegrams and parcel services. State capitals offer telex services, as do the larger hotels, but this is often non-existent in the smaller centres. Some large city hotels also have facsimile services. Telephone systems are efficient. Public telephones are available in all towns and even in small villages. Local calls cost 10 cents. Long-distance calls within Malaysia and Singapore can be dialled direct with STD (Subscribers Trunk Dialling); they are best made from your hotel where the receptionist can assist you with area codes. IDD (International Direct Dialling) is available to Britain, Australia, Hong Kong, Japan, West Germany, Switzerland, the United States, Italy, the Netherlands, Taiwan and Indonesia. Consult the phone book or ask the operator for the dialling codes.

Language

Bahasa Malaysia (Malay) is the official language of Malaysia. As the mother tongue of the entire region, Malay can be understood from southern Thailand, throughout Malaysia, the Indonesian archipelago and into the southern

PEJ BAT
POS
CENDO

Philippines. As it is a tonal language and written in the Latin alphabet, some basic phrases are easy enough for the visitor to pick up (see Basic Malay Vocabulary, page 183). Some words have been taken from the English but adapted to Malay spelling. Familiar examples include *bas* (bus), *klinik* (clinic), *polis* (police) and *pejabat pos* (post office). English is quite widely spoken, especially in the more popular tourist centres, and in banks, hotels and government offices. Chinese dialects are also widely spoken, with Hokkien and Cantonese being dominant in the urban centres. Tamil is used by the Indians who originated from southern India, and the Portuguese Eurasians of Malacca still speak an antiquated Portuguese. Language is never a problem, however, as even in the most out-of-the-way places there is generally someone who understands a little English and can help out with basic directions.

What to Pack

In a land of perpetual summer the most comfortable clothing is that which is light and preferably pure cotton. Man-made fibres, although non-crush, don't breathe, and for those not used to the tropics synthetics can be uncomfortable and even bring on heat rashes. Casual, light, loose clothing is suitable for most occasions. Jeans are often too hot and take too long to dry for those on the move. It is best to leave your mini-skirts, backless sundresses and plunging necklines at home, for most Malaysians dress modestly and expect visitors to do likewise. Swimsuits and shorts are quite acceptable at beach resorts but are not suitable in most other places. For more formal occasions, invitations usually specify 'batik' as the dress code. This means a long-sleeved batik shirt for men, readily found in boutiques and handicraft centres throughout Malaysia. Women can dress as they choose. Light, comfortable slip-on shoes or sandals are handy, as shoes must be removed before entering homes, mosques and some temples. For walking longer distances a well-worn-in pair of running shoes or soft leather loafers are best. For jungle treks and mountain climbs, canvas shoes are better than leather as they dry easily. In the hill resorts and in the early morning in the jungle it can be cool, so pack a tracksuit and a light sweater. Visitors to Mount Kinabalu should bring along plenty of warm, waterproof clothing as temperatures can drop to zero at night.

Most of the popular brands of toiletries and patent medicines are widely available and some locally-made products are excellent. Those labelled *halal* are made from non-animal products especially for Muslims but are widely used by vegetarians and the health-conscious. Bring along sunscreen oil and sunblocks, vitamins and tampons as these are not so readily available. Most of the popular colour print films are available everywhere, as is cheap colour processing, but slide film, especially Kodachrome, is hard to come by and expensive. Safety razors, even the disposable kind, are a better idea than electric razors as only the luxury hotels have outlets to fit. Malaysian current is 220 volts, 50 cycles. Both round and square plugs are used, so it is advisable to pack an adaptor if you plan on bringing electrical gadgets. English-language newspapers, magazines and books are available. There is a wide range of topical books on Malaysia, including reprints of old historical works that make for interesting travel reading.

Climate

Situated between latitudes 1° and 7° North, Malaysia is a hot and humid country where the mercury hovers between 20° and 30°C (68°–86°F) the year round. In the towns and cities it is noticeably hotter than in the villages, where coconut palms and fruit trees shade the houses. The climate of Malaysia is governed by the northeast and southwest monsoons which blow alternately during the year and whose existence in the days of sailing ships made the country the natural meeting and exchange point for traders from East and West. The northeast monsoon blows from approximately November until April and the southwest between May and October. The northeast winds which blow across the South China Sea bring heavy rain and frequent flooding to the east coast of the peninsula between December and February. Sabah and Sarawak also have their wettest season at this time. The southwest monsoon is a drier time, but — being a tropical country — showers can occur any day of the year. The heat frequently builds up around mid-afternoon, erupting in a tropical downpour which leaves the country cool and refreshed in the evening. The highlands are noticeably cooler the year round. As there is no real dry season, Malaysia is always green and this has the psychological effect of making one feel cooler than in a dry desertscape.

Shopping

From airconditioned city boutiques to bustling night markets and roadside handicraft stalls, Malaysia is a lot of fun for the shopper. Duty-free shops in the Kuala Lumpur and Penang international airports and at Pulau Langkawi and Bukit Kayu Hitam in Kedah stock all the usual duty-free items, but Malaysian handicrafts are the best bet for a traveller looking for something different. As with most Asian countries, bargaining is all part of the fun but don't expect too much off the first quoted price, especially in the east coast cottage industries where the prices are reasonable to begin with. At the larger government craft stores it is 'fixed price'. Kuala Lumpur and most of the capital cities have an Indian district where brassware, saris and prayer rugs prevail, and a Chinese area where jade, porcelain and curios can be found, but Malay handicrafts are the only real traditional buys.

Batik is synonymous with Malaysia. Goods range from traditional stamped batik sarongs to elegant hand-painted silk scarves and dress lengths. In Terengganu and Kelantan you can buy direct from the workshop. Kraftangan, the government handicraft shops offer a diverse array of batik gifts, including ready-made clothing, tablecloths, bags, hats and smaller gifts.

Kain songket, a luxurious cloth of handwoven silk shot with gold or silver thread, was once the prerogative of royalty, but it is now popular for weddings and formal wear. Each piece is handwoven, mainly by village women on small looms. In Kelantan, Terengganu and Pahang the cloth is available from workshops and government-run craft shops. Boutiques in Kuala Lumpur also stock it, but it is noticeably more expensive than on the east coast. This luxurious cloth is also available in smaller items such as handbags and cushions.

Silverware is still hand-crafted in Kelantan. Filigree work, where fine silver wire is twisted into delicate tracery, is popular in earrings, brooches and necklaces. Repousse technique, where silver sheet is hammered into relief, is used for tea sets, spoons and bowls. Silverware can be bought direct from the Kelantanese workshops or from Kraftangan in Kuala Lumpur.

Selangor pewter is renowned as the best-quality pewter ware in the world. Pewter is made of refined tin, antimony and copper — an obvious offshoot of Malaysia's tin industry. Visit the factory for the best buys, out along Jalan Pahang on the outskirts of Kuala Lumpur. Beer mugs, vases, cigarette cases, trays, coffee and tea sets and miniature animal knick-knacks make beautifully crafted souvenirs.

Basketry and other crafts are found throughout Malaysia in markets and handicraft shops. Baskets, mats, bags and hats are woven from rattan, bamboo and pandanus. Sarawak and Sabah have some of the best-crafted bags and mats. These are available also at craft shops in Kuala Lumpur, Kuching and Kota Kinabalu or at airport souvenir shops. There is also locally produced pottery in Sarawak and at Ayer Hitam in Johor, and colourful paper kites from Kelantan which make attractive wall hangings.

Kuala Lumpur — Pulse of a Nation

Affectionately known as KL, Kuala Lumpur, Malaysia's capital city, stands at the hub of national life. Growth is happening faster than city planners can keep up with: the city's building boom rivals that of Singapore and Seoul, and these days skyscrapers are as commonplace as palm trees. But for all these outwardly modern trappings, KL is still a city of character, although her history is but a scant 130 years. In the rough-and-ready pioneer days, Kuala Lumpur — meaning 'muddy estuary' — was an apt description for the squalid, lawless, tin-mining settlement, but the name hardly does justice to the elegant, cosmopolitan city of today.

When travellers arrive at KL's Subang International Airport and are whisked along expressways to their luxury high-rise hotel they may wonder why they left home, as it all looks so familiar. On the other hand, if they arrive at the crowded and noisy Puduraya bus station during the heat of the day, they may wish that they were back home. If possible, the perfect way to arrive is by train. To disembark at the 'Moorish'-inspired Central Railway Station at dusk, when the minarets and cupolas are silhouetted against a golden sunset and the muezzin's call to prayer echoes from the National Mosque, is to see the city in its most exotic mood. Even during the day, this 'Moorish' feeling is apparent, as many of the early buildings were the forerunners of KL's Islamic-style architecture which endures in the modern skyscrapers of today and gives the city an integrated look.

Although at first the city looks Islamic, it is very much a cosmopolitan metropolis. In Chinatown, under the faded stucco of turn-of-the-century shophouses, the traffic buzzes past traditional medicine shops and paper stores where artisans reproduce earthly goods in paper for burning at lavish Chinese funerals. Only a block away, sari-clad Indian girls enter a Hindu temple where a Brahmin priest conducts the morning puja.

Like all growing cities, KL is also somewhat chaotic. At peak hour, when the city often grinds to an exasperating halt, the minibuses are crammed with commuters and armies of motor bikes weave through the congested lanes. But for all the city's teething problems, none are as pressing as those of its neighbouring capitals: her pollution is mild compared with that of Bangkok, her housing is splendid compared to Manila's, and there is a freedom in the air which highly-organized Singapore lacks. Unlike most other cities, KL is not far from the countryside, and even from the downtown area jungle-clad hills can be seen in the distance — a constant reminder of Malaysia's great green heartland right at the capital city's doorstep.

Background

As recently as 130 years ago, Kuala Lumpur did not exist; there were only the swampy, jungle-clad banks of the Gombak and Klang rivers. Two Chinese traders, Hei Siew and Ah Sze Keledek, noticed a clearing as they were poling upriver; deciding that it was as good a spot as any other, they set up shop on the site in order to supply the tin miners of nearby Ampang. The outpost grew, and ultimately thrived, against great odds. Of the 87 original prospectors, 70 died of fever within the first month. Further discoveries of tin swelled the population of the shanty town, which reeled from epidemics, devastating fires and gang wars. Secret societies warred over tin holdings and only the toughest and fittest survived. Tin czar, gambling boss and brothel-owner Yap Ah Loy, the town boss, apparently remarked after offering M$100 for his enemies' heads, 'It has been as much as I could do to count out the money fast enough.'

In 1868, Yap Ah Loy was made the *Kapitan Cina*, the Chinese headman of Kuala Lumpur, a move welcomed by the British who were eager to end the gang wars and stabilize the tin industry. Meanwhile, Sultan Abdul Samad of Selangor was having problems with the defiant Raja Mahdi, who refused to remit his revenues from the Klang valley tin mines. Tengku Kudin, the Selangor sultan's son-in-law, was recruited to oppose the defiant raja and from 1869 Yap Ah Loy supported him. When Tengku Kudin gained the support of the British, the Klang valley, after a series of disputes, came under his control. When the British Resident, Frank Swettenham, Tengku Kudin and Yap Ah Loy joined forces and took control of the squalid town, they literally put Kuala Lumpur on the map. Less than 40 years after the original shopkeepers stepped ashore, the town became the state capital. Wooden shanties were pulled down, brick kilns were built, and like a phoenix rising from the ashes a planned new town arose. In 1896 Kuala Lumpur became the capital of the Federated Malay States.

Tin, the city's *raison d'être*, created many millionaires, and their great mansions designed by European architects and embellished by imported craftsmen were crowded along Jalan Ampang. A railway line was constructed in 1886 to connect the capital with Port Klang, and the fanciful Arabian-inspired Central Railway Station was the first example of Kuala Lumpur's 'Moorish' architecture. By 1891 the population stood at 43,786, of whom 79 percent were Chinese. An expanding Chinese community was valued by the British administration because it provided a guaranteed source of revenue through taxes levied on opium, port, pawnbroking and the sale of spirits. Meanwhile, the English were educating the Malay nobility at the prestigious Victoria Institute as a conciliatory move, but the Malay commonfolk were generally left to their own devices in the countryside. Early this century, Kuala Lumpur's cosmopolitan character was further strengthened when

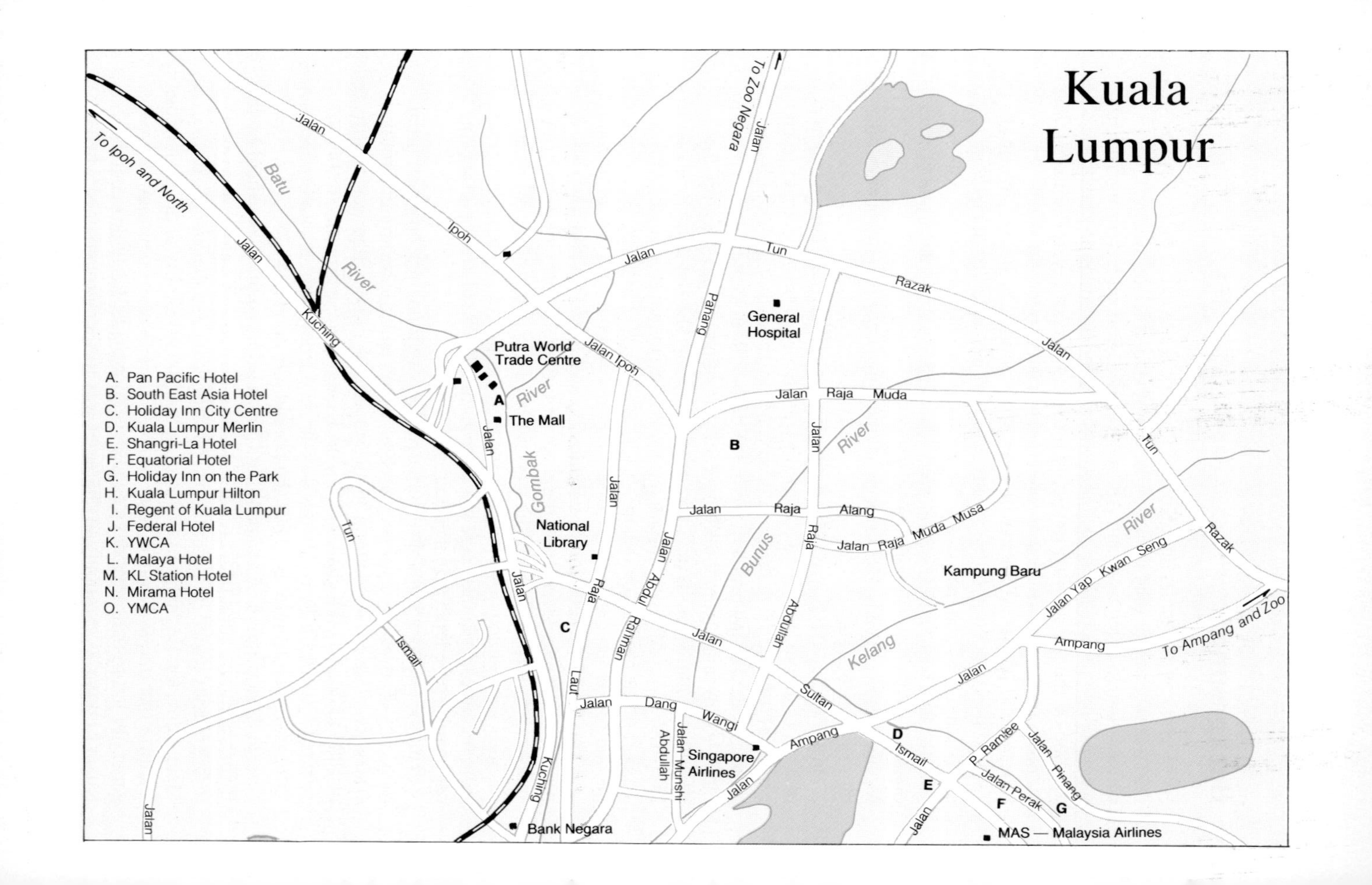
Kuala Lumpur
A. Pan Pacific Hotel
B. South East Asia Hotel
C. Holiday Inn City Centre
D. Kuala Lumpur Merlin
E. Shangri-La Hotel
F. Equatorial Hotel
G. Holiday Inn on the Park
H. Kuala Lumpur Hilton
I. Regent of Kuala Lumpur
J. Federal Hotel
K. YWCA
L. Malaya Hotel
M. KL Station Hotel
N. Mirama Hotel
O. YMCA
To Ipoh and North
To Zoo Negara
To Ampang and Zoo
Jalan Ipoh
Jalan Tun Razak
Jalan Pahang
Jalan Kuching
Jalan Raja Muda
Jalan Raja Alang
Jalan Raja Muda Musa
Jalan Raja Abdullah
Jalan Abdul Rahman
Jalan Raja Laut
Jalan Dang Wangi
Jalan Munshi Abdullah
Jalan Sultan Ismail
Jalan Ampang
Jalan Yap Kwan Seng
Jalan Tun Ismail
P. Ramlee
Jalan Pinang
Jalan Perak
Batu River
Gombak River
Bunus
Kelang River
Putra World Trade Centre
The Mall
General Hospital
National Library
Kampung Baru
Singapore Airlines
Bank Negara
MAS — Malaysia Airlines

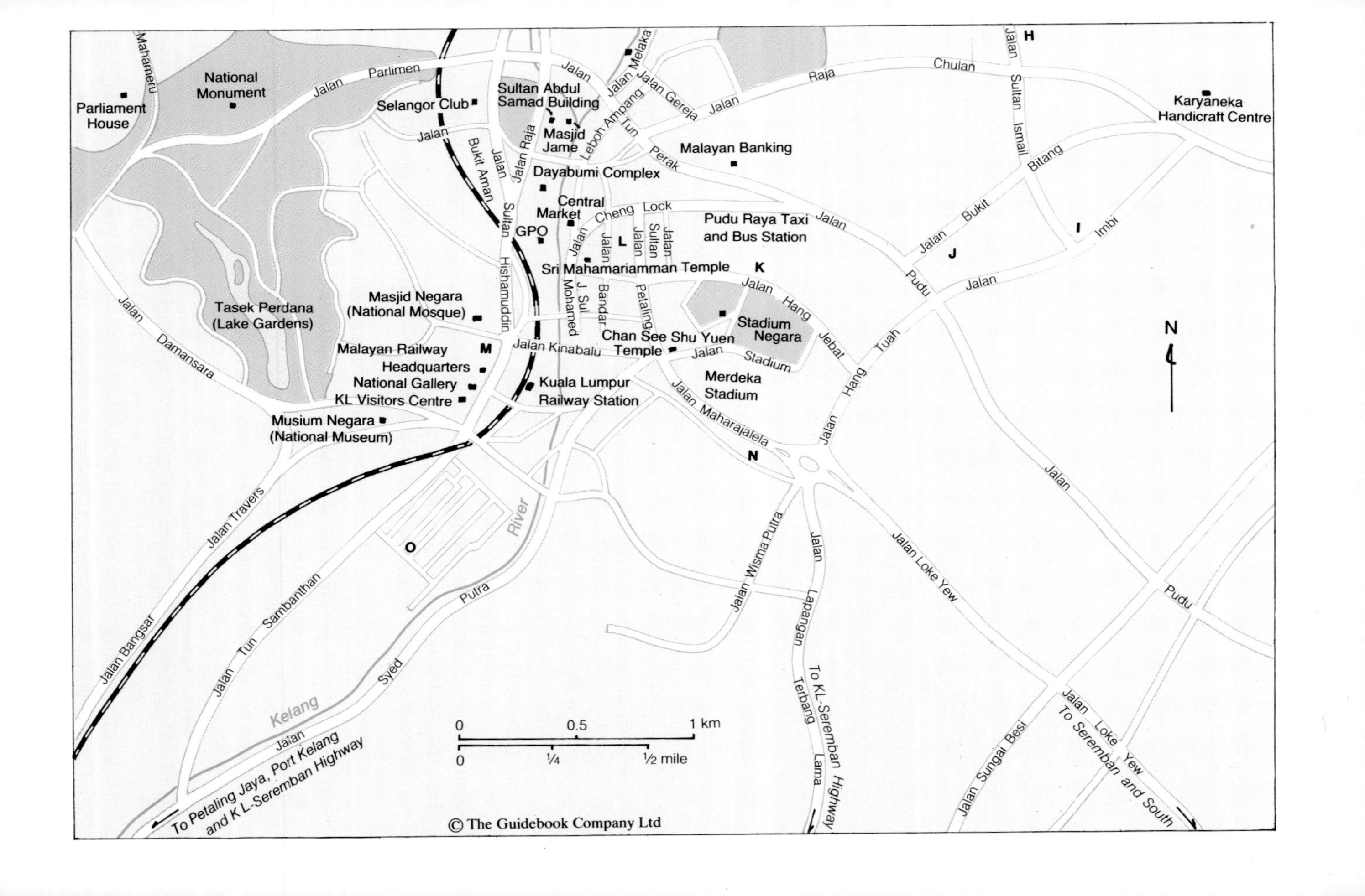

Parliament House
National Monument
Jalan Parlimen
Selangor Club
Sultan Abdul Samad Building
Masjid Jame
Jalan Melaka
Jalan Gereja
Jalan Tun Perak
Lebuh Ampang
Jalan Raja Chulan
Jalan Sultan Ismail
Karyaneka Handicraft Centre
Malayan Banking
Jalan Bukit Aman
Jalan Raja
Dayabumi Complex
Central Market
GPO
Jalan Cheng Lock
Jalan Sultan
Jalan Bandar
Jalan Petaling
J. Sul. Mohamed
Pudu Raya Taxi and Bus Station
Jalan Pudu
Jalan Bukit Bitang
Jalan Imbi
Sri Mahamariamman Temple
Jalan Sultan Hishamuddin
Masjid Negara (National Mosque)
Tasek Perdana (Lake Gardens)
Jalan Damansara
Jalan Hang Jebat
Stadium Negara
Chan See Shu Yuen Temple
Jalan Kinabalu
Jalan Stadium
Jalan Hang Tuah
Malayan Railway Headquarters
National Gallery
KL Visitors Centre
Kuala Lumpur Railway Station
Merdeka Stadium
Jalan Maharajalela
Musium Negara (National Museum)
Jalan Travers
River
Jalan Wisma Putra
Jalan Lapangan Terbang Lama
Jalan Loke Yew
Jalan Tun Sambanthan
Jalan Bangsar
Putra
Syed
Kelang
Jalan
To Petaling Jaya, Port Kelang and K L-Seremban Highway
To KL-Seremban Highway
Jalan Sungai Besi
To Seremban and South
H
I
J
K
L
M
N
O
N
0 0.5 1 km
0 ¼ ½ mile
© The Guidebook Company Ltd

thousands of Indians poured into the country to work the rubber plantations. Temples and Indian businesses cropped up in the capital's streets, and today the descendants of these first settlers number 8.6 percent of the population.

In 1942 the English suffered a humiliating surrender to the Japanese. After three years of occupation, when they stepped back into Malaya, the scene was vastly different as a result of the growth of Malay nationalism. Kuala Lumpur was the venue in 1946 for the formation of UMNO (the United Malays National Organization) in opposition to the Malayan Union proposed by the British. When Independence was finally announced on 30 August 1957, the Union Jack was lowered at the Selangor Club for the last time. On the following day at the Merdeka Stadium, shouts of *merdeka* (freedom) roared over the capital as Independence was formalized. Since then, the capital has been the hub of the nation's energy and action, the skyline keeps expanding upwards, the suburbs keep creeping outwards, and the up-country folk, like the early tin miners, continue to be drawn to the capital by their dreams of riches.

Getting around Kuala Lumpur

As cities go, Kuala Lumpur is still quite small, and as most of the city's sights are clumped together in the downtown area it is quite easy to see most of them within a day. A city map, comfortable walking shoes and some kind of protection from the fierce tropical sun are all that is required for the independent sightseer who prefers to browse through museums and markets at his or her own pace. For those who are not so independent, there are many tours available which show you the city's attractions from the comfort of an airconditioned bus. However, these tours often introduce you only to other tourists and not to the locals. Walking is much more rewarding. If you are confused about directions simply stop and ask for help. If you appear to be lost, the local people will often approach and ask if you need assistance. KL is not too big and the people are not in too much of a hurry to find time to offer help.

Taxis are the most convenient means of reaching attractions a little further out of the way or for travelling downtown from your hotel. Taxis can either be hired from taxi stands or hailed by the roadside. Rates are moderate, with airconditioned taxis being a little more expensive. Meters are fixed on some taxis and not on others, and it is advisable to fix the fare before getting in. For close hops through the downtown area, the fare should be around M$3. For airport taxis, expect to pay M$15. Share taxis for out-of-town trips are available upstairs at the Puduraya Bus Terminal on Jalan Pudu. The fares for these rides are fixed and each of the four passengers pays the same. Most drivers know enough English to understand destinations and prices.

The city's bus service is also efficient if you are a little more adventurous.

Buses enable you to see a lot of the city at little cost. Avoid peak hours and carry plenty of small change. Bus fares are calculated at 20 cents for the first kilometre (just over half a mile) and 5 cents for each additional two kilometres (1.2 miles). The minibuses which ply the city charge a standard fare of 50 cents. These are not for the faint-hearted as minibus drivers are a breed apart and are notorious both for their speed and lurching stops.

For the visitor experienced at city driving there are many hire-and-drive car services available, most of which have offices in the leading hotels. Expect to pay from M$70 to $100 a day for unlimited mileage. If you are not familiar with the city it is better to leave the driving to someone who is, as KL's streets are confusing and it is very easy to become stuck on an expressway and end up far from your destination. Hire cars are an excellent choice for excursions to Fraser's Hill, the Genting Highlands and Carey Island, as you have the freedom of being able to stop at any time to take photos and to explore at your own pace.

Sights and Walks

The **downtown history and architecture walk** covers a dozen or so sights located along both sides of the downtown riverbank area in a north to south direction.

Masjid Jame, undoubtedly one of the city's most beautiful buildings, is a fitting start to a KL tour as it was at this site — the confluence of the Klang and Gombak rivers — that the city began. The promontory was the landing place for boats journeying upriver with miners' supplies and back downriver with tin from the Ampang mines. This classic Arabian-style mosque, built in 1907, houses a triple-domed prayer hall surmounted by two soaring minarets. The whole is built of pale terracotta-pink bricks embellished with white archways, cupolas and balustrades and surmounted with sparkling silver domes. Although Masjid Jame is in the centre of the downtown area it is surprisingly cool and serene. Coconut-palms rustle overhead in the breeze and the white marble floors underfoot are a welcome retreat for the urban workers who gather here for their afternoon prayers. Masjid Jame is open to all visitors, who must remove their shoes before entering and be dressed modestly. Out of respect, it is best to visit between prayer times. The main entrance is on Jalan Tun Perak.

The **Sultan Abdul Samad Building** is the imposing copper-domed building directly behind and across the river from the Masjid Jame. Previously known as the State Secretariat, construction of this forerunner of KL's 'Moorish' architecture began in 1894 when the Governor of the Straits Settlements, Sir Charles Mitchel, placed a yen note, several Straits coins, a hunk of tin and a copy of the *Selangor Journal* under the foundation stone. It was generally acknowledged that its design was 'too far ahead of its time',

UNITED ASIAN BANK

HongkongBank

with its 41-metre (135-foot) -high clock tower, curving archways and bulbous onion-shaped copper domes. It now houses the Judicial Department and the High Court.

The **Selangor Club**, the black and white mock-Tudor building directly across the road from the Sultan Abdul Samad Building, was the focus of life during the English colonial days. Out-of-town rubber planters and government officials would sip their *stengahs,* a half-shot of whisky and water, on the spacious verandas while watching cricket matches on the Padang. The club became known as thc Thc Spotted Dog, apparently because the wife of one of the members used to tie up her dalmation dog at the club steps. Here the British made gallant efforts to quell the monotony of life in the tropics. Tea parties, soirées, amateur theatricals, bridge nights, and cricket and football matches enlivened their days. During the annual flooding of the Klang River two prominent lawyers, on a wager, had a swimming race between the Selangor Club and the Sultan Abdul Samad Building.

The **Central Market**, a pastel-pink and blue gem of art deco architecture, is situated on the opposite side of the river. The Central Market was once the city's major 'wet market', stocking everything from live chickens to tropical fruits, but when the population moved out into the suburbs the market declined and at one stage was even slated for demolition. Saved by a concerned public and some conservation-minded officials, the old market has today been revamped and revitalized into a hive of boutiques and restaurants and is the unofficial meeting-place for the city's artisans and craftsmen. Spread over an entire city block, the market is entirely free of central structural supports and has a superb skylight running the entire length of the building. Sunlight pours through, flooding the shopping mall with natural light, and the large geometric leadlight windows surrounding the building give the interior a bright and airy feel. The marble-topped counters on the handicrafts stalls are the original slabs on which the old 'wet market' butchers used to carve up chickens and display fish. Here you can have your portrait painted, your fortune told, watch a glass-blowing demonstration and browse through the most interesting collection of shops in the capital. Every Sunday the pavement outside the market plays host to the city's artistic talents at the Sunday Art Market, KL's answer to Paris's Montmartre.

Dayabumi, a stunning modern high-rise complex, towers over the river. A walkway connects it with the Central Market across the river. The glistening white 34-storey tower, the Menara, is 32-sided with open-fretwork and high vaulted arches, giving it a striking Islamic appearance. The neighbouring square building, of the same design, is the General Post Office, Pejabat Pos Besar. Adjoining this complex which fronts Jalan Sultan Hishamuddin are some 'Moorish' buildings which now house **Infokraf**, the exhibition centre of the Malaysian Handicraft Development Corporation. Handicrafts exhibited here are also for sale.

Masjid Negara — The National Mosque is located further down Jalan Sultan Hishamuddin. The 73-metre (239-foot) -high minaret looms into view, towering over the 5.2-hectare (12.8-acre) complex which comprises the Grand Hall, library, meeting hall, ceremonial rooms and a mausoleum. The marble mosque is surrounded by verandas screened by white grilles in traditional Islamic style, similar to the mosque at Agra Fort in India. Completed in 1965 after five years in the making, the National Mosque cost an estimated M$10 million. Inside the Grand Hall, built to accommodate 8,000 worshippers, the vast marble floors are flanked by pools which reflect the blue glow of the stained-glass skylights. Visitors are welcome from Saturday to Thursday from 9 am to 6 pm and on Fridays from 2.45 to 6 pm. As with all mosques, visitors must remove their shoes on entering and ladies must be decently attired.

Kuala Lumpur Railway Station is without a doubt one of the most architecturally interesting railway stations in the world. Surmounted with minarets and cupolas and decorated with keyhole arches and scalloped eaves, the building is straight out of an *Arabian Nights* fantasy. It is directly diagonal to the National Mosque, further along Jalan Sultan Hishamuddin. Designed and built at the turn of the century, it replaced the original station which dated from 1885. Beneath the Islamic exterior the building is similar to the glass and iron railway stations constructed in England during the Victorian era. Across the road is the **Railway Headquarters Building**, another interesting edifice, built in the same style. This building is of grey stone and is slightly more reserved in tone than the whimsical white and gold station. On the ground floor of the headquarters is a sweeping corridor of keyhole archways and an elegant circular staircase.

The **National Art Gallery** is just a little further down the road from the Railway Headquarters Building. Housed in the former colonial-style Hotel Majestic, the gallery has a permanent collection of fine works by Malaysian artists. Exhibitions by local and international artists are held throughout the year. The gallery is open daily from 10 am to 6 pm, but is closed from 12.15 to 2.45 pm on Fridays.

Musium Negara — The National Museum is situated a short walk from the National Art Gallery and sits on a rise between two expressways. The steep-sided overlapping roofs are based on traditional Malay architecture. On both sides of the entrance are two immense murals in Italian glass mosaic, each 35 metres (114 feet) in length and five metres (16 feet) high, depicting traditional cultural activities and episodes from Malaysian history. History buffs could easily lose a few hours here, either studying the different arts and crafts of the indigenous *orang asli* people, or ogling royal relics from the Malay sultanates. Whole scenes of Malaysian life are depicted with wax models, original costumes and furnishings. One gallery shows a Malaccan Chinese house complete with bridal chamber, a walk-through Malay

kampung house, and a shopfront of a Baba store from Malacca. Other displays include weaponry, currency, Malaysian birds and mammals, entomology, and exhibitions on the rubber and tin-mining industries. Open daily from 9 am to 6 pm and closed on Fridays between 12.15 and 2.45 pm. Admission is free.

Lake Gardens, Kuala Lumpur's undulating green parkland, is virtually at the museum's gate. In the early morning and late afternoon the twisting park road becomes a haven for the city's joggers. Beside the lake, under the shade of tropical trees, Malaysians come to picnic, lovers to linger, and energetic youngsters to paddle aquabikes on the lake. Surrounded by a moat and fountains, the **National Monument** is dedicated to those who died during the 12-year Emergency against the communist terrorists. Sculpted in bronze, the monument depicts the Malaysian security forces in combat. One holds the Malaysian flag, another gives aid to a wounded soldier, and below are depicted fallen terrorists. Designed by the American sculptor Felix de Weldon, who created the Iwo Jima Memorial in Washington DC, the monument provokes a lively discussion as the figures look decidedly un-Asian.

Parliament House stands on elevated grounds in the northern part of the Lake Gardens. Commanding an excellent view of the surrounding lawns and gardens, this 18-storey building houses the Senate and the House of Representatives as well as various offices and committee rooms. With prior arrangements, visitors are permitted to watch sittings of Parliament.

Cultural Sights

Chinatown, roughly bordered by Jalan Petaling, Jalan Bandar and Jalan Sultan, bustles with commercial activity any time of the day or night. During daylight hours the old pastel-coloured turn-of-the-century shophouses carry on generations-old businesses. Dry goods stores with rattan baskets full of an exotic array of preserved eggs, sharks' fins and dried fish spill on to the pavements. Here *sinsehs*, Chinese druggists, still weigh up a weird cornucopia of seeds, barks and roots on old brass scales when dispensing their traditional medicines. It is rewarding to spend some time browsing around the shops to observe the fascinating day-to-day life of Chinatown. At dusk, the mid-section of Jalan Petaling is closed to vehicles and the street turns into an open-air night market. Food stalls spring up, interspersed with cassette hawkers and clothing booths. The air is pungent with cooking aromas and alive with the beat of the latest in Cantonese opera or Malay heavy metal. Under the glare of fluorescent tubes and pressure lamps the bazaar hums on until the early hours.

Chan See Shu Yuen Temple, the most elaborate Chinese temple in Kuala Lumpur, is situated at the corner of Jalan Petaling and Jalan Stadium. Built in

1906, the façade and roof ridges of the temple are decorated with elaborate glazed ceramic sculptures of dragons and other mythical creatures, giving an extremely ornate effect. Paintings and wood-carvings embellish the interior, which has features of typical Chinese temples — open courtyards and symmetrically arranged pavilions. Like many Malaysian Chinese temples, it serves as a venue for both religious ceremonies and meetings.

Sri Maha Mariamman Temple on Jalan Bandar, close to Chinatown, is the oldest Indian temple in Kuala Lumpur. It was founded in 1873 by Indians from Tamil Nadu who had come to Malaysia as contract labourers to work in the rubber plantations. Located initially on the site of the present Central Railway Station, the temple was relocated to Jalan Bandar in 1885. The tiered *gopuram*, or gateway, depicts the universal pantheon of Hindu deities and is one of the most ornate in Malaysia. Gold, precious stones and Spanish and Italian tiles are incorporated in the decorations.

Kampung Baru — Weekend Market, or *pasar minggu*, is an open-air market which comes alive on Saturday nights. Malays refer to it as the Sunday market as their Sunday starts at dusk on Saturday, not at midnight. Kampung Baru, a predominantly Malay section of the city, is only ten minutes from the centre of town along Jalan Raja Muda. The night market is an essential part of Malaysian life, and in towns and villages throughout the country it is often the only nightlife available. Batik sarongs, bamboo birdcages, traditional handicrafts and a variety of stalls selling cut-price shoes and clothing compete for space with dozens of food stalls. Spicy *satay*, fresh corn on the cob, and cakes made of coconut milk and rice flour and wrapped in banana leaves are only a few of the delicacies that can be found at the *pasar minggu*. If you miss the Saturday night market the handicraft stalls are still open on weekday nights, or you can head to the **Chow Kit Market** area on Jalan Raja Bot which operates every night of the week.

Jalan Melayu is another interesting area for browsing and taking in the passing parade. From the Jame Mosque, cross the road and follow the river to the start of Jalan Melayu. Indian shops filled with silk saris, brass pots and bolts of colourful cloth line both sides of the road. The first turn on the right is Jalan Masjid India where, opposite the Indian mosque, the sidewalk is crammed with Indian and Malay shops specializing in *songkok* (the velvet Malay cap), *baju Melayu* (the traditional loose outfit for men), prayer rugs from Arabia, herbal medicines from Java, perfumed oils from the Middle East and framed gold-leaf inscriptions from the holy *Koran*. In the evening, a large outdoor eating market, specializing in Malay food, is held at the end of Jalan Masjid India in a converted carpark.

Shopping

Central Market on Jalan Hang Kasturi has the best range of Malaysian handicrafts in the capital. Craft stalls specialize in hand-crafted items and cheap souvenirs. Boutiques range from Aslicraft, where you can purchase the unique wood-carvings of the Mah Meri tribe, to those specializing in basketry, hand-painted silk batik, local watercolours, Kelantanese kites, Sarawak woven goods and many others. At the Karyaneka Handicraft Centre on Jalan Bukit Bintang, pavilions representing each state sell specialized crafts from each region. The large central showroom features a wide variety of ready-made clothing and gifts in batik and elegant evening bags made of *kain songket* brocade. Batik Malaysia on Jalan Tun Perak also stocks batik cloth by the metre and a variety of ready-made men's shirts, sarongs, beachware and the traditional women's *baju kurung*. At the Kutang Kraf Batik Factory in Damansara Heights you can purchase batik at warehouse prices.

Out-of-town Drives

Unlike many of the world's capitals, Kuala Lumpur is close to the surrounding countryside and has a rugged National Park literally on its doorstep. Hill resorts and other places of interest are within a few hours' drive from the city.

Templer Park, a real Malaysian jungle, is only a half-hour drive of about 21 kilometres (13 miles) north of the city. Covering an area of 1,214 hectares (3,000 acres), the park was named after Gerald Templer, the last British High Commissioner, whose idea it was to lay aside a 'vast jungle retreat for the public'. Paths wind through this jungle reserve past waterfalls and alongside boulder-clad streams. Monkeys are abundant and a large variety of butterflies can be found here, including the world-famed Raja Brooke's Birdwing which is usually found beside the streams. Bamboo clumps, tree ferns and towering rain forest trees draped with lianas fringe the paths that lead into the interior, where two towering limestone outcrops rear 305 metres (1,000 feet) from the jungle floor. Known as **Bukit Takan** and **Anak Takan**, these sheer-sided hills are riddled with caves containing a large number of fossils. Templer Park is a popular picnic spot for urban folk on weekends, but during the week the trails are quite deserted.

Batu Caves, 13 kilometres (eight miles) from Kuala Lumpur on the road north to Ipoh, are a group of caves set high in the cliff-face of a limestone massif. In 1891 Hindu priests set up a shrine to Lord Subramaniam in the main or Cathedral Cave and since then the caves have been sacred for Malaysia's Hindus. The cliff-side cavern is reached by an arduous climb of 272 steps or by a small rail-car which runs to the 240th step. Inside the aptly-

named Cathedral Cave, shafts of light pierce the gloom and stalactites drip from the vast ceiling. Each year, at the end of January or in early February, around 100,000 Hindu pilgrims congregate here to celebrate the festival of Thaipusam. Astrologically, this is a most propitious time, for it was on this day that Lord Subramaniam received the invincible spear known as Vel with which he overthrew the forces of evil. Thousands of the pilgrims perform acts of penance, carrying *kavadis* containing bowls of milk, which cannot be spilled, and decorated with peacock feathers. Chains from these are hooked into the penitents' flesh and skewers pierce tongues and cheeks. In a trance state the devotees mount the steps to the temple. After splashing the milk on the deity, the ordeal is over and their penance and prayers are accepted. At ground level, one cave has been converted into a museum, with several hundred garishly-painted statues depicting the legendary exploits of Lord Subramaniam and other Hindu deities.

Zoo Negara is 13 kilometres (eight miles) from the capital on the road to Ulu Kelang. Open daily between 9 am and 7 pm, the zoo is set in over 16 hectares (40 acres) of forest surrounding a lake. Here are found most of Malaysia's famed wildlife, including tigers, bears, tapirs, *seladang* (wild buffalo) and the cute mouse-deer. The latter, also known as *kancil*, frequently appear in Malaysian folklore as clever heroes. The zoo is renowned for its collection of snakes and primates.

Mimaland, 18 kilometres (11 miles) north of the city, may not appeal to everyone, but children love it. There is a huge free-form swimming pool fed by mountain streams, landscaped with lotus ponds and surmounted by a Big Splash. A mini-zoo, roller-skating rink, tennis courts and a lake for boating provide plenty of activities. Accommodation is available in native-style houses built on stilts over a lake, in chalets or in a lakeside motel. The park has several restaurants. A direct bus service leaves at regular intervals from the ENE Plaza off Jalan Pudu. Mimaland is open from 9 am to 10 pm.

Genting Highlands, a hill resort which boasts Malaysia's only casino, is another 40 minutes' drive from Mimaland. Genting can also be reached directly from KL by helicopter in ten minutes. At an altitude of 1,828 metres (6,000 feet), travellers can try their luck at roulette and blackjack, keno or tai sai. However, if you are looking for peace and quiet there are other more suitable hill resorts, as Genting is rather ugly, brash and commercial. There are hotels, a man-made lake, an indoor heated pool, tennis and squash courts, and a cable car which drops from the casino to a golf club.

Fraser's Hill, or Bukit Fraser, 101 kilometres (63 miles) northeast of the city, is a quiet hill retreat that still has a colonial air about it. Built on seven hills 1,524 metres (5,000 feet) above sea level, the resort is named after its first European resident, Louis James Fraser, a mule skinner who ran a gambling shack and traded in tin and opium. English colonials found it a pleasantly cool retreat from the humid lowlands and their greystone bungalows adorned with rose gardens still dot the hilltop resort. Fraser's Hill has one of the few public golf courses in the country. Green fees are only M$8 per weekday and $12 on weekends. Bicycles can be hired at the Merlin Hotel and there are public tennis courts. At the **Jeriau Waterfall** is a natural swimming pool in a jungle setting. Many jungle trails surround the hills and climb the surrounding peaks. 'The Tavern', a colonial-style restaurant, is a favourite spot to gather after dark around the roaring log fire. Fraser's Hill Development Corporation runs chalets and bungalows and there is an international-standard hotel. It is rather difficult to get to Fraser's Hill without a car. One way is to travel to **Kuala Kubu Baru** by rail or road, from where buses and taxis run to Fraser's Hill. The last eight kilometres (five miles) from the Gap Road to the resort are along a narrow winding road which works on a one-way system open for 40 minutes in each direction. The road from the coast to Fraser's Hill is a winding jungle road which gives a marvellous vista of jungle-clad hills.

Selangor State Mosque — Masjid Sultan Salahuddin is Malaysia's newest and most spectacular mosque. Situated at the Selangor state capital of **Shah Alam**, halfway between Kuala Lumpur and Klang, the mosque is Southeast Asia's largest and was completed in 1988. Its shimmering blue dome is an imposing 91 metres (300 feet) high and 52 metres (170 feet) in diameter, making it the largest dome in the world. Four blue and white minarets soar 137 metres (450 feet) above the complex, which cost M$160 million. The mosque can accommodate 20,000 worshippers and the entire structure is decorated with coloured glass grilles of traditional Islamic geometric patterns. At night the Main Prayer Hall is lit with four giant chandeliers, and during the month of Ramadan the entire mosque is floodlit at night, creating marvellous reflections in the adjoining lake.

The **Orang Asli Museum**, 25 kilometres (15 miles) north of Kuala Lumpur on the Gombak Road, preserves the traditions of Malaysia's *orang asli*, the 'original people'. There are around 70,000 *orang asli* in peninsular Malaysia, split into some 18 tribes who have been living here since the dawn of time. The museum was set up to preserve their arts and crafts and traditions before they are lost in the inevitable march of progress. Displays depict the different tribes and where they live and there are miniature models of their various homes. Baskets, fish traps, blowpipes, musical instruments and beautifully carved ornaments are amongst the items displayed. Two of the *orang asli* tribes, the Mah Meri and the Jay Hut, are renowned for their wood-carvings, and there is a section devoted to their work. Crafts are on sale at the handicrafts shop at the museum.

Carey Island, where most of the Mah Meri carvers live, is a two-hour drive from Kuala Lumpur. Take the highway to Klang and turn south towards Port Dickson, then turn off to Kampung Sungai Bumbun. Expatriates from Kuala Lumpur drive out here to order custom-made wood-carvings. One popular carving is 'tiger in chains', which is based on the legend of a tiger which fell into a pig trap. The carvers have a battered volume of anthropologist Werner's compilation of *orang asli* carvings which fulfils the function of a sales catalogue. Wood-carving contributes to the welfare of the *orang asli* whilst keeping alive their traditional crafts.

Port Dickson, a popular stretch of coast on the Malacca Straits, is 96 kilometres (60 miles) from Kuala Lumpur. It is the best and closest beach to Kuala Lumpur and is popular with the weekend crowd. If you are not planning to visit the east coast and its superior beaches, Port Dickson is a reasonable compromise. The fastest way to get there is to take the tollway to Seremban and turn off on the Port Dickson turnoff.

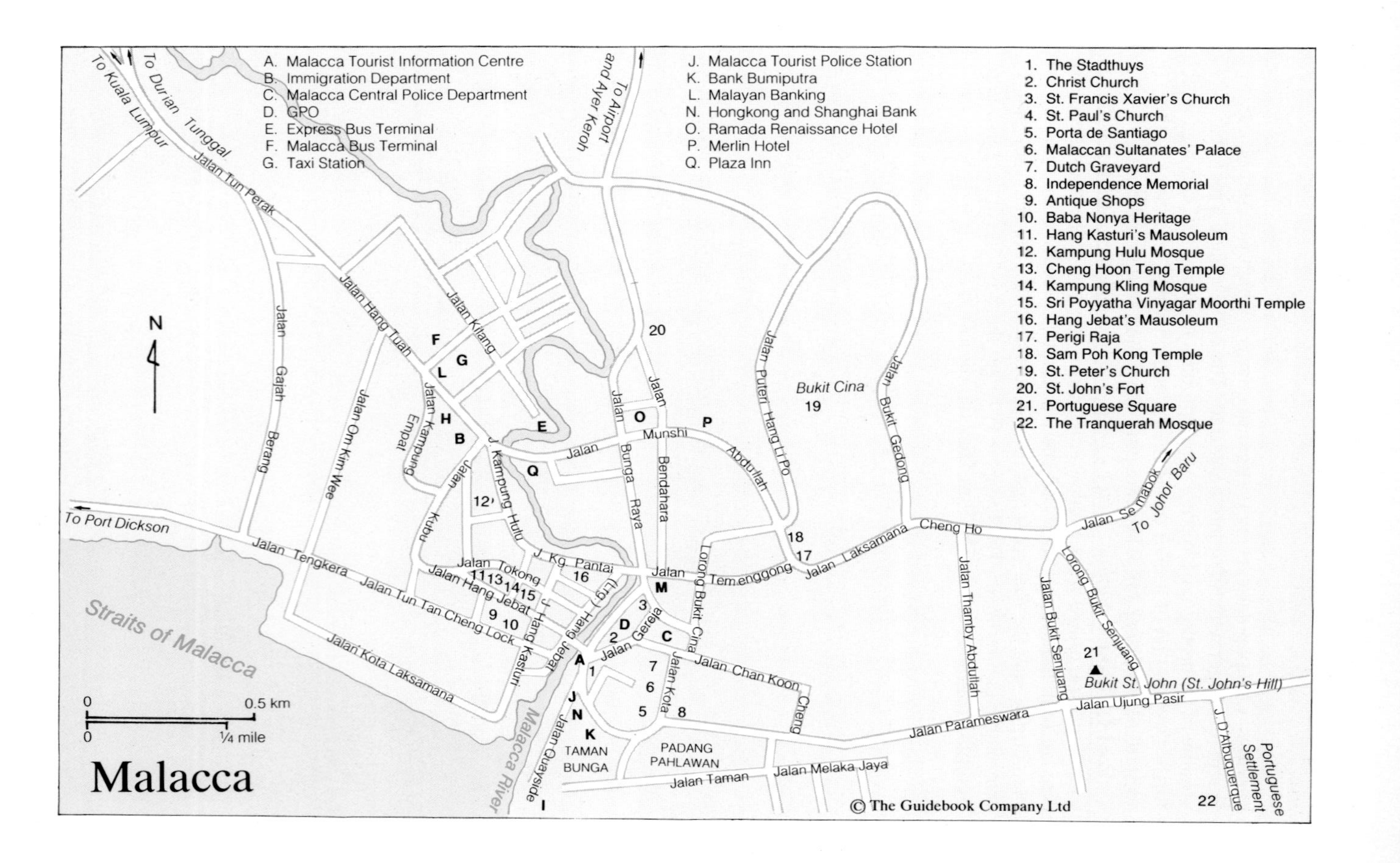
Malacca
A. Malacca Tourist Information Centre
B. Immigration Department
C. Malacca Central Police Department
D. GPO
E. Express Bus Terminal
F. Malacca Bus Terminal
G. Taxi Station
J. Malacca Tourist Police Station
K. Bank Bumiputra
L. Malayan Banking
N. Hongkong and Shanghai Bank
O. Ramada Renaissance Hotel
P. Merlin Hotel
Q. Plaza Inn
1. The Stadthuys
2. Christ Church
3. St. Francis Xavier's Church
4. St. Paul's Church
5. Porta de Santiago
6. Malaccan Sultanates' Palace
7. Dutch Graveyard
8. Independence Memorial
9. Antique Shops
10. Baba Nonya Heritage
11. Hang Kasturi's Mausoleum
12. Kampung Hulu Mosque
13. Cheng Hoon Teng Temple
14. Kampung Kling Mosque
15. Sri Poyyatha Vinyagar Moorthi Temple
16. Hang Jebat's Mausoleum
17. Perigi Raja
18. Sam Poh Kong Temple
19. St. Peter's Church
20. St. John's Fort
21. Portuguese Square
22. The Tranquerah Mosque
To Kuala Lumpur
To Durian Tunggal
Jalan Tun Perak
To Airport and Ayer Keroh
To Port Dickson
To Johor Baru
Jalan Hang Tuah
Jalan Kitang
Jalan Gajah Berang
Jalan Om Kim Wee
Jalan Kampung Empat
Jalan Kubu
J. Kampung Hulu
Jalan Munshi Abdullah
Jalan Bunga Raya
Jalan Bendahara
Jalan Puteri Hang Li Po
Jalan Bukit Gedong
Bukit Cina
Cheng Ho
Jalan Laksamana
Jalan Temenggong
Lorong Bukit Cina
Jalan Tengkera
Jalan Tun Tan Cheng Lock
Jalan Tokong
Jalan Hang Jebat
J. Kg. Pantai
(Lrg.) Hang Jebat
J. Hang Kasturi
Jalan Kota Laksamana
Jalan Gereja
Jalan Chan Koon Cheng
Jalan Kota
Jalan Quayside
Malacca River
Straits of Malacca
TAMAN BUNGA
PADANG PAHLAWAN
Jalan Taman
Jalan Melaka Jaya
Jalan Parameswara
Jalan Thamby Abdullah
Jalan Bukit Senjuang
Lorong Bukit Senjuang
Jalan Semabok
Jalan Ujung Pasir
Bukit St. John (St. John's Hill)
J. D'Albuquerque
Portuguese Settlement
N
0 0.5 km
0 ¼ mile
© The Guidebook Company Ltd

Malacca and the Southwest

Isabella Bird, the intrepid Victorian traveller who visited Malacca in 1879, remarked in her book *The Golden Chersonese*, 'Malacca fascinates me more and more daily. There is, among other things, a medievalism about it. The noise of the modern world reaches it only in the faintest echoes.'

Progress, of course, caught up with the town long ago, but the medievalism that so fascinated Isabella Bird lingers even now in the heart of the old port town and reaches out into the surrounding countryside.

Malacca is unique amongst Malaysian towns in that it has experienced all the major phases of the nation's history. Ruled in turn by the majestic Malaccan Sultanate, the spice-hungry Portuguese, the grim Dutch reformists, the colonial English and the occupying Japanese, the city finally reverted to Malay rule in 1957 after almost four-and-a-half centuries of foreign domination. Malacca is a kaleidoscope of Malaysian history: the old port on the river still bustles with fishing craft and the narrow lanes of old Chinatown still harbour traditional family businesses and ancient temples. Stalwart Dutch 17th-century buildings, romantic Portuguese 16th-century ruins and some of the nation's oldest mosques are found here. The countryside surrounding the town is one of the nation's most picturesque regions. Green paddy-fields surround wooden houses built on stilts and shaded by coconut groves. Bullock carts amble along the beachfront where fishermen sit mending nets in the shade, and out on the placid Malacca Straits an Indonesian sailing *perahu* drifts along like a phantom from the past.

From its beginnings Malacca has been a most cosmopolitan place. A Portuguese chronicler of the 16th century remarked that 84 languages were heard on the streets of the town. Today the region is still multicultural; apart from the large Malay, Chinese and Indian populations, there are a number of fascinating minority groups, including the Portugese Eurasians (descendants of the early Portuguese settlers), the *baba* and *nonya* (Malaysianized Chinese), and the Chitty Indians, who are descended from the early Indian traders. As a result of this multicultural and multi-religious community, the festival calendar is crammed with events. With a little luck, travellers may find that their visit coincides with the Easter candlelit processions at St Peter's, the Pesta Datuk Chachar of the Chitty Indians, the Malays' Hari Raya or the week-long festivities of the Chinese New Year.

The Journey South

Since the opening of the tollway (Lebuhraya) from Kuala Lumpur to Ayer Keroh near Malacca, the trip from the capital to Malacca has been shortened considerably. For those with limited time, the new highway is a boon, but the journey is somewhat lacking in interest as the tollway traverses mainly rubber and oil-palm estates and misses all the picturesque *kampung* (villages) and small Chinese-style towns along the way. If your time is not so limited, it is worthwhile to drive south along the tollway (follow the *selatan*, meaning 'south', signs) from Kuala Lumpur to the Seremban exit. From Seremban the inquisitive traveller can drive to Malacca along smaller country roads. Note that Malacca appears on all maps and signs as 'Melaka', this being the spelling in Bahasa Malaysian.

Seremban is a picturesque town set amongst hills 66 kilometres (41 miles) from Kuala Lumpur. It is the capital of **Negri Sembilan** state, which means 'nine states' (the nine states under different Malay rulers federated in 1773). Seremban is essentially a colonial town dating from the late 19th century. Chinese shophouses interspersed with Victorian public buildings line the main street of this town, which owes its existence to the tin-mining boom. Negri Sembilan's population has its origins in the matriarchal Minangkabau of Sumatra, who settled here during the 16th-century Malaccan Sultanate. Minangkabau, loosely translated, means 'buffalo horns', and their distinctive architecture, found all over the state, uses this symbol in the upswept roof design.

The **Istana Ampang Tinggi**, an old palace in Seremban, is an excellent example of this design. Once the residence of a Malay prince, the wooden palace was transported from its original site and reconstructed in Seremban. Set on stilts, the building displays some fine wood-carvings of the 19th century.

A rewarding trip into the Negri Sembilan interior can be made by following the road to Kuala Pilah, 37 kilometres (23 miles) due east of Seremban. About eight kilometres (five miles) before Kuala Pilah, turn off to **Sri Menanti**, the royal capital, another ten kilometres (six miles) further on. Here is the remarkable traditional-style palace of the Yang di-Pertuan Besar, possibly the best surviving example of Minangkabau architecture. Wooden shingles cover the upswept roofs of this elaborately-carved palace which is now a museum.

Also along the Kuala Pilah road are **megaliths**, upraised stones of mysterious origin, which also occur at Pengkalan Kempas on the Port Dickson–Malacca road and throughout Malacca state. Known to the Malays as *batu hidup* (living stones), these huge hand-hewn stones dating from the Stone Age are believed to be still growing. They are similar to monoliths of the same antiquity in Europe. From Seri Menanti, the road winds through Negri Sembilan to Tampin, on the border of Malacca state. Malacca town is 37 kilometres (23 miles) from here.

Background

Malacca is Malaysia's oldest town and the site of the classical empire of the Malays. Founded in around 1400 by Parameswara, a fugitive Sumatran prince, Malacca in the course of only 100 years became the greatest trading port of the region and the centre of the vast Malay world. Situated on the Straits of Malacca, halfway down the west coast of the peninsula, the port was ideally placed at the crossroads of the monsoons. Merchants from Arabia and India came across the Bay of Bengal on the southwest wind, and the traders of China and the Spice Islands sailed down on the northeast monsoon. Malacca became an entrepôt, where spices, scented woods and jungle exotica were exchanged for Indian textiles, and porcelains, silks and metalware from China. Dominant among the traders were the Muslim Indians, wealthy and respected traders whose religion commanded considerable prestige in the region. When Parameswara converted to Islam he became the first sultan of Malacca.

Overlooking the harbour, on the hill now known as St Paul's, the sultans and their court enjoyed a life of medieval opulence, residing in gilded palaces, borne aloft on silk-caparisoned elephants, seated on golden thrones and waited on by hundreds of beautiful slave girls. Sultan Mansur Shah's reign (1459–77) marked the pinnacle of Malay power and culture. Legendary happenings, intrigues, scandals and the exploits of Hang Tuah, Hang Jebat and Hang Kasturi (the three musketeers of Malay history) enlivened these golden days of the Malaccan Sultanate.

By the end of the 15th century Malacca was, in the words of a Portuguese historian, 'the richest sea port with the greatest abundance of shipping that can be found in the whole world.' Tales of the 'wonderous Golden Khersonese' and the 'city where the winds meet' were heard by the Portuguese, who were lusting to overtake Arab domination of the spice trade. After an abortive first attack on the city in 1509 the Portuguese were forced to retreat, but they returned in full force two years later under the command of Alfonso de Albuquerque, the Governor of Portuguese India. Their timing was perfect, for the Malaccan Sultanate was in chaos under Sultan Mahmud who had executed his *Bendahara* (Prime Minister) on suspicion of treachery and had lost the support of the *orang laut*, the sea tribes vital for a naval battle. Although the Malays fought furiously, led by Mahmud on his war elephant, they were overcome and forced to flee south to Johor. Initially trade flourished under the Portuguese, but their zealous crusading for the cross alienated the wealthy Muslim traders who defected to Sumatran ports. From their massive stone fortress, 'A Famosa', the Portuguese ruled Malacca for 130 years, constantly warding off attacks by the Malays and others who on several occasions blockaded the harbour and brought the city to the brink of starvation. The Portuguese retaliated by burning the Johor capital in 1587.

MELAKA
JALAN LAKSAMANA

When the Dutch attacked Malacca in 1640 the Malays assisted them. After a five-month siege which left thousands dead of malaria and dysentery, the Portuguese were forced to surrender. The victory was bittersweet, for Malacca was ruined. Countless wars had decimated the population and traders had sought greener pastures elsewhere. The Dutch proceeded to rebuild Malacca in the image of a Dutch trading town, but they kept the town subordinate to their capital Batavia (Jakarta).

The English were Malacca's next caretakers and, except for a brief period from 1814 to 1824 when it was restored to the Dutch, they ruled until Independence. Under the British, Malacca remained an economic backwater, overshadowed by Penang and Singapore. However, later in the century, wealthy Chinese and English planters started growing rubber and the town's fortunes revived. Tan Chay Yan planted the first rubber garden on the outskirts of Malacca in 1895; 20 years later Malaysia was producing over half the world's rubber. The Japanese Occupation during the Second World War irretrievably damaged the English colonial scene, and nationalism made its appearance after the war. In 1956, on his return from England, Tunku Abdul Rahman, later to become Malaysia's first Prime Minister, chose to deliver the news of his successful negotiations for independence in Malacca. Cries of *merdeka* (independence) were first heard on the Padang, the playing fields opposite historic St Paul's Hill. On 31 August 1957 the last British Resident of Malacca stepped down and the Malays resumed control.

City Sights and Walks

Wherever you wander in Malacca there is always some new corner awaiting discovery in the town's old and mystery-filled streets. Historic sites, mosques, temples, traditional family businesses, markets, food stalls and all the bustle expected of such an old port town can be found here.

Historic Sites Walk

Many of Malacca's important historic spots are all within the old part of the town and can easily be visited on foot. An alternative is to take a trishaw ride, which is slow enough for you to absorb the city's sights and sounds. Trishaws can be picked up in the **Town Square** beside the river, or anywhere in the downtown area. Trishaw drivers are often self-proclaimed tourist guides, providing an interesting tour peppered with a lively narration.

The **Malacca River Bridge** on Jalan Hang Jebat is a fitting place to begin the walk, for this is where it all began back in the 14th century. The present bridge, which replaced an older wooden one built last century, is the site of the original bridge that Sultan Mahmud lost to the Portuguese. Indonesian sailing *perahu* and wooden barges crowd the nearby docks where Sumatran seamen still carry on a brisk barter trade, much the same as in Malacca's historic past.

The **Stadthuys**, one of the oldest surviving Dutch buildings in the east, dominates the town square by the river which is also known as the Red Square because of the terracotta colour of the old surrounding buildings. Once the home of the Dutch governors, it was built between 1641 and 1660 utilizing the foundations of the Portuguese fort. It is now the **Musium Sejarah** (Historical Museum) and houses artifacts from every era of Malacca's colourful past, including Dutch sideboards, *nonya* wedding costumes, and porcelains and coins dating from the Malaccan Sultanate.

Christ Church, on the left of the square, is the oldest Protestant Church in Malaysia, built by the Dutch between 1741 and 1763. Red bricks were specially shipped from Holland for its construction. Huge rafters in the nave, measuring 15 metres (48 feet) in length, were each carved from a single tree. Sunday worshippers still use the original pews. The church, whose records date back to 1641, houses a fine collection of silver-plate.

In the centre of the square is the **Tan Beng Swee Clock Tower**, built by a wealthy *baba* family in 1886. Beside the tinkling waters of the **Queen Victoria Jubilee Fountain**, trishaw drivers await customers, an Indian drink-seller serves refreshing *cendol*, a local drink, and outdoor clerks pound away on battered typewriters.

Porta de Santiago (Santiago Gate), the only remaining ruin of the 16th-century Portuguese fortress 'A Famosa', is on Jalan Kota at the base of St Paul's Hill. Originally the fort covered the entire hill and housed the Portuguese nobility. Within its massive stone walls were five churches, two hospitals, and administrative buildings. Porta de Santiago was restored by the Dutch after their bombardment of the fortress and the date 1670, together with the Dutch East India Company's coat of arms, was added. 'A Famosa' fortress appears on many old etchings and engravings. It survived fairly intact until the British decided to destroy it so as to prevent it from falling back into Dutch hands. The timely arrival of Stamford Raffles, the founder of modern Singapore, halted the destruction, but only in time to save one gate. Munshi Abdullah, a famous Malay writer, bemoaned its passing: 'The fort was the pride of Malacca and after its destruction the place lost its glory, like a woman bereaved of her husband, the lustre gone from her face.'

St Paul's Church, atop the hill of the same name, overlooks the old section of Malacca — a sea of low red-tiled roofs along a maze of narrow streets. Originally the church was the site of the palace of the Malaccan sultans and was built using stones from earlier buildings. Built by the Portuguese in 1521, the church was known as 'Nossa Senhora da Annunciada' (Our Lady of the Anunciation). Inside the roofless church are 36 granite headstones dating from the Dutch colonial times when the church was renamed St Paul's. An empty vault in the centre of the church once contained the body of St Francis Xavier, who died off the coast of China in 1552. Apparently in 1614, when the Pope requested the right arm of the saint to be severed from his corpse and sent to Rome, blood gushed from the wound even though he had been dead for 62 years. St Francis visited Malacca four times and the town abounds with legends of his doings. In 1953 a marble statue of the saint was erected on St Paul's Hill. One quiet night a huge tree fell, burying the statue; when the branches were cleared away the statue was intact except for the right arm which had broken off. The statue of St Francis Xavier, minus one arm, stands in front of the church tower.

The **Proclamation of Independence Memorial**, once the Malacca Club, stands directly opposite Porta de Santiago. Known as 'The Town House', the old colonial building topped with onion-shaped domes was once the hub of social life for the English colonials. Somerset Maugham, the famous English novelist, visited the club and used it as the setting for one of his tales in *Malayan Short Stories*. Today it houses a permanent exhibition relating the story of Independence.

Malaccan Sultanates' Palace, located at the base of St Paul's Hill, is the superb reconstruction of Sultan Mansur Shah's 15th-century *istana* (palace). Built in 1985 using traditional methods of construction and Malaysian hardwood, it is the biggest wooden palace in Southeast Asia. It was reconstructed from written accounts in the *Sejarah Melayu*, the classical history of Malacca's golden age. According to this text, the *istana* was the finest royal palace in the world but was destroyed by lightning in around 1460. Although the roof is of wooden shingles, not metal as in the original, the reconstructed palace is a magnificent example of traditional Malay architecture and wood-carving. It houses the collection of the Malaccan Sultanates and an Islamic museum.

A **Protestant Cemetery** dating from Dutch times is a little further down from the *istana* and contains many interesting gold headstones from the Dutch and English colonial eras. The walk back along Jalan Gereja takes you past the back buildings of the Stadthuys, where massive terracotta walls front the curving street.

Chinatown Stroll

Opposite the Town Square, on the other side of the river, is the start of Chinatown. The faded stucco walls of centuries-old shophouses line the riverbank where, in the heyday of this old port town, merchants and traders ran the bazaars and filled their warehouses with oriental exotica. Interspersed between the temples and historic sites, blacksmiths, goldsmiths, basket-makers, coffin-makers, kite-makers and others still carry on their businesses in tiny shopfronts along the narrow streets, making a stroll through Chinatown a memorable experience.

Jalan Tun Tan Cheng Lock, the ancestral home of Malacca's unique Straits-born Chinese, the *baba* and *nonya*, is the one-way street that runs off the bridge. Lined with Chinese-style townhouses, it was known as 'Millionaires Row' when the street came to prominence during the rubber boom at the turn of the century. Many houses date from 18th-century Dutch times, and others were specially contracted and built by immigrant craftsmen from China in the 19th century. Footways lined with ornamental tiles, carved and gilded teak swing-doors, and decorations of porcelain dragons and flowers bedeck the exterior of these houses. At one time, the only way to see the interior of these houses was to know a *baba* family, but now one of the most opulent homes has been converted into a museum.

The **Baba Nonya Heritage**, at 50 Jalan Tun Tan Cheng Lock, offers a rare look into the unique lifestyle of the Straits-born Chinese. The house was built in 1896 by the millionaire rubber planter Chang Cheng Siew and is elaborately decorated in the flamboyant Straits-Chinese style — a fusion of High Victorian, Chinese and the tropics. At least 30 metres (100 feet) deep and two storeys high, the house contains four airwells which open to the sky, lighting up the interior and providing ventilation. Every surface of the interior is either gilded, carved, inlaid, lacquered or embroidered. A huge panelled screen, intricately carved and gilded, separates the main hall from the *tian gelap*, the room where young unmarried women could peer out at male guests. A magnificent teak staircase, gleaming with gold leaf, winds upstairs,

and gilded dragons coil up the sides of the ornate ancestral altar. William Chan, whose ancestors built the house, gives tours through his family home three times daily at a cost of M$7 per person.

The **Chee Family Mansion** is another unusual *baba* palatial home. Set back from the street, further down Jalan Tun Tan Cheng Lock, it is a private mansion still occupied by descendants of Chee Yam Chuan, the founder of the Overseas Banking Corporation. An eccentric and unusual blend of Dutch, Portuguese, Chinese and English styles, the mansion is crowned by a tower on the roof, which was for many years the highest structure in Chinatown. Beside the front driveway is an old breadfruit (*nangka*) tree, heavy with the pendulous tropical fruit.

Cheng Hoon Teng Temple, translated as the 'Abode of the Green Merciful Clouds', is the oldest Chinese temple in Malaysia. Situated in Jalan Tokong, the temple has been the centre of Chinese religion and culture in Malacca for more than 300 years. It was founded in 1645 by Li Kup, a political refugee who fled from China to escape the Manchus. The temple is built in the southern Chinese architectural style, which traditionally placed a great deal of emphasis on the design and embellishment of the roof. The tiled roofs are heavily decorated with mythological characters, and the flowers and birds made of coloured glass and porcelain are still bright after centuries of tropical sunlight. Devotees shake the I Ching fortune-sticks, light joss-sticks and place offerings before Kwan Yin, the Goddess of Mercy, to whom the temple is primarily dedicated. Cast in solid bronze, the image of the goddess was brought from India during Victorian times, and oddly enough it looks rather like the colonial queen herself.

Kampung Keling Mosque is a little further up the road at the corner of Jalan Tukang Emas and Jalan Lekiu. Built in 1748, this elegant mosque has a three-tiered roof and an unusual pagoda-style minaret. Dominating the white-tiled prayer hall is a huge Victorian chandelier. Dutch religious control relaxed during the mid-18th century and many of Malacca's most beautiful mosques were built during that period.

Sri Poyyatha Vinyagar Moorthi, the oldest Hindu temple in Malaysia, is just a few doors further down Jalan Tukang Emas. Built in 1781, the temple's main festival is the Masi Magam, held on the full moon in late February or early March. The statue of Lord Subramaniam is taken from the temple in a chariot to the Nagarathar Temple in Cheng on the outskirts of Malacca. Devotees carrying *kavadis* parade around the temple. After dark, the chariot returns to the Sri Poyyatha Vinyagar Moorthi.

Jalan Hang Jebat, formerly known as Jonkers Street, is one of the busiest thoroughfares of Chinatown and the antique centre of Malacca. Wares from 300 years of history crowd the many shops along this ancient street. Some establishments specialize in *nonya* porcelain, Malaccan-style 'red and gold' carved furniture, wooden opium beds, and blackwood furniture inlaid with mother-of-pearl. Goldsmiths display a glittering variety of Straits-Chinese silver, and in the dark recesses of junk shops it is still possible to discover the odd bargain. Some of the older businesses started collecting antiques during the Depression when the price of rubber plummeted, forcing the wealthy *baba* to sell their family heirlooms. When shopping here, don't hesitate to bargain as it is expected.

Trishaw Tours

Below is a list of sights which are a little further afield but still within the city area. These locations are best seen by hiring a trishaw for a few hours as the bus system is often overcrowded and confusing for a newcomer to Malacca.

Bukit Cina (Chinese Hill) fronts the main roads of Jalan Munshi Abdullah and Jalan Laksamana Cheng Ho. Covering 42 hectares (104 acres), the hill contains the oldest and largest Chinese graveyard (12,500 graves) outside mainland China. In the early morning and late afternoon, joggers descend upon the hill from the steps on Jalan Puteri Hang Li Poh. A well-marked path winds up and down for about three kilometres (1.8 miles), passing graves dating back to the Ming Dynasty and some huge horseshoe-shaped tombs of the Kapitan Cinas, heads of the Chinese community in colonial times. Two 15th-century Malay rulers are buried on Bukit Temperong Plain and several old *keramat,* sacred Muslim graves, are found on the northeastern foot of the hill. On the eastern side of the summit, look out for some unmarked flat stones which once formed part of the Madre de Dios, a Franciscan Monastery built in 1581 by the Portuguese. From the top, the view is magnificent — a full-circle panorama of Malacca.

Sam Poh Kong, the Chinese temple dedicated to Admiral Cheng Ho, the Muslim admiral of the Ming fleet who sailed to Malacca in the 15th century, is situated at the foot of Bukit Cina at the junction of Jalan Munshi Abdullah and Jalan Puteri Hang Li Poh. The brilliant red, gold and white temple was originally built as a place of worship for those who had relatives buried on Bukit Cina. Outside, a huge gnarled tree shades souvenir stalls and, inside, old women in *samfu*, the traditional Chinese pantsuit, sit on carved blackwood chairs, listening to Chinese opera on the radio and selling incense sticks and paper for offerings.

Perigi Rajah (The Sultan's Well) is located at the foot of Bukit Cina, next to the Sam Poh Kong Temple. It is said to have been constructed in Sultan Mansur Shah's reign (1459–88), apparently for the Chinese princess Hang Lih Poh and her entourage during their residence at Bukit Cina. Legend has it that during one of his visits to Malacca, Admiral Cheng Ho of the Imperial Chinese fleet, who was said to possess saintly powers, drank from the well. Its importance as a freshwater supply for early Malacca can be gauged by the Dutch-built fortifications around the well.

The **Portuguese Settlement** (Medan Portugis) is about three kilometres (1.8 miles) south of Malacca town along Jalan Parameswara. This unique settlement is the home of the descendants of those early Portuguese who ruled Malacca over 300 years ago. Although it may look like any other *kampung*, it has a distinctly Latin flavour. Easter, Christmas and the Festa de San Pedro, held each year on 29 July in honour of the patron saint of fishermen, are the best times to visit the settlement as the Portuguese Eurasians throw 'open house' and are famed for their hospitality. On weekends, Malaccans and tourists alike flock to the Portuguese Square, or 'Medan', on Jalan Albuquerque where outdoor cultural shows are often performed featuring traditional songs and dances, including the famous *branyo* in which everyone participates. Also in the square beside the Malacca Straits are outdoor restaurants which serve Portuguese-style seafood and are open to the wee hours. This is a favourite after-dark venue for Malaccans.

St John's Fort is the only remaining Dutch fort in Malacca. Atop a hill on Jalan Bukit Senjuang, the white-walled bastion built in the early 18th century provides a sweeping view of the city and the Malacca Straits. Legend has it that a secret tunnel connects St John's Fort with Porta de Santiago about 1.5 kilometres (a mile) away. Apparently, so the story goes, the Dutch built the tunnel while they were repairing the Santiago Gate, the rationale for such a claim being the inordinate length of time that the repairs took — over 20 years, whereas the Stadthuys took only 19 years to build. Also, so the tale goes, the existence of the tunnel was known to Raffles, hence his order to save the gate. However, it remains undiscovered to this day.

St Peter's Church is the traditional place of worship for the Portuguese Malaccans. Built in 1710, it is the oldest Catholic church in use in Malaysia. Easter is celebrated with pomp and tradition dating back to 1587 when the first Augustinian fathers arrived in Malacca. On Palm Sunday and Good Friday the mass culminates in a huge candlelit procession when a life-sized statue of Christ is borne in procession around the grounds of the church.

Out-of-town Drives

Surrounding the town of Malacca are some of the most picturesque rural scenes to be found in Malaysia. Amongst coconut groves and rice paddies are traditional Malay *kampung* homes set on stilts, with long shuttered windows that open generously to the breeze. In this region are many of the best examples of traditional architecture in the country.

The **drive north** to Tanjung Bidara, a good swimming beach 35 kilometres (21 miles) north of Malacca, takes the traveller past idyllic rural scenes, fishing villages, and some historic sites before finishing up with a pleasant swim. From the Malacca River bridge, follow the one-way Jalan Tun Tan Cheng Lock which turns into Jalan Tengkera, lined with old ornamental

Kampung — Village Life

Hidden in Malaysia's green heart are the villages or *kampung*, hamlets of tradition often untouched by the mainstream of progress. Away from the highway, along the red dirt roads where palm fronds almost touch overhead, gaudy turquoise kingfishers dive into canals and a feathery mist rises in the early morning air. The *kampung* is another world, far from the noise and bustle that characterize the towns and cities.

Here life goes on in a gentle, traditional way, and from the beating of the drum before dawn, to the evening prayer, Islam — a way of life— pervades all. While the sun is still a faint glow in the east, the musical thud and chink of mortars and pestles echoes through the *kampung* as wives pound the spices that flavour the breakfast rice. Radios crackle with news or current hits, but in the traditional households unmarried girls don't sing along with the tunes, for singing in the kitchen is taboo — they may have difficulty in finding a husband.

Kenduri — the Malay feasts held to celebrate weddings or auspicious occasions such as the *potong jambul* (the baby's first hair-cutting), the *sunat* (or circumcision ceremony) and many others — are always a good excuse for a get-together. For a wedding celebration, out-of-town relatives arrive days beforehand to help with the preparations, and all over the vast kitchen floors women sit peeling, cutting, chatting and laughing. Mounds of pineapples are reduced to slices, cucumbers are slivered for pickles, and chillies and more chillies are pounded and sliced to garnish almost every dish in the Malay cuisine. Outside, the fires are lit, and the men gather to help the *kenduri* chef (always male) who presides over the cooking of the *nasi minyak*, a rich spicy rice dish, and the curries that form the basis of the feast. Huge cauldrons are brought out of storage, glassware and crockery are unpacked (or borrowed from neighbours for a big event), furniture is stacked away, and woven *pandanus* mats are spread on the floor to accommodate the often hundreds of guests.

At a wedding, when all is prepared, the Javanese *kompang* players roll their drums and the bride and groom, resplendent in traditional *kain songket* — a silk brocade woven with silver thread — mount the bridal dais, and the *bersanding*, a remnant of the 12th-century Hindu court of Srivijaya, begins. Arrayed before them are traditional gifts displayed in modern fashion: new shoes on a silver platter, silver paper flowers in a vase made of bathtowels, toothbrush and deodorant surrounded by quail's eggs in pink satin ribbons. *Bunga rampai*, flower petals mixed with aromatic thinly-shredded leaves, are showered on the hands of the couple. Henna is smeared on their palms and *air mawar*, rose water, is sprinkled over them to ensure good luck in their married life. The formalities over, the guests and relatives get down to the real business of eating, which lasts until evening, when satiated with food they head off home to their own *kampung*.

Everyone hurries home before sunset, an hour that brings all village folk indoors, for even before the Malays converted to Islam and the hour became sacred for prayer, sunset was a time when the malingering yellow spirits of the west were lurking, their livers acid from the bilious glow and ready to harm anyone they found alone. *Mata hari*, the sun (literally 'the eye of the day'), slips behind the oil palms, over the mosque and across the Indian Ocean to Mecca. 'Allahu Akbar', 'God is Great', echoes from the mosque, and another day in the *kampung* has ended for sunset, not midnight, is the end of the day for Malays.

Kampung Tanjung

Chinese shophouses. **Tengkera Mosque** is on the right. Built in the Sumatran style, this 18th-century mosque is distinguished by a three-tiered roof and a pagoda-like minaret. In the grounds of the mosque is the tomb of Sultan Hussein Shah of Johor who signed over Singapore to Raffles in 1819.

Continue north on this same road which becomes Jalan Klebang. Along the seafront are old Chinese mansions, originally owned by rich *baba*. Some, in ruins, are thought to be haunted, but many others are still beautifully maintained. At **Klebang Besar** beachfront, Malay food stalls offer delicious cold fruit juices and *ayam percik*, barbecued chicken in peanut sauce.

About ten kilometres (six miles) from town take the left turn at the yellow **Tanjung Kling Mosque**, another historic mosque with an unusual octagonal minaret. A little further on down the road is an old Muslim graveyard overlooking the sea where **Hang Tuah**, the legendary 15th-century warrior, is said to be buried. From here the road leads to the seafront at **Pantai Kundor**. Picturesque Malay *kampung* homes, shaded by coconut palms, overlook the Straits of Malacca. Shrimp paste, known as *belacan*, is dried here on racks in the sun. The beach is lined with *atap* thatched-roof chalets which offer cheap accommodation for budget travellers. Pantai Kundor is a fishing village and if you are lucky to arrive when the boats have returned you can buy fresh fish, crabs, and stingray from the fish market on the beachfront. Fishermen mend their nets on the beach and have their hair cut in the thatched hut that serves as a seaside barber's shop. In the evening, when the sun sets behind the offshore fishtraps, the local men arrive on their bicycles with their *langgiang*, a shrimp net on a long pole. Just after the sun has set, the men push their nets through the shallow waters illuminated by their headlamps which resemble miners' lights.

At the Pantai Kundor sign, turn right to join up with the main road north, Jalan Sungai Udang. Here, paddy-fields flank the road and water-buffaloes wallow in the mud — classic scenes of Malay country life. On reaching Masjid Tanah, a large market town, follow the road north and the signs to **Tanjung Bidara Beach** for the best swimming on the straits. The long beach with its rocky outcrops and large shade trees is perfect for a picnic by the sea. Malay food stalls offer cheap local snacks and drinks, or the Tanjung Bidara Beach Resort nearby has a bar and restaurant, tennis courts and swimming pool at five-star prices if you feel inclined to stay overnight. To return to Malacca direct it is only a 30-minute drive if you take the main road south.

The **drive west**, another interesting jaunt from Malacca town, combines a drive through rural villages and rubber and oil-palm plantations with a mountain climb at the end for those who are energetic, or a short stroll through the jungle to a spectacular waterfall.

The legendary **Gunung Ledang**, formerly known as Mount Ophir, is about 50 kilometres (31 miles) from Malacca. Take the road south towards Muar and at Kandang take the right turn to Jasin. Keep an eye out near the

18-kilometre (11-mile) stone on the right for a superb Malaccan-style traditional house. Known as a *rumah serambi*, the house features a steep double-pitched roof tiled in classic terracotta tiles, carved panels on the gables and brilliant blue staircases leading up to the veranda. At **Jasin**, a quaint rural town dominated by old Chinese shophouses, take the road right to **Tangkak**. The countryside opens up here and Gunung Ledang, its peak swathed in cloud, is seen up ahead. Just over the border of Johor state, only five kilometres (three miles) from Tangkak and on the left-hand side of the road, is a bizarre old brick mansion. This crumbling folly looks most incongruous in the Malay countryside. The two-storey ruin contains huge circular columns, a large family crest of two lions embracing a shield and, on the roof, a huge statue of a vulture-like bird with its wings outstretched. Tree roots entwine the walls and ferns drape the bricks of this long-empty rubber planter's home. Local legend has it that the house has been abandoned since the Japanese occupied it during the Second World War.

To reach the mountain of Gunung Ledang, go through Tangkak and take the turnoff to Segamat. At the sign 'Air Terjun' (which means 'waterfall'), turn left and follow the road to the base of the mountain. The path up to the waterfall winds alongside the rocky stream where giant rain forest trees loom overhead. From the top of the falls there is a stunning view of the evergreen countryside. The path deteriorates from here on and the summit climb is recommended only for the very fit. According to legend, there is a secret cave at the peak where the fabulous *puteri*, or guardian princess of the mountain, resides. In the 15th century, Sultan Mansur Shah tried to woo this beautiful princess, who demanded a dowry of seven trays of mosquitoes' hearts, seven trays of mites' hearts, a vat of juice from sapless young areca palms and a cup of the sultan's blood and another of his son's. The sultan managed to assemble this impossible dowry save for the cup of his son's blood, which he did not have the heart to ask for, thus losing the suit. A famous *bomoh*, a Malay medicine man, from the nearby town of Muar swears that he learnt his secret arts from the *puteri* of Gunung Ledang.

Other out-of-town Drives

At **Umbai**, eight kilometres (five miles) south of Malacca, take the turn on the right to the jetty. Across the straits is **Pulau Besar** (The Big Island), offering white sandy beaches, good swimming, and jungle walks. Boats can be chartered from the jetty and overnight accommodation can be arranged in a *kampung* house. Legends abound on the island, which also contains some old and sacred graves. If you don't want to annoy the local spirits it is advisable not to eat pork before making the crossing.

One of Malaysia's most famous traditional homes, the **Merlimau Penghulu's House**, is situated another eight kilometres (five miles) further on, just outside the town of Merlimau. Don't take the turnoff to the town; instead, take the next turn on the right. This ornate Malayan chieftain's house, built in 1894, is still in its original state. An elaborate art nouveau tiled staircase leads to the veranda where the eaves and balustrades are beautifully carved. Set along the veranda walls are built-in wooden couches, painted blue and white, and hat racks made of antler horns.

Other places of interest can be reached by returning along this road towards the town and taking the right-hand road to **Perigi Hang Tuah** (Hang Tuah's Well), four kilometres (2.5 miles) from Malacca. The soul of Hang Tuah, the great court warrior of the 15th-century Malaccan Sultanate, is said to reside here in the form of a white crocodile. Apparently, however, only spiritually enlightened people can glimpse it.

This road leads to **Mini-Malaysia**, a new concept in outdoor museums, featuring 13 different houses from the different states built in the traditional manner. In each house, mannequins portray the different customs and traditions peculiar to that state. In the Melaka (Malacca) house, for example, visitors are given an insight into aspects of a traditional Malay wedding ceremony. In the Perlis house is a 'Hari Raya' scene, with womenfolk preparing cakes and cookies, and in the Perak house a circumcision ceremony is depicted. The architecture in each house is as close to the original as possible, with the Sabah and Sarawak houses being built with bamboo and logs.

South to Johor

Johor, the southernmost state in the peninsula and also one of the most developed, is linked to Singapore by a causeway across the Straits of Johor at Johor Baru, the state capital. From Malacca to Johor Baru is 217 kilometres (135 miles). The road south to Muar winds through *kampung* scenes where traditional Malaccan-style houses are set close to the road which is overhung with coconut palms and fruit trees. If it is fruit season, the road is lined with stalls selling durian, rambutan or *duku*, and many Singaporeans make the drive north just to stock up on fresh fruit.

Muar, a riverine town 42 kilometres (26 miles) from Malacca, has some dignified neo-classical government offices and a superb mosque dating from the reign of Sultan Abu Bakar at the turn of the century.

Batu Pahat, another 50 kilometres (31 miles) south, is a large market town usually bypassed by travellers but which has some of the best eating in Johor. There are plenty of open-air eating stalls beside the river — try the Malay *satay* or the Chinese oyster omelette. From here the southbound traveller can either continue down the coast on a lesser road to **Pontian**, or go inland to **Air Hitam** and the main trunk road south. Although Air Hitam has some interesting pottery kilns south of the town and the market beside the road is well known for its fruit, the road is always crowded with diesel-belching trucks. The Pontian road is slightly longer but is a much more leisurely drive as it passes through fishing villages and coconut and pineapple plantations.

Johor Baru, the bordertown to Singapore, is also the royal residence. Although the outskirts of this growing town are not very attractive, the drive along the shorefront known as 'The Lido' is worth a visit. Atop a hill overlooking the Straits of Johor is the elegant white **Sultan Abu Bakar Mosque,** built in 1892. The cosmopolitan Sultan Abu Bakar made several trips abroad, was received by Queen Victoria and the Emperor of Japan, and was an accomplished polo player. In 1866 he took up residence in the newly named Johor Baru (new Johor), made it the state capital, and built the palatial *istana*, a palace equipped with every European comfort. The *istana* is now a museum housing the priceless royal collection of the Johor Sultanate. Singaporeans flock to Johor Baru to take advantage of the spicier nightlife and the cheaper food and liquor. If you want to take a side trip to Singapore, the city centre is only 27 kilometres (17 miles) away.

Desaru is a 25-kilometre (15-mile) stretch of golden beach, 102 kilometres (63 miles) from Johor Baru. Turn off at Kota Tinggi. There are resort hotels, golf links, tennis courts and water sports at the beach, which is a favourite with Singaporeans.

Traditional Malay Architecture

Totally in harmony with the environment, the traditional Malay house reflects and expresses Malay culture and lifestyle. Basically a timber house, it is raised on stilts with wooden or bamboo walls, many windows and a large, dominant *atap* thatched or tiled roof. Wooden carvings embellish panels, grilles, railings and balustrades, which apart from their aesthetic appeal provide ventilation and light. Chinese merchants remarked on the *bumbung panjang* — the original and most common house form — back in the 15th century, and the hybrids and regional variations of today evolved from this early design.

The **Malacca house** is characterized by a unique tiled staircase leading up to a large open-sided veranda. Courtyards which link the *dapur* (kitchen) with the *rumah ibu* (main house) are found only in Malacca. Many of Malaysia's most beautiful historic homes are found in the Malacca region.

The **Minangkabau house** of Negri Sembilan has unique curved roof-ends, a feature imported from Sumatra by the early Minangkabau settlers. In palaces and chiefs' homes, the doors were purposefully built low so that visitors had to bow in respect upon entering. Unmarried girls used to sleep in the attics, but these days the attics are used as storage space.

The **bumbung Perak**, also known as *bumbung potongan Belanda*, is derived from colonial Dutch houses, and is found in the northwest states, especially Perak. The gambrel roof gives more headroom than the original *bumbung panjang* which was in vogue when the Malays had minimal furniture and sat on the floor. The *bumbung Perak* evolved to accommodate later trends.

The **east coast house** of Kelantan and Terengganu differs from that of the west coast in the common use of tiled roofs with gables showing Thai, Laotian and Kampuchean influence. Columns are larger and there is more headroom and fewer windows. Wall-panelling resembles traditional Thai houses and both the panels and thick framing timbers are well-carved.

The **Selang house**, a variation of the original *bumbung panjang*, is most commonly found in the northern states of Kedah, Perlis, Penang and Perak. The *selang* is a covered walkway used to join different sections of the house, usually the *dapur* (kitchen) with the *rumah ibu* (main house) which is used for sleeping, sewing, praying, and for marriage and festival feasts.

The **Gajah Menyusu house** is so-named because it has the appearance of a baby elephant (the kitchen addition) sucking from its mother (the *rumah ibu*, which literally means 'mother house'). Additions are easily added to the original house as the main roof overlaps the new. These homes are commonly found in the northern states of the west coast.

The Malacca House

Close up of windows on veranda

Bumbung Perak House

Minangkabau House

East Coast House

Gajah Menyusu House

Selang House

Close up of Selang

Penang and the Northwest

Introduction

Up in the northwest where the Indian Ocean meets the Straits of Malacca, close by the border of Thailand, lie some of the most idyllic islands of the tropics. Penang (Pulau Pinang), known as the 'Pearl of the Orient', has a reputation that far outweighs its size; the island is a mere 24 kilometres (15 miles) in length. During the 1960s Penang lay smack in the middle of the 'Hippie Trail', the overland odyssey from Europe to Southeast Asia undertaken by the restless youth of the affluent West. Penang was a resting spot on the 'trail', a place in which to soak up the sun on palm-fringed tropical beaches while recovering from or preparing for the rigours of India.

Patrick Balfour, who travelled here in 1935, remarks in his book *Grand Tour*, 'Here I met people who lived in Penang, as one might live on the Mediterranean, for no other reason but that they liked it. It was the first time since leaving Europe that I had found a place where Europeans lived from choice.' The Penang of both Balfour and the hippies is long gone; today the island leads northern Malaysia in commerce and progress. But the beaches are still the mecca of tourists the world over, and although high-rise luxury hotels loom overhead, the charm of Penang persists. Downtown Georgetown, a sea of red-tiled roofs, turn-of-the-century shophouses, and bazaars, temples and mosques, is still intact. And in the rural towns of the interior and the fishing villages of the southwest, life goes on practically undisturbed by the island's progress.

If all this action sounds a little too frenetic; if you long for deserted beaches, lonely country roads, a place untouched by industry and where the biggest town is strung out along only one main road — Pulau Langkawi, an archipelago of 99 islands right at the Thai border, may be just the thing. Here, where legends outnumber the towns, it is still possible to ride bicycles along lonely country roads and to swim on completely deserted beaches.

But the northwest is not just all islands; there are plenty of other attractions, from Kedah — the rice bowl of the north — to the rambling state of Perak, with its royal town of Kuala Kangsar and the bustling city of Ipoh, the tin capital of the world. Perak is a most rewarding state to drive through for the scenery is magnificent — the main mountain range, known as the Barisan Titiwangsa, runs parallel to the coastal plain creating a soaring backdrop of blue hills, many of which are still covered with jungle.

North through Perak

From Kuala Lumpur follow the signs saying 'Ipoh', or *utara*, which means north. The highway passes through some ugly new industrial suburbs before leaving a spectacular cutting in the hills; from here the countryside opens up and the city becomes no more than a memory. Gently undulating hills of rubber and oil-palm plantations line the road north through **Selangor** state, interspersed with small rural towns with the ubiquitous Chinese shophouses and temple downtown and the mosque and Malay *kampung* on the outskirts. Over the border into **Perak** state the hills become mountains, the closer peaks purple, then violet and blue before fading out on the horizon.

At **Bidor**, 141 kilometres (68 miles) from Kuala Lumpur, there is an interesting alternative drive to the main trunk road north. This smaller road passes through the riverine market town of Teluk Intan and along the Perak River valley, affording a more in-depth look at Perak away from the commercial development which envelops the main road north.

Teluk Intan, 42 kilometres (26 miles) from Bidor, is a quaint old town on the banks of the sluggish Perak River, peninsular Malaysia's second longest river. Steamy, lowland Teluk Intan, slumbering in the tropical sun, is a town where it is rare to meet other travellers. Dominating the centre of the town is a most unusual leaning clock tower, Malaysia's answer to the Leaning Tower of Pisa which was built by a rich Chinese tin baron in 1885. The eight-tiered circular tower, built of bricks with a red-tiled roof and balustrades of Chinese green glazed tiles, is an architectural incongruity. Swallows nest under the eaves of the tower while on the seventh floor is a clock with roman numerals, a distinctly English colonial touch. At sunset, when the old clock tower takes on a rich golden hue, the adjacent town square comes to life. At the outdoor food stalls — the favourite eating spot in town — you can sample the unusual *gado gado* (prawns and beanshoots cooked in batter and smothered in peanut sauce). Opposite the town square is an old covered market-place, a maze of stalls stocked with everything from curry spices to singing pigeons in bamboo cages. At the end of a lane opposite the market is a tiny Chinese temple with enormous circular coiled joss-sticks dangling from the ceiling. Teluk Intan is a good overnight stop as accommodation is plentiful, including a Rumah Rehat (Government Rest House) that serves half a dozen different types of fried rice.

When travelling in Malaysia, as in the tropics generally, it is best to follow the example of the locals and rise with the sun. If your hotel is near a mosque you can often do so without the aid of an alarm clock, as the muezzin's amplified call to morning prayer is often loud enough to wake even the most heavy sleeper. The very early morning is a rewarding time to drive — the air is fresh and cool, and as you cross the Bidor River on an antiquated one-lane bridge shared by a railway line you can watch the sun rise over rice paddies

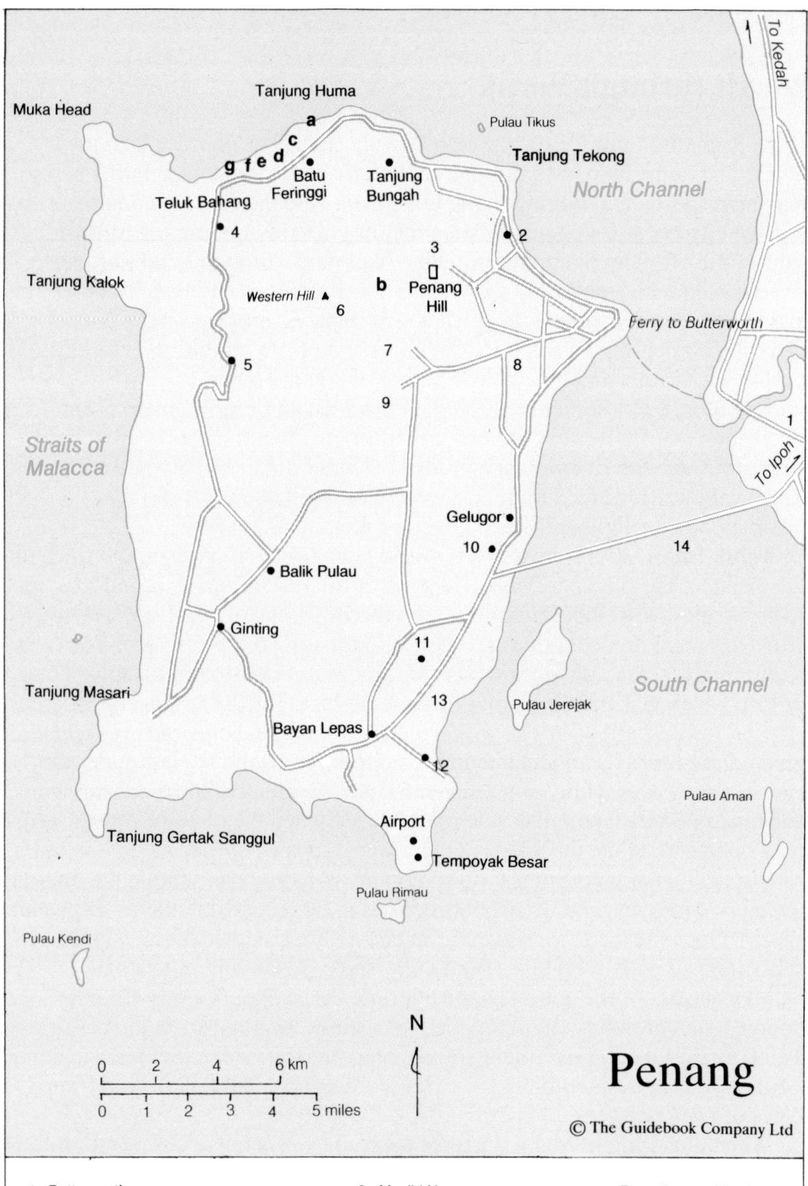

1. Butterworth
2. Bagan Jermal
3. Botanical Gardens or Waterfall Gardens
4. Penang Butterfly Farm
5. Titi Kerawang
6. Walking Paths
7. Funicular Railway
8. Masjid Negara
9. Kek Lok Si Temple
10. University Sains Malaysia
11. Bandan Bayan Baru
12. Batu Maung
13. Snake Temple
14. Penang Bridge

a. Rasa Sayang Hotel
b. Bellevue Hotel
c. Golden Sands Hotel
d. Lone Pine Hotel
e. Holiday Inn Hotel
f. Casuarina Beach Hotel
g. Bayview Beach Hotel

with canals full of pink flowering lotus. Typical Perak wooden houses are set high on stilts, presumably so as to keep dry in times of flood, but one Victorian writer asserts that this was to keep the occupants safe from tigers. As these houses are also found in the more hilly regions where flooding is not a threat there may be some truth in this theory.

Kampung Gajah, although not prepossessing at first sight, was the scene of one of Malaysia's first anti-colonial incidents — the murder of J.W.W. Birch, the unpopular first British Resident of Perak, in 1875. Birch, an intolerant and tactless man, was in the habit of giving the Malay chiefs 'a good dressing down', which probably hastened his demise more than his controversial tax and slave policies. After he was murdered in a bathhouse on the Perak River the British overreacted, pursuing the sultan into exile and killing the conspirators. The Malays realized that their rulers, once answerable only to God, were now answerable to the British. Birch's grave is nothing special, but the road beside the river and the *kampung* where the incident took place provide a rare look at a traditional Malay village which remains almost unchanged since Birch's time.

Just before Kampung Gajah, take the turnoff to Pulau Besar and follow the winding soft dirt track beside the river to the graveyard. Cocoa plants and banana and other fruit trees grow in abundance around the old wooden houses in the *kampung*. Village women row the long thin *sampan* across the wide, sluggish river to an old wooden mosque. An antiquated ferry chugs downstream, stopping at wooden jetties to take on village folk on their way to market. Not so long ago, such river 'roads' were the only means of access to most parts of Malaysia.

The road north to **Parit**, which runs parallel to the river, is known as the **Valley of the Kings**, for here can be found the tombs of many of Perak's past rulers. The graves are well marked and indicated by signs. It is not hard to imagine why this was a favoured final resting place, for surrounding the town of Parit are some of the most idyllic rural scenes in the country. Here the 'Perak' house is at its most spectacular — wooden carvings adorn the eaves of these huge rambling country homes, which are still oiled in the traditional manner. Durian, the king of fruits, grows in abundance here; some trees are 45 metres (150 feet) high and festooned with trailing parasitic ferns. Coconut palms, mango trees and cut hedges of red and orange ornamental shrubs surround the immaculately kept houses. In the evening, housewives sweep their yards with brooms made of the spines of coconut palms — a loving task, for the Malays believe that the cleaner and brighter a house, the more blessings God will bestow on its occupants.

Batu Gajah, just off the road north to Ipoh, was the leading town of the **Kinta Valley** during the English colonial days. There are some fine examples of neo-classical architecture on the hill overlooking the present town, for the colonials always built on hills in order to escape the heat. Out of town, on the road to Gopeng, are the remains of **Kellie's Castle**. Had it ever been finished, it would have been the most palatial of all the planters' bungalows. The castle, complete with ramparts, a four-storey tower and cavernous hallways arched in the Islamic style, was apparently near to completion when the owner made a trip to England and never returned.

Pulau Pangkor (Pangkor Island), a popular resort, is another alternative destination on the Straits of Malacca easily accessible from the Kampung Gajah–Parit road. A ferry links **Lumut** on the mainland to Pangkor. This group of islands, known as the Dindings during the colonial days, has white coral sand beaches, clean green waters which are excellent for swimming, and a partially restored 17th-century Dutch fort. According to legend, Pangkor's most famous beach, Pantai Puteri Dewi or 'The Beach of the Beautiful Princess', was named after a distraught princess who threw herself from a nearby cliff on hearing the news of her betrothed warrior's death. Accommodation ranges from Malaysian-style chalets to airconditioned first-class hotels.

Ipoh, recently designated a city and the capital of Perak state, is renowned throughout Malaysia for its Chinese food and unusual Buddhist cave temples. Ipoh is a commercial city populated mainly by Cantonese Chinese, many of whose ancestors manned the pumps and dredges of the tin mines on which the city's fortunes were made. Opulent tin barons' mansions still abound in the leafier suburbs. Protruding from the landscape both north and south of the city are some unusual limestone outcrops. These sheer-sided buttresses are pitted with caves, some of which have been converted into Chinese and Hindu temples. **Perak Tong**, six kilometres (four miles) north of the town, houses a massive Buddha and other deities, and a lotus pond containing tortoises. The biggest temple, **Sam Poh Tong**, is six kilometres (four miles) south of Ipoh. The temple dates back to the start of this century when the first monk took up residence. There is an excellent view of the surrounding countryside from the top of a rather gruelling flight of 246 steps.

Kuala Kangsar, home of the Sultan of Perak and the location of one of Malaysia's most famous mosques, is situated 50 kilometres (31 miles) from Ipoh along the old highway or considerably less if you take the new expressway (Leburaya). This elegant royal town overlooks a looping bend of the Perak River, where along the shoreline is the *istana* or palace of the Sultan of Perak and the fabulous **Ubadiah Mosque**. Like an apparition from an *Arabian Nights* tale, the mosque is dominated by a huge copper onion-dome flanked by lesser domes and cupolas, with minarets on all four sides. It was built by Sultan Idris of Perak between 1913 and 1917. Another kilometre (just over half a mile) further down the river road is the **Musium Di Raja**, a 19th-century traditional wooden raja's palace adorned with elaborate carvings. It now houses the royal collection of the sultans of Perak.

Taiping, 37 kilometres (23 miles) from Kuala Kangsar and set amongst cloud-wreathed hills, lays claim to the most prodigious rainfall on the peninsula. As its name implies, the town is populated largely by Chinese and owes its existence, as do most Perak towns, to tin mining. In its early days it was a lawless town and the scene of fierce fighting between rival clans, but since the Pangkor treaty of 1874 the town has remained quiet. Taiping was the first British capital of Perak until 1935 and still has some fine colonial buildings. The pride of the town is the **Lake Gardens**, once an old tin mine and now a landscaped parkland and golf course overlooking a lake, where Taiping's joggers and sportsmen congregate. Looming over the park is **Bukit Larut**, formerly known as **Maxwell's Hill**, Malaysia's oldest hill resort. Atop the hill in the cool bracing air of 1,020 metres (3,346 feet) you can relax in front of a log fire in a comfortable bungalow and look down through the clouds to Taiping and out to the Straits of Malacca below. There is also an excellent and most moderately priced Government Rest House, where each room has a balcony overlooking the lake and the hill. In the evening, after the inevitable afternoon rainshower, the lights of Bukit Larut can be seen glittering atop the hill.

From Taiping follow the road north to **Penang**, 90 kilometres (56 miles) away. Visitors to the island have the option of driving over the spectacular new Penang Bridge or taking the ferry from Butterworth. The bridge affords sweeping views of the island, whereas the ferry provides a touch of nostalgia, as passengers alight in the very heart of old Georgetown. Travellers arriving by train automatically link up with the ferry.

Penang (Pulau Pinang)

Background

Some 200 years ago according to legend, Francis Light, Penang's founding father, in an attempt to hasten the clearing of the jungle, filled cannons with gold and silver coins and blasted the treasure into the undergrowth. This monetary encouragement spurred the locals into action — the jungle was hacked back and the fledgling colony of Penang began her chequered career. Light had long hankered after Penang, for the English needed a base for their sailing ships engaged in the lucrative China trade. A harbour was needed to refit the East Indiamen which plied from Madras to Canton bearing their precious cargoes of opium and tea, and the British required a port where a squadron could be stationed to guard the Bay of Bengal during the northeast monsoon. Penang was the perfect choice, situated on the protected west coast at the entrance to the Straits of Malacca and providing an ideal deepwater anchorage.

When Light stepped ashore on 11 August 1786 and raised the British flag, it was somewhat premature as he had only a vague letter signed by the Sultan

of Kedah and not a treaty of cession. It wasn't long before Sultan Abdullah realized that he had been tricked by an old colonial ruse and demanded compensation for his land. Light tried to humour the sultan, entrusting him with 20 chests of opium, but disgusted at Light's attempt to put him off the sultan assembled a force to recapture Penang. His forces were quickly repelled by Light's troops, but he did manage to extract a treaty awarding him 6,000 Spanish dollars a year for the legal occupation of the land.

Francis Light selected a site near his landfall for the capital and named it Georgetown after the reigning monarch of England, King George III. The original town grid planned by Light is still evident in the older part of the city, where some of the island's most renowned historic buildings are to be found. Georgetown's population grew rapidly as immigrants were lured to the new port which was tax and duty free. Chinese, Indians, Arabs and Bugis from Sulawesi flocked here to try their luck in the 'Pearl of the Orient', as Penang became known. Many of the early immigrants were *baba*, the Straits Chinese from Malacca. Their home port had been declining under the restrictive trade policies of the Dutch and they thrived in the free-port atmosphere of Penang.

Meanwhile in the south, Raffles had raised the British flag on the island of Singapore and in no time this more centrally located port became the new centre of British trade and commerce, sounding the death-knell to Light's hopes of Penang's supremacy. In 1832 Singapore replaced Penang as the capital of the Straits Settlements. But a new boom occurred in the 1850s when tin was discovered nearby on the mainland, and some of the palatial mansions built during that time can still be seen on the island. Another period of prosperity hit Penang during the rubber boom early this century, spawning in the process another period of grandiose architecture.

Penang today continues to prosper — the 65-storey Komtar tower looms over old Georgetown, the new Penang Bridge (the longest in Asia and third-longest in the world) links the island with the mainland, and multi-million dollar projects abound at the tourist mecca of Batu Ferringhi. But despite this inevitable onslaught of concrete jungle, Penang still manages to be an easy-going and relaxed place, where old-world charm blends successfully with modern sophistication.

City Sights and Walks

A Stroll through Georgetown

Downtown **Georgetown**, a labyrinth of narrow streets and alleyways, is so compact that the easiest way to explore the city is on foot. Trishaws provide an equally rewarding experience, especially when it is raining and you peer out from under the canvas cover. Many of the downtown streets have covered arched pavements, known as 'five foot ways'; designed to shade the pedestrian from both sun and rain, they make walking a pleasure even in the noonday sun. Georgetown is a hard-working city and nowhere is this more obvious than in bustling Chinatown, where amongst the faded, pastel-coloured shophouses family businesses still thrive in the conglomeration of hawkers' stalls, coffee shops, bazaars and temples. 'Little India', in the shadow of the Kapitan Kling Mosque, abounds with goldsmiths and cloth merchants, and the tang of curry spices wafts from roadside restaurants.

Weld Quay, at the bustling waterfront, is an appropriate place to begin a walk around thc city for it was here, in the grand old days of sailing ships, that it all began. Nearby are the **Clan Piers**, a village built on stilts over the harbour. Seven Chinese clans of fisherfolk, numbering around 2,000, have lived on these wooden jetties for generations. Apparently the residents believe that the deities they worship protect the village from nature's wrath. Surprisingly enough, even the most dilapidated of these houses seem to survive.

The **Penang Clock Tower**, a Georgian edifice in the middle of a traffic turnabout, is found at the junction of Lebuh Light and Lebuh Beach (*lebuh* means 'a broad street'). A Chinese millionaire presented the tower to Georgetown in 1897 during Queen Victoria's Diamond Jubilee celebrations. The tower is 60 feet (18 metres) high — one foot for each year of the Queen's reign.

Fort Cornwallis, opposite the clock tower, was originally a wooden stockade, built shortly after Light's arrival in 1808. It was later rebuilt, as it stands today, with convict labour. Named after Charles Marquis Cornwallis, a Governor General of India, the fort had a rather inglorious history; considered inadequate to defend the harbour, not one shot was ever fired from its poised and polished cannon. Today, amongst the cannon embrasures, children play in the gardens and slide down the cannon barrels. One cannon, the famous **Seri Rambai**, was presented to the Sultan of Johor by the Dutch in 1606. Later, after being passed through Portuguese and Javanese hands, it ended up in Penang. The island folklore holds that childless women can become fertile by placing flowers in the barrel and offering special prayers.

The **Eastern and Oriental Hotel**, Penang's 'grande dame' establishment, is a little way down Lebuh Light from the Fort. Affectionately known as the 'E and O', this century-old hotel still exudes a unique and distinctive old-world charm while keeping abreast with the times. Originally owned by the Armenian Sarkies brothers, who also owned Raffles Hotel in Singapore, the hotel has played host to a number of famous guests including Somerset Maugham and Rudyard Kipling.

The **Penang Museum and Art Gallery**, where Lebuh Light meets Lebuh Farquhar, was originally the Penang Free School. Built in 1816 to educate future government servants, it was the oldest school east of the Suez. In the museum is a kaleidoscope of Penang's history: bejewelled wavy-bladed *kris*, the short Malay dagger; beaded trousseaus of the Straits Chinese; and old paintings and etchings of the Penang of yesteryear. At the entrance is a statue of Francis Light, whose features were cast from the portrait of his son, Colonel William Light, the founder of Adelaide, in South Australia.

St George's Church on Lebuh Farquhar, built in 1818, is a gem of Georgian architecture and one of the most classic buildings in Asia. In the church cemetery, amidst the dappled light of old frangipani trees whose roots entwine the gravestones, is the **Tomb of Francis Light**. His is a simple tomb compared with neighbouring monuments built in the style of mini Greek temples. Penang's founding father died of malaria only eight years after he proclaimed Penang for the Crown on 21 October 1794.

The **Cheong Fatt Tze Mansion**, situated on Lebuh Leith around the corner from Lebuh Light, is now a state monument. During the 1880s Penang's wealthy businessmen vied to outdo one another in architectural opulence. Built by Thio Thiaw Siat, a Kwangtung businessman who imported craftsmen from China, this stately home is one of only three surviving mansions of this type in the world; the other two are in Manila in the Philippines and Medan in Indonesia. Inside the rambling 24-room building are cobblestone courtyards, a spiral staircase, teak screens with gold-leaf carvings, tapestries, embroideries and a collection of rare porcelain.

The **Kwan Yin** (or **Goddess of Mercy**) **Temple**, built at the beginning of the 19th century, is Penang's oldest and most popular temple. Situated in Lebuh Pitt, the temple, although renovated and redecorated, remains a unique testimony to the artisans of a bygone era. Two guardian dragons dominate the massive roof, and the front of the building is decorated with intricate traditional Chinese carvings. Inside the temple are six images, the principal one being Kwan Yin Hwut Chia, or the Virgin of the Lotus Flower. The second is Mah Chow Poh, the Patroness of Virgins and the Queen of Heaven, while the remaining four figures are attendants. Kwan Yin is strongly associated with fertility, peace and good fortune, and while she is invoked virtually every day, on the 19th day of the second, sixth and ninth months of the Chinese lunar calendar the temple is thronged with devotees offering food, flowers and oil while burning joss-sticks to seek consolation for various ills.

Kapitan Kling Mosque, further up Lebuh Pitt, was named after the *kapitan*, or headman, of the Kling or south Indian community in the 19th century. The free-standing minaret, topped with the crescent moon and star (the symbol of Islam), is an easy-to-spot downtown landmark. Some of the Muslim congregation are the descendants of the original Indian soldiers who arrived with Francis Light.

Khoo Kongsi, the most famous Chinese clan house in Malaysia, is located further down Pitt Street and is approached through a lane under an archway. Alongside this cobblestone lane are 19th-century Chinese townhouses whose

Baba and *Nonya* — Across Two Cultures

One of Malaysia's most intriguing ethnic minorities are the Straits-born Chinese, or *peranakan* (meaning 'born here'). Their story began 500 years ago when the first Chinese traders put up in Malacca while awaiting the monsoon winds which would sail them home. A few intermarried with the local women, who proved useful guardians of their businesses during their absence. Some early settlers even had royal blood, for according to the 16th-century *Malay Annals*, a Ming emperor sent his daughter Princess Hang Li Poh in marriage to the Sultan Mansur Shah. Some 500 'youths of noble birth' accompanied the royal bride and the entourage took up residence at the foot of the hill, since named 'Bukit Cina' or Chinese Hill. It is from these regal beginnings that they claim their roots, and from this early marriage of Malay and Chinese they evolved their unique culture which persists today.

Nonya, as the woman are called, and *baba*, the males, were wily and clever at trade. They soon became exceedingly wealthy and developed an opulent, glittering lifestyle — a combination of the Chinese talent for making money and the Malay love of enjoyment. Their 'Golden Age' was from the mid-19th to the early 20th century, when *peranakan* families made fortunes from spices, timber, tin and the new boom crop, rubber. Pampered by servants, the wealthy *nonya* spent their time visiting, gossiping, gambling with chikky cards and chewing *sireh* (betel nut). At home, their time was spent refining the arts of home-making, at which they excelled. Beadwork was their passion. These intricate colourful works of art were made from tiny glass beads stitched on velvet. It was customary for *nonya* to bead most of their trousseau, including wedding slippers, pillow ends, belts and bed hangings, for the most spectacular of events — the *nonya* wedding. The traditional wedding ceremony, rarely seen these days, ran for 12 days, with each day reserved for special rituals. The elaborate Chinese-style, heavily-embroidered wedding gowns were crowned with a head-dress of gold and diamonds.

The *peranakan* love of spicy and piquant food sets them apart from the other immigrant Chinese. A unique cuisine developed, using coconut milk and *belacan* (dried shrimp paste), chillies and other spices. Delicate cakes, pastries and sweets were laboriously prepared, as skill in cooking these delicacies was considered a great asset in the marriage stakes.

Even their porcelain was different, for they ordered expensive custom-made sets directly from China. Nonyaware, as it is called, is distinguished by its brilliant bold colours and the predominant theme of phoenix birds and blossoming peonies. This porcelain was reserved for ceremonial use and, like other *peranakan* artifacts, today they are prized collectors' items. *Baba* and *nonya* were great Anglophiles, as they thrived under the English free-ports of the Straits Settlements. Their porcelain shows this leaning, as eggcups, sugar jars, soup tureens and soap boxes never occur in traditional Chinese porcelain.

The *baba* and *nonya* taste was also catered for in silverware. A curious blend of Chinese motifs and Islamic design evolved. Produced locally by immigrant Chinese craftsmen to satisfy the *nonya* fondness for ostentatious display, this unique silverware is found only in the old Straits Settlements of Malacca, Penang and Singapore. Even though most *nonya* could afford to wear gold they preferred silver, as they believed it kept away evil spirits.

In all aspects of their material culture the *peranakan* expressed themselves richly, and their architecture and interior design were no exception. Nowhere is this more evident than in Jalan Tun Tan Cheng Lock, the street named after Malacca's most famous *baba* son, Tan Cheng Lock, a reformist and founder of the Malaysian Chinese Association. Once named Heeren Street and dubbed 'Millionaires Row', the street is dominated by Straits Chinese ancestral homes. About 20 are still owned and maintained by the original families, although many family members have long since left Malacca for Kuala Lumpur or Singapore. Beyond the tall, heavy doors in the front hall are elaborate ancestral altars symbolizing filial piety. Throughout the narrow, deep two-storey houses, built in Southern Chinese style; are carved and gilded doors, screens, panels and blackwood furniture inlaid with mother-of-pearl.

Fortunately, *peranakan* culture has experienced a revival of sorts. Although many of the rituals and customs are no longer practised, Malaysians of Straits-born descent have become more conscious of their heritage. *Nonya* food continues to be popular; there has been a spate of nostalgic books by *baba*; and top dollars are now being paid for *nonya* porcelain and Straits Chinese silver.

Baba Nonya silverwork

owners' nameboards — gold calligraphy on lacquer — are mounted above old, teak swing-doors. Turn a corner and the clanhouse appears across Cannon Square, a vast open courtyard paved with granite slabs. Facing the opulent *kongsi* is a lesser building, the opera stage, and on the left is an old office building where clan office-bearers issue free visitor passes. Both outside and inside, the clanhouse is unbelievably ornate, especially the massive tiled roof — reputed to weigh 25 tons (25.4 tonnes) — which is decorated with cobalt-blue dragons and fanciful urns full of flowers. Elaborately carved wooden lanterns covered in gold foil hang from the ceiling, and on the exterior walls are ornate friezes and embossed panels depicting characters from Chinese folklore. In the interior are three halls, the most splendid of which contains the image of the Khoo clan's patron saint, Tua Sai Yeah, a famous general of the Ch'in Dynasty (221–207 BC). The God of Prosperity resides in the left hall, while the right is reserved for the ancestral soul tablets of the Khoo clan, dating back to 1840. The original clanhouse, built as a replica of the Imperial Palace, was burnt down not long after its completion. It is universally believed that its ornateness offended the gods, so a lesser structure was built. The Dragon Mountain Hall of the Khoo clan, today's clanhouse, is so sumptuous that its forerunner must have defied description.

Sights on Georgetown's Outskirts

Northam Road Mansions A favoured location for the homes of Penang's rubber czars after the boom of 1911–20, Northam Road was generally known as 'Millionaires Row'. Manicured lawns slope down to the seafront, where gothic follies adorned with plaster curlicues, Doric columns, wrought-iron gazebos, turreted roof-tops, copper domes and intricately carved shutters and balconies stand as monuments to prosperity. Northam Road is lined with huge angsana trees which almost meet overhead. Many of the mansions were owned by Straits Chinese who embraced the style of their English rulers and built palatial homes, the most famous being 'Homestead'. Dubbed by contemporaries a 'mini Buckingham Palace', it is still occupied by descendants of its founder, Yeap Chor Ee.

Wat Chayamangkalaram, in Lorong Burmah off Jalan Burmah, is Penang's Thai Buddhist Monastery. In its gigantic hall lies the third largest statue of its kind in the world — a 32-metre (105-foot) -long reclining Buddha. At the entrance of the meditation hall, mythical serpentine creatures, known as '*naga*', coil up the balustrades. In the courtyard outside, guarding the complex, are the mythical Thai '*kinnara*' with the head and torso of a man and the legs and wings of a legendary Himalayan bird. Anyone wishing to photograph the reclining Buddha must obtain permission beforehand, in writing, from the Home Ministry and present it to the Head Monk.

The **Penang Botanical Gardens**, seven kilometres (four miles) from the city at the end of Jalan Kebun Bunga, were established in 1844 by Charles Curtis. The 30 hectares (74 acres) of greenery are surrounded by jungle-clad hills. Waterfalls, fern rockeries, tropical flowering plants, and the inquisitive *kera* (Common Leaf Monkeys) that roam the spacious grounds make the gardens a favourite place for Penangites and travellers alike.

Penang State Mosque, at the junction of Jalan Air Hitam and Jalan Masjid, is one of the most spectacular in Malaysia. From the 52-metre (170-foot) minaret are panoramic views of Georgetown and the surrounding countryside, but permission to ascend must first be obtained from the State Religious Council. Suspended from the ceiling in the main prayer hall is a magnificent chandelier measuring six metres by 4.8 metres (20 by 16 feet).

Around the Island

The island of Penang itself is very different from bustling Georgetown for, as in most of Malaysia, the Chinese and Indians flocked to the cities and towns but left the countryside to the Malays. Scattered over the verdant island are picture-postcard *kampung*, fishing villages and the best beaches on the west coast. The best way to see the island is by car as you can stop at deserted beaches for a swim, take photographs and explore the countryside at your leisure. Hire cars are available at very moderate cost from the tourist complex at Batu Ferringhi or you can rent a taxi for the day. Bicycles can also be rented here, which are ideal for exploring the coast and bays close to Batu Ferringhi. The distance around the island is about 70 kilometres (43 miles).

Batu Ferringhi, Penang's most famous beach, is situated 14 kilometres (nine miles) from Georgetown along a winding seaside road. Splendid old villas sit crouched in little bays beside the pale blue waters, and at **Tanjung Bunga**, in a tiny cove beside a waterside mosque, a fishing fleet of gaily-painted wooden *sampan* floats in the translucent sea. Off shore is a rocky outcrop, known as Lovers Isle, and beyond in the distance are the misty blue mountains of Kedah on the mainland. Luxury high-rise hotels abound at Batu Ferringhi, the tourists' mecca. At the 'Rasa Sayang' and other palatial beachside towers are swimming pools and Western-style restaurants which pamper to the less-adventurous tourist. On the beach, windsurfing, para-gliding, waterskiing and other activities are available for those who don't want just to sprawl in the sun. Restaurants and souvenir shops abound here but the prices, as to be expected, are inflated.

Teluk Bahang, a picturesque fishing village which is only now getting its first high-rise hotel, is six kilometres (four miles) further on. From Batu Ferringhi the road is relatively deserted except on weekends, and there are plenty of secluded coves for those who want to leave the crowds behind. At the southern end of Teluk Bahang is a rickety wooden jetty that leads to a village of fishing boats. Dusk is the best time to visit, when the fishermen are preparing to go to sea and the beach and jetty are a hive of activity as ice, lanterns and nets are ferried out to the trawlers. From here you can take a footpath or hire a boat to get to **Muka Head**, where there is good fishing and snorkelling.

The **Penang Butterfly Farm**, home to 4,000 native Malaysian butterflies, is one kilometre (0.6 miles) from the roundabout at Teluk Bahang. Here in a huge, caged-in, landscaped garden visitors can mingle with the butterflies. Billed as the world's largest butterfly farm, it has extensive breeding facilities as a butterfly's lifespan is but a mere two weeks. There is also a glass cage where visitors can observe butterflies breaking out of their pupal skins, laying eggs and sunbaking on rocks. The park is open daily (including public holidays) with a M$2 admission charge.

Titi Kerawang, a freshwater pool filled from the surrounding waterfalls, is another ten kilometres (six miles) further on. The road meanders snakelike through the high country, the untouched heartland of Penang. Where the road crests the hills and the trees clear, a panorama of a verdant island dropping away to the sea below is revealed.

Balik Pulau, a quiet rural town known as the 'durian capital of Penang', is 32 kilometres (20 miles) from the city. The main street is lined with old Chinese shophouses shaded by split bamboo blinds, known as 'chicks', which protect the goods on display from the harsh noonday sun. Surrounding the town are some idyllic *kampung* scenes: gaily-painted wooden houses perch on stilts on freshly-swept sand, and brilliant pink bougainvillaeas trail over their latticed and carved verandas.

The Snake Temple, the popular name for the 'Temple of the Azure Cloud', is just outside Bayan Lepas on the circular route back to the city. Coiled around the altars, shrines and incense burners of the temple are dozens of pit vipers. Although poisonous, these particular snakes are harmless as they are heavily drugged by the incense smoke. After dark they feed on eggs left by worshippers. The temple was built in 1850 for the dedicated worshippers of Chor Soo Kong, a Taoist deity. Worshippers refer to the snakes as 'holy representations' of the deity. Each July, on the birthday of the deity, the snake population is said to increase. Local photographers will drape a serpent around your neck for a souvenir photograph, if you dare.

Penang Bridge, the island's latest and most expensive wonder, can be seen on your right on the road back to the city. Linking the mainland with the island, the bridge is the world's third longest, with a span of 13.5 kilometres (eight miles). Snaking across the channel, the bridge hugs the waterline until it arches in the centre where four Moroccan-style minarets top the massive supports.

Kek Lok Si Temple, home of the 10,000 Buddhas Precious Pagoda,

Fruits of Malaysia

Blessed with a warm and moist climate, Malaysia abounds with a wide variety of delicious tropical fruits. Apart from the more well-known pineapple, mandarin oranges, limes and watermelon, the nation grows over 40 varieties of bananas, ranging from the tiny sweet **pisang mas** to the large green cooking variety. Less recognizable to the traveller are the many local tropical fruits, some of which are listed below.

Durian, a football-shaped, spiky fruit is the undisputed king of Malaysian fruits. The obnoxious smell puts off many first-timers, but once you have sampled the creamy, rich, fruity pulp, addiction is sure to follow. The fruit is in season from June to August and from November to February, but *durian* aficionados will pay outrageous prices out of season. Wild jungle fruit is even more coveted.

Rambutan, a small, hairy red fruit indigenous to Malaysia, is a traveller's favourite. The sweet white flesh is similar to the lychee. The best are the type whose flesh easily comes off the pip. The main season is between June and September.

Mangosteen (*Manggis*) is a circular, purple-skinned fruit with a pinky-white segmented flesh. It has a delicate, sweet, acidic flavour and is believed to have beneficial 'cooling' qualities. Its seasons follow the *durian* and *rambutan.*

Jackfruit (*Nangka*) is probably the largest of all cultivated fruits, reaching 39 centimetres (15 inches) in length. The yellow flesh is tangy and rather chewy and the seed is also boiled and eaten. *Nangka* is available year round but is best in June and December.

Duku is a small, round, pale-brown fruit with a white flesh. The taste can vary from sweet to slightly sour, but don't bite the seed as it is bitter. *Duku* take 15 years to bear fruit from seed.

Mango comes in a wide variety of species, from the sweet, orange-fleshed *kuini* to the sour *bacang* which is pounded with spices to make sambal. Many varieties are called 'plum' by Malays and grow in every *kampung* home and in many urban yards.

Starfruit (*Belimbing*) is so-named because when cut the slices are star-shaped. The greeny-gold flesh is very juicy with a slightly tart flavour. Starfruit stalls abound south of Kuala Lumpur beside the expressway. Available year round.

Papaya (*Betik*) is cheap, highly nutritious and available year round. Apparently it was introduced to Malaysia by the Portuguese who brought it from South America in the 16th century. Papaya is an important source of vitamins A and C.

Soursop (*Durian Belanda*) has a creamy soft flesh with a sweet, slightly tart, flavour. Although rounder and green, it slightly resembles the *durian* without the thorns and smell. It is also popular when made into a drink.

Rose Apple (*Jambu Air*) is a small, disc-like fruit with a polished pink skin. The crisp, slightly tart skin and flesh are eaten, but not the seeds. It grows in *kampung* throughout Malaysia and is also found in the wild.

Guava (*Jambu Batu*) is estimated to contain five times more vitamin C than orange juice. This green, rock-like fruit can be eaten fresh or made into jams and jellies. It is also sold sliced and iced with a sugar and spice garnish.

Pomelo is a pendulous citrus fruit slightly similar to grapefruit though not as sour. It is popular with the Chinese during their festive seasons and is often used as an offering on altars.

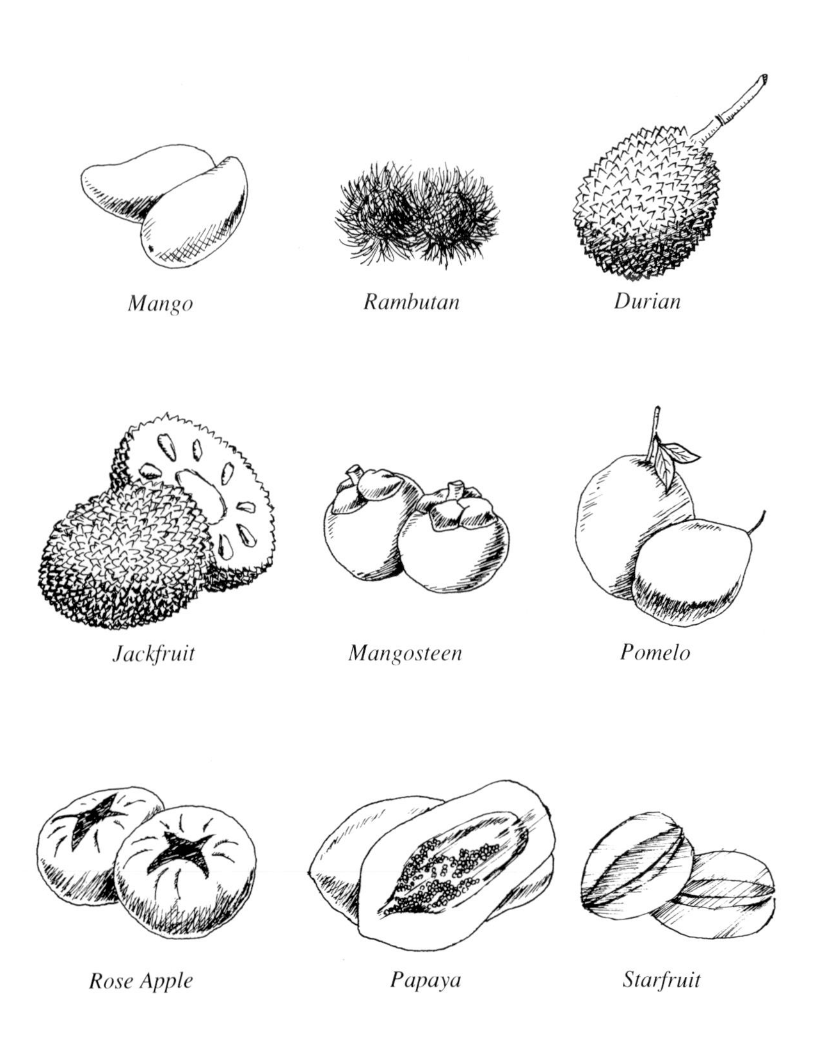

Mango *Rambutan* *Durian*

Jackfruit *Mangosteen* *Pomelo*

Rose Apple *Papaya* *Starfruit*

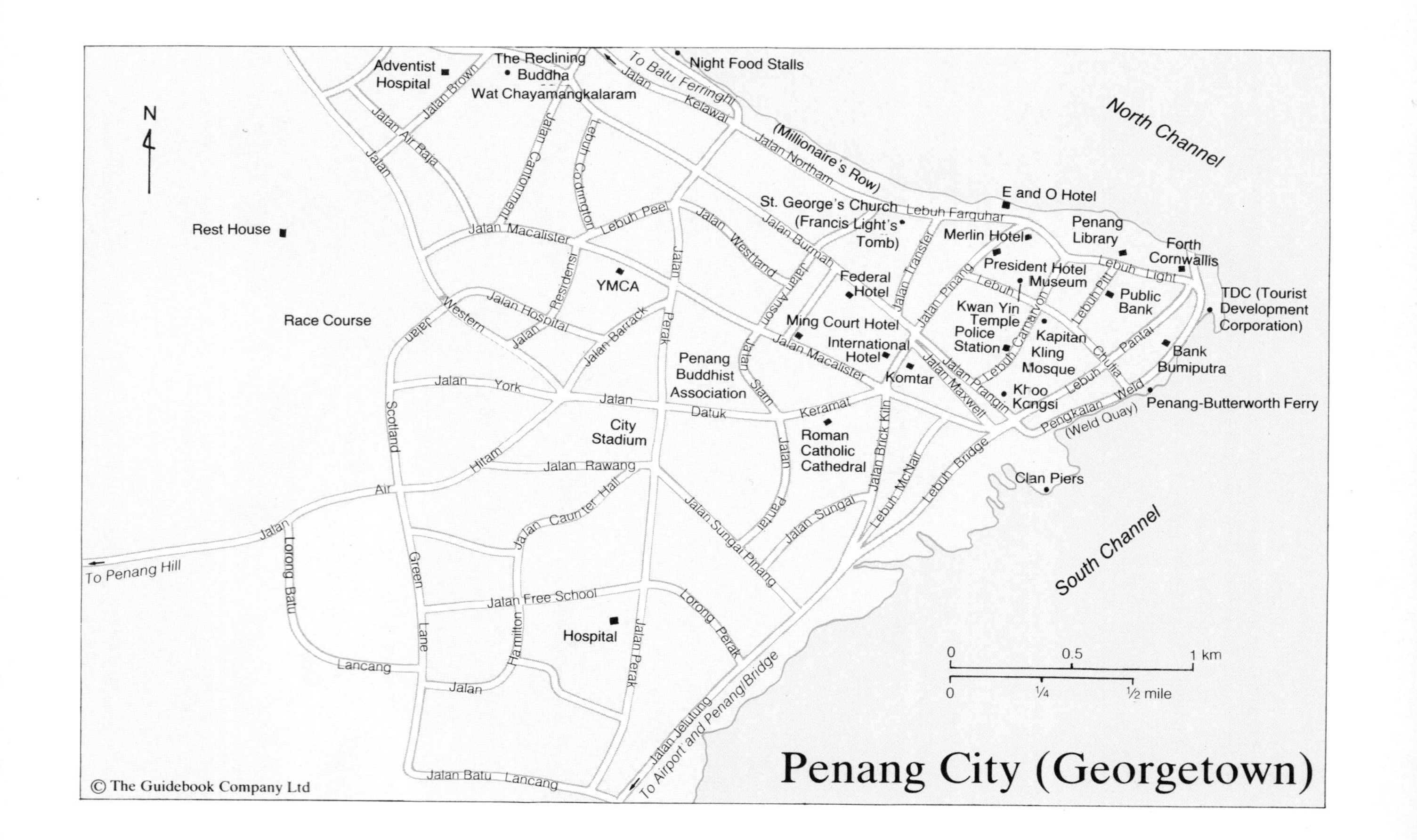

Penang City (Georgetown)
North Channel
South Channel
N
Night Food Stalls
To Batu Ferringhi
Adventist Hospital
The Reclining Buddha
Wat Chayamangkalaram
(Millionaire's Row)
Jalan Northam
E and O Hotel
St. George's Church
(Francis Light's Tomb)
Lebuh Farquhar
Penang Library
Forth Cornwallis
Merlin Hotel
President Hotel
Museum
Federal Hotel
Public Bank
TDC (Tourist Development Corporation)
Kwan Yin Temple
Police Station
Kapitan Kling Mosque
Ming Court Hotel
International Hotel
Komtar
Khoo Kongsi
Bank Bumiputra
Penang-Butterworth Ferry
Pengkalan Weld (Weld Quay)
Clan Piers
Rest House
YMCA
Race Course
Penang Buddhist Association
City Stadium
Roman Catholic Cathedral
Hospital
To Penang Hill
To Airport and Penang Bridge
Jalan Jelutung
Jalan Perak
Jalan Macalister
Jalan Burmah
Jalan Anson
Jalan Westland
Lebuh Peel
Jalan Cantonment
Lebuh Codrington
Jalan Air Raja
Jalan Brown
Jalan Residensi
Jalan Hospital
Jalan Barrack
Jalan Western
Jalan York
Jalan Scotland
Jalan Datuk Keramat
Jalan Siam
Jalan Pantai
Jalan Rawang
Jalan Air Hitam
Jalan Caunter Hall
Jalan Sungai Pinang
Jalan Free School
Jalan Hamilton
Lorong Perak
Green Lane
Lorong Batu Lancang
Jalan Batu Lancang
Jalan Brick Kiln
Lebuh McNair
Lebuh Bridge
Jalan Transfer
Jalan Pinang
Jalan Prangin
Jalan Maxwell
Lebuh Carnarvon
Lebuh Chulia
Lebuh Pantai
Lebuh Pitt
Lebuh Light
0 0.5 1 km
0 ¼ ½ mile

dominates the hillside above the town of Air Hitam. To reach the base of the temple complex take the turnoff to Air Hitam at the junction where the Penang State Mosque is situated. From the market town a covered bazaar of shops lines the steps that mount to the temple. Plastic Buddhas, souvenir t-shirts and all kinds of bric-à-brac crowd the tunnel-like stalls that cater more to Malaysian tourists than to overseas travellers. In 1885, a wandering Buddhist abbot apparently experienced a vision of a crane flying with outstretched wings across the hills and this inspired the creation of the temple. In the gaudy hillside complex, where red and yellow colours predominate, various halls honour Kwan Yin (the Goddess of Mercy), Bee Lay Hood (the Laughing Buddha) and Gautama Buddha (the Founder of the Faith). Sacred turtles, some with red calligraphy on their backs, swim in the temple's rockpools. The crowning glory is the cream and white classical pagoda adorned with thousands of Buddhas and mounted by a spiral staircase. On a neighbouring hill, a huge new white statue of Kwan Yin looms over the trees.

Penang Hill (Bukit Bendera), the island's hill resort, is reached by the country's only funicular railway. To reach the station take the turnoff from Jalan Air Hitam. The track climbs an impossibly steep gradient through a cutting lined with colonial masonry. Jungle trees, bamboo groves and pitcher plants grow alongside the track. On the peak, at 830 metres (2,723 feet), the air is noticeably cooler and the scenery is reminiscent of more temperate zones. Barely one year after Francis Light founded the settlement he built a trail to the top of the hill and erected a house where he grew strawberries imported from his native Suffolk. Penang Hill was regarded as a 'health resort' and after the opening of the railway in 1923 colonial bungalows sprouted all over the hill. When the clouds clear, the views are spectacular. The famous watercolourist Wathen, who visited here in 1811, described the view as 'a charming valley thickly studded with handsome villas and picturesque bungalows and intersected with pleasant carriage roads and meandering streams.' The old Bellevue Hotel on the peak, built in the late 18th century, is a perfect spot in which to enjoy the bracing air, while walking the hill trails and taking in the panorama of sea and island.

Eating Out in Penang

Penangites are passionate about eating out, which is not surprising considering the multicultural array of food available. Many dishes are of Thai, Chinese, Indian and Arabic origins, but all have been influenced by Malay methods of preparation. You can take your choice and dine in roadside stalls, open-air restaurants along the beach or in airconditioned establishments in five-star hotels. The well-known seaside boulevard, **Gurney Drive**, becomes a huge hawker centre after dusk and into the wee hours. *Laksa*,

Penang's famous noodle dish in spicy coconut gravy, can be found here, along with local cakes known as *kuih*, and *cendol* and *ais kacang* — both famous iced desserts. Considered the king of Penang cuisine, *nasi kandar* is steaming white rice served with a wide assortment of pickles, sambals, vegetables, meat, prawns and cuttlefish. A tiny shop wedged between Kapitan Kling Mosque and a goldsmith's shop serves the best in town. Logically enough, the island's seafood is legendary; lobsters, chilli crabs, sweet and sour prawns, and seafood steamboats abound at the many seaside restaurants along Batu Ferringhi, Tanjung Tokong and Tanjung Bunga.

Shopping

Although Penang is no longer a free port, and the laws have become tougher since the 1960s when black-market goods abounded, it is still renowned as a shopper's mecca. Jalan Pinang, in the heart of the old town, hosts a variety of department stores and duty-free shops as well as the Penang Road Bazaar, a covered maze of densely packed shops where you can find just about anything. Jalan Campbell, in the heart of Chinatown, abounds with goldsmith shops, while antique and junk shops are found along Lebuh Bishop and Rope Walk. Memorabilia from 200 years of history, including Straits Chinese silver, cast-iron Dutch lamps, Victorian grandfather clocks and discarded Chinese opera gowns, crowd the old shops. Don't hesitate to bargain here, as all the locals do.

Kedah — Rice Bowl of the North

Kedah, Malaysia's oldest state, is often missed by tourists who assume that Penang is the end of the road. Apart from the obvious charms of the legendary islands of Langkawi, Kedah is the only state that has remains of the early Hindu kingdoms of the eighth and ninth centuries. As Kedah's population is predominantly Malay, the state is one of the most traditional in the nation. Although a vassal of Thailand throughout much of its long history, Kedah's traditional Malay rulers were retained and the present royal family can trace its line back to Hindu times.

Bujang Valley, the site of peninsular Malaysia's oldest Hindu settlement, can be reached from the town of Bedong about 14 kilometres (nine miles) from **Sungai Petani** in southern Kedah. From here take the road to **Merbok**, where the headquarters of the Bujang Valley Historical Park are located. On the southern slopes of **Gunung Jerai**, which was a landmark for ancient mariners navigating across the Bay of Bengal, is a museum and the site of the best-known and largest of all the temples found in the area — **Candi Bukit Patu Pahat** (the Temple of the Hill of Chiselled Stone). The raised four-sided stone edifice contains a circular stone over a hole which resembles a Siva '*lingam*'. The temple was built in the ninth century while Kedah was a vassal of the great Sumatran empire of Sri Vijaya. Little stone caskets containing golden Sivaite symbols were found in the foundations of the temple and a host of other Hindu and Buddhist remains have been unearthed throughout the Bujang Valley.

Alor Star, the capital of Kedah state, lies in a sea of rice paddies. In the town square is the Thai-inspired and beautifully carved **Balai Besar**, or Great Hall, where the Sultan of Kedah holds audience on ceremonial occasions. Close by is the unique octagonal **Balai Nobat**, which houses the royal state orchestra and where it is claimed the sound of drums can sometimes be heard at *subuh*, the morning prayer time. Opposite is the elegant onion-domed **Zahir Mosque**. At **Kuala Kedah**, the nearby port town, are the remains of a historic fort which guarded the Kedah River during the Thai invasion of 1821.

Pulau Langkawi — Island of Legends

Scattered across the northernmost watery boundaries of peninsular Malaysia are the 99 tropical islands which comprise the Langkawi group. Most of the islands are deserted rocky outcrops topped with jungle, though many have enchanting lonely beaches. The bulk of the population live on the big island, Pulau Langkawi. Airconditioned express ferries, complete with wrestling on in-house videos, ply the route from Kuala Kedah and from Kuala Perlis further to the north. The ferry trip, which takes around one hour, costs M$10 one way. Langkawi has its own airstrip and Malaysia Airlines flies daily from Kuala Lumpur via Penang. There is also a ferry service from Penang.

From a distance across the glassy waters of the Malacca Straits the islands seem to hover above the sea and appear as one, but closer up you discover that they are intersected by fiord-like passageways where marble cliffs rear straight up from the water's edge. **Kuah**, the main town of Langkawi, sits in a crescent-shaped bay overlooking a horizon filled with the faint blue silhouettes of other islands. Although Kuah is a duty-free port, it has none of the commercial bustle usually connected with this status. Kuah is basically still a fishing village. Children hunt for crabs on the town beach, men play chequers with shells and bottle tops under spreading trees, and fishermen wander back from their boats with baskets full of fish.

Pantai Cengang and **Pantai Tengah**, the best beaches on the island, can be reached by island taxi. Scattered along the white sandy beaches are Malay-type resorts and chalets, the most luxurious of which is the Langkawi Island Resort, just a mile from the jetty at Kuah. It has swimming pools, restaurants, bars and all the other trappings of luxury resorts, but the beach is unsuitable for swimming. Other cheaper accommodation can be found in Kuah.

The best way to explore this fascinating island is to hire a motor bike or bicycle in Kuah town. There are over 82 kilometres (50 miles) of tarred roads

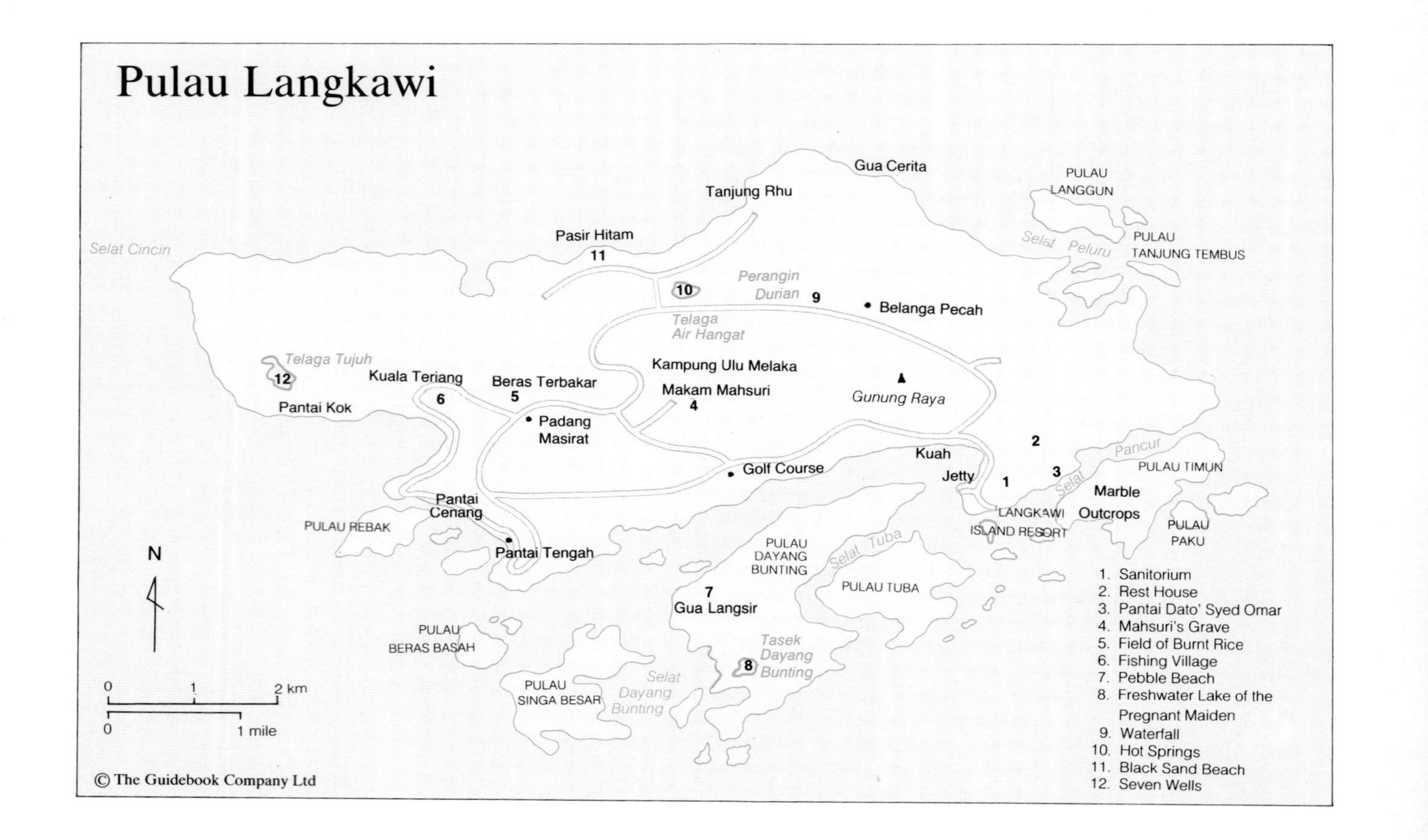
Pulau Langkawi
Gua Cerita
Tanjung Rhu
Pasir Hitam
11
Selat Cincin
PULAU LANGGUN
Selat Peluru
PULAU TANJUNG TEMBUS
10
Perangin Durian
9
Belanga Pecah
Telaga Air Hangat
Kampung Ulu Melaka
Makam Mahsuri
4
Gunung Raya
Telaga Tujuh
12
Pantai Kok
Kuala Teriang
6
Beras Terbakar
5
Padang Masirat
2
Kuah
Pancur
PULAU TIMUN
Golf Course
Jetty
1
3
Selat
Marble Outcrops
Pantai Cenang
PULAU REBAK
LANGKAWI ISLAND RESORT
PULAU PAKU
Pantai Tengah
PULAU DAYANG BUNTING
Selat Tuba
PULAU TUBA
N
7
Gua Langsir
PULAU BERAS BASAH
Tasek Dayang Bunting
8
PULAU SINGA BESAR
Selat Dayang Bunting
0
1
2 km
0
1 mile
1. Sanitorium
2. Rest House
3. Pantai Dato' Syed Omar
4. Mahsuri's Grave
5. Field of Burnt Rice
6. Fishing Village
7. Pebble Beach
8. Freshwater Lake of the Pregnant Maiden
9. Waterfall
10. Hot Springs
11. Black Sand Beach
12. Seven Wells
© The Guidebook Company Ltd

on the island and some of the older roads are paved with marble foundations from Langkawi's hills.

A Bike Ride around the Island

From Kuah follow the main road through the town, past villages and paddy-fields where water-buffaloes lounge in the mud, and on out to the golf club. Opposite the club is the road to **Makam Mahsuri**, the tomb of Langkawi's legendary island beauty and subject of its favourite legend. The story goes that in the tenth century, Mahsuri, a Malay princess, was executed for adultery, but her innocence was proved when white blood poured from her wound. Apparently she was the victim of a plot by the chief's jealous wife who envied her beauty and popularity. Before she died she put a curse on the island which lasted for seven generations. The curse ran its course long ago and the tomb of Mahsuri is now a local shrine. The tomb, 12 kilometres (seven miles) from Kuah, is nothing special, but in the surrounding countryside are timeless scenes reminiscent of an earlier age. Along the road to the tomb, which winds through paddy-fields, villagers fold palm leaves for traditional *atap* roofing and children pluck mangoes with long bamboo poles.

To return from Mahsuri's tomb, take the turnoff on the right to **Padang Matsirat** (The Field of Burnt Rice), 19 kilometres (12 miles) from Kuah. The islanders believe that there is proof here of Mahsuri's curse, for during a Thai invasion shortly after her death the islanders scorched their rice fields rather than abandon them to the invaders. Occasionally after heavy rains, burnt grains appear on these rice paddies. The road winds on to **Kuala Teriang**, a small fishing village in a secluded cove, and from there an untarred road skirts the palm-fringed coastline dotted with traditional wooden houses and fishing lagoons to the resort beaches of **Pantai Cengang** and **Pantai Tengah**.

Another excellent bike ride is the road north of town, which winds up through the centre of the island, past marble cliffs, rubber plantations, Indian shrines, paddy-fields and on up to the northern coast. **Pasir Hitam** (The Beach of Black Sand) is 19 kilometres (12 miles) and **Tanjung Rhu** 23 kilometres (15 miles) from Kuah. This latter beach was once Langkawi's best beach but it has been spoilt by an unfinished and abandoned resort complex.

To explore the other islands and their narrow fiord-like passages you can join a tour or rent a boat for the day. A favourite jaunt is to **Pulau Dayang Bunting**, an offshore island with a freshwater lake where, according to folklore, a childless couple drank the lake water, after which the wife became pregnant. Many Malaysians visit the lake in the hope that they will be similarly blessed.

Kuah has some fine eating-out spots. The food stalls on the waterfront are recommended for 'Langkawi Chicken Chop' and the open-air eating place next to the bridge serves excellent Thai Muslim food, including *tom yam*.

Other stalls are renowned for their baked fish and chilli crabs. As Langkawi is a duty-free port, liquor and cigarettes are much cheaper here than on the mainland and you can also pick up authentic Indonesian *jamu* (traditional herbal medicines).

Across the Top

Not so long ago, the only way to cross the northern part of the peninsula from Penang to Kelantan was to fly, or perhaps to make a month-long jungle trek. But with the opening of the East West Highway, it is now possible to drive from one coast to the other. The road from Penang to Kota Baru passes through the towns of Sungai Petani, Baling, Keroh and Grik, where the highway proper begins. If you are driving from Kuala Lumpur or Ipoh, turn right just after Kuala Kangsar towards Grik. This latter route is the most interesting, for it winds up to **Tasek Cenderoh,** one of Malaysia's most picturesque lakes. The road snakes across a causeway over the lake which is dotted with water-lilies and surrounded by jungle-clad hills. At **Kota Tampan**, a little further north, archaeologists recently discovered the remains of a stone-age workshop, evidence that man has lived here since the dawn of time, perhaps dating to 35,000 years ago. Before this discovery, the earliest evidence of prehistoric man was from Sarawak's Niah Caves.

At **Grik**, the East West Highway begins. There are police checkpoints at the beginning and end of the highway, as this thick jungle territory near the Thai border is still known to harbour the odd band of communist terrorists. For security reasons, travellers are not allowed to start the journey after 4 pm. This new highway is quite an engineering wonder, traversing mountain tops and slicing through entire hills. Erosion is obviously a major problem in the wet season. Viewed from this lofty vantage point the jungle canopy is a riot of colour. In the equatorial forest each species has its own spring and autumn, and trees bud and shed all the year round. Below, in the gloom of the rain forest, these flowering tree-tops can rarely be seen because the canopy is up to 50 metres (164 feet) high. According to local belief, these colourful young shoots and flowers are preserved for the eyes of God alone. The distance from Grik to Jeli is 115 kilometres (71 miles), and Kota Baru is a further 94 kilometres (58 miles). Just before Grik is the **Pergau Falls**, a boulder-lined stream which is an excellent spot to cool off. All told, the distance from Penang to Kota Baru is 373 kilometres (224 miles) and from Ipoh, 369 kilometres (231 miles). Allow at least ten hours for the journey and stock up on petrol, drinks and snacks at Grik.

The East Coast

A Journey through Time

A curious crescent-shaped boat, with an upraised bow and stern, cuts through the glassy waters of the South China Sea. Along the foreshore, a golden beach fringed with coconut palms stretches to the horizon. Fishing villages perch on stilts at the water's edge, and — off shore — wooded isles encircled by coral reefs float in a turquoise-coloured sea.

From Kelantan in the far northeast, through the states of Terengganu, Pahang and Johor, stretches the east coast — a timeless region where traditional lifestyles are the rule, not the exception. Not so long ago this coast was cut off from the rest of the country by the mountainous interior. Spared the rampant colonialism of the west coast, the east is Malaysia at its most unhomogenized and the heartland of Malay arts and crafts. There is a quietness that is immediately apparent — a feeling of timelessness. It is a place that appeals to romantics, to travellers in search of peace and of time stood still.

During the months from December to March, the northeast monsoon descends upon the east coast. These rainy months are a time of hibernation, for the fishing fleets are port-bound and floods often cut off the villages and even the main roads for days on end. If your visit coincides with the monsoon season, Malaysia Airlines operates daily flights from Kuala Lumpur to Kota Baru, Kuala Terengganu and Kuantan and from Penang to Kota Baru and Kuala Terengganu. By road, Kota Baru is linked to Penang by the East West Highway, and Kuantan to Kuala Lumpur by another cross-country highway. There is also a train line through the undeveloped centre, from Gemas in Negri Sembilan state to Kota Baru. Express buses regularly ply the east coast route from towns all over the peninsula and even from Singapore.

Kelantan — Land of Lightning

Hemmed in by mountainous terrain to the south and west, Kelantan — peninsular Malaysia's most traditional state — has always tended to look northwards to the fertile coastal plain and the South China Sea for its livelihood. Northern Kelantan is bordered by miles of white-sand beaches and fishing villages and the broad coastal plain is covered with rice fields, but further to the south much of the state is covered by vast stretches of lush tropical jungle where monkeys, deer, tigers and elephants still roam.

Because of this isolation, Kelantanese culture thrived, and although development projects are transforming the lifestyle of many people, traditional Malay arts continue to flourish. The *makyung*, a Malay court

dance, is now found only in Kelantan. After the rice harvest, kite-flying, top-spinning and drum-beating contests are popular entertainments and no celebration is complete without the *wayang kulit* or puppet-shadow play. Hidden amongst the *kampung* are tiny workshops where the famed Kelantanese silversmiths, wood-carvers, batik artists and silk brocade weavers ply their crafts.

This rich cultural tradition springs from an equally rich history, for Kelantan's roots go back to the legendary second-century empire of Langkasuka. Scholars still dispute its location, but according to a Chinese history of AD 502, the kingdom — famed for its camphor wood — took 30 days to cross from east to west. Langkasuka survived for seven centuries and appears on ancient Chinese maps together with Terengganu, Pahang and Kelantan. Even the location of Srivijaya, the forerunner of Malacca and formerly thought to have been at Palembang in Sumatra, is now supposed by some historians to have been somewhere in the vicinity of Kelantan.

In the 14th century most of the east coast fell under the rule of the great Javanese kingdom of Majapahit, but Hayam Wuruk, the ruler of Majapahit, was a conqueror not a statesman, content to empire-build not to colonize. Javanese influence from these times is still strong in Kelantan, where Javanese words are included in the local dialect. In more recent times and up to the first decade of this century, Kelantan lay under Thai control, but was ruled by its own sultans. Thai overlordship often amounted to nothing more than the sending of a yearly tribute called the *bunga mas dan perak*, a small tree of silver and gold flowers. In 1909 the British conceded a treaty with Siam, putting Kelantan under British rule and relinquishing Patani, a neighbouring Muslim kingdom, to Thailand, thus severing this old Islamic centre from the rest of the Malay world.

Kelantan came to the attention of the world in 1941 when, 95 minutes before the attack on Pearl Harbour, Japanese troops landed at Pantai Dasar Sabak and started their march to Singapore. In 1948 Kelantan became part of the Federation of Malaysia.

Kota Baru — Sights and Beaches

Situated at the very top of the state, Kota Baru, the capital of Kelantan, sprawls along the banks of the river of the same name. Hub of the populous agricultural plains, Kota Baru is also the centre for most of the traditional arts and crafts. A traveller coming from the west coast, where most of the businesses are run by the Chinese, will notice the difference in Kota Baru where the Malays predominate, as they do along the whole of the east coast. Cut off from the west coast for so long, the eastern states were spared the massive influx of Chinese and Indian immigrants under the British colonial system.

The **Central Market** of Kota Baru is the best and most colourful in all of Malaysia. In 1830 a Malay writer, Munshi Abdullah, commented on the number of women hawkers who bring their garden produce to market in baskets on their heads, and even today in the Central Market the male merchants are far outnumbered. A pale yellow light filters through the translucent roof of the octagonal market building, and bathed in the glow, like players at centre stage, the Kelantanese women sit surrounded by a dazzling display of fresh fruit and vegetables. The huge arched roof somehow muffles the din, and the noise becomes melodic. Dressed in batik, with delicate veils over their heads, the women sit nestled amongst fern shoots from the riverbanks, pink lotus blossoms from the rice fields, bright green *petai* beans from the jungle, exotic banana flowers that taste of artichoke, and piles of dazzling red chillies, the mainstays of Malay cuisine. The women chew their betel nut, strike a bargain, and tend to their babies in the easy timeless east coast manner.

Gelanggang Seni (The Kelantan Cultural Centre) is opposite the stadium, off Jalan Mahmood. This centre for Kelantanese performing arts is probably the only venue in Malaysia where these traditional activities can be seen. Shows featuring the *rebana ubi*, giant drums made from hollow logs, are held every Saturday afternoon. On the first day of May each year, the Giant Drum Festival attracts drummers from all over the state who gather here to drum up a storm. Also held on Saturday afternoons are kite-flying competitions. Kites, known as *wau*, were popularized during the 15th-century Malaccan Sultanate and are a popular Kelantanese sport. The colourful paper kites can sometimes measure up to 3.5 metres (11 feet) from head to tail. *Wayang kulit*, the puppet-shadow play, is staged at the Cultural Centre every Wednesday night. The *tok dalang*, the puppeteer, sits behind the screen working the puppets and narrating the story. A traditional orchestra provides the background music. Top-spinning competitions are held on Wednesday and Saturday afternoons, when competitors pit their skills and expertise against one another. The *gasing*, or top, is about the size of a dinner plate and can weigh up to 5.5 kilograms (12 pounds). Other traditional performances of *silat*, the Malay art of self-defence, and *berdikir barat*, described as verbal fencing in wit and verse, are sometimes held here, but check beforehand at the Tourist Development Corporation Office in Jalan Sultan Ibrahim.

Istana Balai Besar (The Palace with the Large Audience Hall) is situated in the northern part of town, in the square formed by Jalan Hilir Kota and Jalan Hulu Kota which was originally a fort. Inside the palace, built in 1844 during the reign of Sultan Muhammad II, are beautifully executed wood-carvings. The old palace houses the Throne Room, the Hall of Audience and the State Legislative Assembly Hall and is still used for important occasions such as royal wedding ceremonies. At the first royal ceremony ever held here, the sultan received a letter from the King of Siam recognizing him as

the ruler of Kelantan. Also housed here is the Royal Barge, with a splendid figurehead in the image of a legendary bird with a gilded head and tail. The barge was used only once, when Sultan Muhammad IV went for a pleasure cruise down the Kelantan River in 1900.

Istana Jahar, situated just beside the Balai Besar, is now the Kelantan State Museum. The superb craftsmanship of the Kelantanese wood-carvers is evident in the intricate carved beams and wooden panelling that embellish this old palace. Built in 1889 by Sultan Muhammad IV, the museum is open to the public from 10.30 am to 6 pm and is closed on Wednesdays.

The **State Mosque** is virtually next door to the State Museum. Construction of the mosque began in 1916 and was completed ten years later during the reign of Sultan Ismail. Architecturally, it is similar in style to the Abu Bakar Mosque in Johor. Adjacent to this is the State Religious Council Building, built during the reign of Sultan Muhammad in 1914.

Out-of-town Drives

'The coast of Kelantan is an unbroken stretch of magnificent beach, fringed with coconuts, where the breakers of the South China Sea pound the white sand and cloud the air with a mist of spray.' Although this description was written in 1935, not much has changed, and this idyllic coast is within easy reach of Kota Baru.

Pantai Cinta Berahi (The Beach of Passionate Love), situated ten kilometres (six miles) north of town, is the most famous of all Kelantan's beaches. Along the narrow road that winds out to the coast, along which sway Kelantanese women with fruit-filled baskets balanced on their heads, giant bamboos almost meet overhead. At Kampung Penambang, four kilometres (2.5 miles) along, watch for the clothes-lines tied to coconut palms on which brilliantly coloured, newly-washed batiks are put out to dry. In backyard sheds, artisans are at work applying wax to cotton cloth stretched over a pad of banana leaves. Traditional stamped batik sarongs and the freehand batik painted cloth can be bought from the little shops that front the workshops. This *kampung* also specializes in weaving the *kain songket*, a rich silk brocade shot with silver or gold thread. Many of the village women have a loom set up to work on between their household chores. This rich silk cloth can be purchased from the cottage-craft factory in Kampung Penambang. Kite-makers also abound on this road and if it is the kite-flying season; after the rice harvest, you may glimpse the kites soaring high over the dried rice paddies. Located just before the beach is the Local Handicraft Centre, where batik, *kain songket*, silverwork and other crafts can be purchased. Close by is the beach, which offers resort- and motel-style accommodation. The swimming is good and the Thai-style local food delicious, but the prize of the day is a lurid, glorious sunset over a fiery sea.

Tropical Underwater World

Malaysia's offshore islands, particularly the more remote east coast groups, are fringed with coral reefs rich with animal and plant life. Reefs slope gently away from the shore and at low tide are covered by only 1.5 metres (five feet) or less of water. Even the novice snorkeller can safely glimpse this fascinating underwater world. Some of the more commonly encountered animals and plants of the reef slope community are listed below.

(a) **Stinging or Fire Coral** (*Millepora platyphylla*) form massive colonies up to a metre (3.2 feet) across of yellowish upright plates, pillars or branches. A microscopic fuzz growing on its surface produces a temporary stinging sensation on contact.

(b) **Butterflyfish** (*Chelmon rostratus*) have flat, disc-shaped bodies, beautifully striped with yellow, silver and black, and a false eyespot. This 10–20-centimetre (four–eight-inch) -long fish has a beak-shaped mouth.

(c) **Bottlebrush Worms** (*Family Serpulidae*) have a calcareous tube embedded in the coral and feather tentacles arranged spirally on two lobes, each one–two centimetres (0.3–0.7 inches) in length. Colours are intense blue, red, orange, black or white.

(d) **Sea Nettle** (*Aglaophenia*) is a pinkish brown, fern-like growth with branches 20 centimetres (eight inches) long. Contact with the skin produces a sharp sting and raises welts which disappear with time.

(e) **Feather Duster Tube Worm** (*Sabellastarte indica*) lives in a flexible membranous tube attached to corals from which protrude feathery feeding tentacles, speckled brown and white and measuring eight centimetres (three inches) across.

(f) **Featherstar** (*Himerometra*) have up to 30 graceful feathery arms which undulate through the water as they swim. They often attach to (g) **Gorgonian Sea Fan**, a brightly-coloured tree coral when they are young, but break free when mature.

(h) **Neptune's Cup Sponge** (*Petrosia*) is a large, pinkish-brown sponge whose glass-like spicules can cause temporary skin irritation if touched.

(i) **Anemonefish** (*Amphiprion ocellaris*), a colourful orange and white striped fish, lives safe from predators among the stinging tentacles of pastel-coloured reef anemones (j) (*Radianthus*).

(k) **Sea Whips** are a hard, tree-like coral lacking cross connections. They range from single white strands (*Junceella*) to white, red and purple candelabra-like structures (*Otenocella*).

(l) **Angelfish** (*Pomacanthus annularis*) are disc-shaped like the closely related butterflyfish, but bigger — 20–60 centimetres (eight–24 inches) — and more colourful. Adults have a long spine which is used for fighting.

(m) **Crown of Thorns Starfish** (*Acanthaster planci*) favours grazing on (n) **Staghorn Coral** (*Acropora*). Measuring 40 centimetres (16 inches) across and covered with poisonous spines, this notorious starfish can devastate reefs if numerous.

(o) **Moray Eels** are snake-shaped fish about 1.5 metres (five feet) long and most often seen peering out from corals waiting to snatch passing fish. Their past bad reputation is being refuted by divers who claim that they are doglike and friendly.

Pantai Dasar Sabak, three kilometres (two miles) past the airport, is renowned not only for its beach but also for its colourful fishing fleet. At mid-afternoon, when the fleet is just returning to shore, a hundred or so rainbow-painted fishing boats bob in the shallow waters as one by one they are hauled by chanting crews, straining under bamboo poles, up on to the beach. The fishermen, heads wrapped in turbans Kelantanese-style, unload their catch into baskets on the beach. Their wives, arms heavy with gold jewellery, sort the fish and barter with fishmongers on the hot sandy beach. Atop the prows of these colourful boats are elaborately carved and painted *bangau*, spar holders made in the likeness of the *bangau*, Malaysia's egret; or fashioned into figures from the *wayang kulit,* the shadow-puppet play. These lavishly decorated boats are not ornamented for tourist appeal, nor are they 'art for art's sake'; they are adorned so as to appease the spirits of the sea, for it is in the *bangau* that the soul, known as *semangat,* resides. A well-disposed *semangat* can mean the difference between a good and a bad catch and can even keep adverse weather at bay.

Wat Photivihan, a Thai temple, is situated across the Sultan Yahya Bridge over the Kelantan River in the **Tumpat** district, about 12 kilometres (seven miles) from Kota Baru. The road traverses the rice fields where water-buffaloes lounge in the mud and houses perch on stilts high above the flood-prone fields. In most Kelantanese house compounds you will notice bamboo birdcages suspended from high poles. These cages house the prized *merbok*, a songbird especially popular on the east coast. Every Friday morning bird-singing contests are held in these outer villages. There are several Buddhist temples in this vicinity, but the most famous is Wat Phothivihan, which houses a 40-metre (131-foot) -long reclining Buddha.

Masjid Kampung Laut, Malaysia's oldest mosque, is located at **Kampung Nilam Puri**, ten kilometres (six miles) south of Kota Baru. The mosque was originally located opposite Kota Baru town on the banks of the river, but because of the constant flood danger it was dismantled and moved to its present location. Built by Javanese craftsmen using the prized *cengal* hardwood and constructed without the use of nails, the mosque is a superb example of 18th-century woodwork.

Terengganu's Offshore Islands

About 20 kilometres (12 miles) off shore from the Kelantan/Terengganu border are the untouched islands of the Perhentian group. At Jerteh, 60 kilometres (37 miles) south of Kota Baru, take the turnoff to Kuala Besut, a fishing port and jumping-off place for **Pulau Perhentian**. The islands offer excellent coral-reef snorkelling and miles of untouched beaches; be prepared to rough it, though, for there are no fancy resorts. On Pulau Perhentian Besar there is a Government Rest House, but bookings must be made in advance through the Pejabat Daerah (District Office) in Kuala Besut (tel. 09–976235). Small thatched-roof chalets are available, but the Rest House is by far the better bargain as a beachside room for four, complete with bathroom, is only M$20 per night. While there is a tiny coffee shop, it is best to take along your own supplies. Wooden fishing trawlers operate from the main wharf. There is no set timetable and it's all rather vague, but as tourists are still a novelty here everyone is willing to give directions.

Kuala Besut is an interesting fishing port to explore while you wait for the boat. Cars can be left at the police station free of charge. Friday, Terengganu's weekend, is the best time to go to the islands as local families often go out overnight and the boat service is assured. On market day the whole dockside is swamped with covered stalls selling black-market jeans from Thailand, local batik, woven pandanus mats and a succulent array of local fruits and freshly cooked *keropok*, deep-fried fish crackers. The estuary is clogged with boats, for Kuala Besut is a working port with plenty of dockside activity. Once on board, the journey to Pulau Perhentian Besar takes just under two hours, chugging along through a jade-green sea. Pulau Perhentian Besar (*besar* means 'big') has a sister island, Pulau Perhentian Kecil (*kecil* means 'small'). On this smaller isle is a traditional fishing village famous for its prowess at *berdikir barat*, a verbal art form traditionally performed at weddings.

On arrival at the jetty, which protrudes from a palm-fringed white beach, travellers will find the Rest House just to the right, and Pak Daham's and other chalets a short walk along the beach to the left. The snorkelling off this beach is superb: pink tabletop corals, green bulbous brain corals and delicate grey and violet soft corals fringe the channel that drops off between the two islands. Rainbow-hued parrotfish, damselfish and clown fish abound in the tepid waters and when you re-emerge on the surface the jungle noises sound intense after the silent underwater world. Thick virgin rain forest grows right to the water's edge and there are trails for those interested in trekking. Other islands, such as Pulau Redang further south, offer splendid diving and fishing but they are even more remote than Perhentian and getting there is a problem. It can all be organized for a price, however.

Kuala Terengganu

Kuala Terengganu, the capital of the state of the same name, has an old-world quality to it. Old Chinese shophouses line the river, trishaws weave through the back lanes and the market spills out along the riverbank. The island-studded estuary throbs with marine activity. Ferry boats criss-cross the waters and fishing fleets chug downstream and out into the South China Sea. Islam first came to Malaysia 32 kilometres (20 miles) upstream from Kuala Terengganu, where a stone pillar was found inscribed with the oldest-known

Malay text in the Arabic script. The 'Terengganu Stone' records the Muslim laws put forward by a raja and is dated 1326, well before Malacca's conversion to Islam. Terengganu is still an Islamic stronghold and the state's population is predominantly Malay. In its early days, Terengganu had a reputation as a pirate-free port. The Thais believed that the port was protected by a compassionate Buddha who sent fierce winds to drive away their enemies. These gales were the northeast monsoon which annually drenches the land and keeps the fishermen at home to mend nets, repair their boats and wait for the winds to die down.

The **Terengganu River** is where the action of the town is centred. Along the riverfront next to the jetties is the **Pasar Besar**, the town market. Here vegetable and fruit sellers, fishmongers, chicken and meat sellers, dry goods vendors and craftsmen gather to sell their wares. The market spills on to the pavement outside, where women hawkers sit amidst mounds of a dozen different varieties of bananas.

Pulau Duyung, an island in the middle of the Terengganu River famed for its traditional boat building, is a short 40-cent boat ride from the town jetty. The island's boat builders are internationally renowned for their expertise in crafting boats from the famed tropical hardwoods of the interior. The noise of power saws and electric planers fills the air — the tools are electric but the work is still traditional. Workshops fringe the island where every type of craft, from custom-built American yachts to fishing trawlers, is constructed. There are no roads on the island, where wooden *kampung* houses stand high on stilts above the tidal flats. For those wishing to stay here overnight there is a unique thatched roof cottage called 'Awis Yellow House', where you can rent a cheap room only ten minutes from downtown Kuala Terengganu.

Other attractions include some interesting examples of traditional Terengganu-style wooden homes in Kampung Dalam Kota, near the market area; the **Istana Mazia**, the palace of the sultan built in the French style; and the carefully preserved **Istana Tengku Nik**, a fine example of traditional Malay architecture, which is found on the way south out of town. At **Kampung Tanjung**, brass workers pour white-hot metal into moulds for casting, and batik makers stamp their waxed designs on cloth, following traditional occupations passed down through the generations.

South along the Seashore

South of Kuala Terengganu the road hugs the South China Sea which laps the shores of a seemingly endless stretch of empty beach, broken here and there by fishing villages. If the noonday heat gets too much, the beach is close by for a refreshing dip, and for those wanting to linger on this delightful coast there are beachside chalets and bungalows and, a little further down the coast, some of Malaysia's best-known resort hotels.

Traditional Malay Pastimes

For centuries, Malays have made full use of their leisure time. Many of their traditional pastimes evolved during breaks in the agricultural calendar and others became specialized entertainments at festivals and celebrations. Some of these traditional pastimes are now staged only in Kelantan, Kedah and Terengganu on special occasions, but others have caught on throughout the nation and have become popular sports.

Gasing, or **top-spinning,** contests are often held between neighbouring Kelantanese villages, especially after the rice harvest. The tops, weighing about 5.5 kilograms (12 pounds) and measuring as wide as a dinner plate, are polished, streamlined works of art. Some master spinners' tops even have spindles of inlaid silver. Spinning the top is an art in itself, requiring manual dexterity, timing and strength. Once the *gasing* is spinning, it is scooped off the ground with a thin wooden bat and transferred on to a little wooden post with a metal surface. It is then left to spin. Experts can set a top spinning for two hours and villagers believe that if a *semangat*, or spirit, enters the top it can twirl for 24 hours.

Kite-flying has been a popular seasonal sport in Kelantan for centuries. After the rice harvest, when the hot arid winds blow, farmers gather on the stubble of the rice plains to match their kites in inter-village contests. These elaborate kites, known as *wau*, measure up to two metres (6.5 feet) across and soar up to 152 metres (500 feet). Made of glazed coloured paper and mounted on a bamboo frame, with a bow-shaped device fixed to the neck, they emit a humming sound when aloft. *Wau* may resemble fish, swallows, cats and even frogs, but the moon kite, *wau bulan*, is the most popular and elaborate with its distinctive crescent-shaped tail. Kelantanese contestants who have the highest-flying and most belligerent kites are the winners in a contest which originated in the 16th-century court of the Malaccan Sultanate.

Wayang kulit, the **shadow-puppet play,** was the favourite after-dark entertainment of the Malay village before cinemas became widespread. Even today on the east coast, *wayang kulit* is performed on auspicious occasions such as weddings, births or after a successful rice harvest. The puppets, crafted from buffalo hide and mounted on bamboo sticks, are held behind a white cloth, and an oil lamp creates the flickering shadows on the screen. The skilled puppeteer, called *To' Dalang* (Father of the Mysteries), moves the puppets and narrates the story which often involves dozens of different characters. A Malay band plays a haunting accompaniment to tales of the classic Indian epics, *The Mahabharata* and *The Ramayana*, which first came to Malaysia from the medieval Javanese kingdom of Majapahit.

Silat — the **Malay art of self-defence** — like most Asian martial arts, calls for graceful, disciplined movements and inner power. Its exponents of old practised deep meditations so as to invoke help from the spirits in warding off evil blows, but today it is more likely to feature as part of a wedding celebration than as a fight to the death. Exhibition *silat*, enacted by the *Pendekar*, or expert, is a highly-stylized, electrifying performance, backed by the beating of gongs and drums.

Sepak takraw, sometimes referred to as 'aerial soccer over a net', is one of Malaysia's most popular sports. All that is required is a small rattan ball and an open space. Contestants can use heels, soles, insteps, thighs, shoulders and heads — everything but hands — to keep the ball aloft. Other Southeast Asian countries play variations of this same game, which apparently derives from a 14th-century contest between four Malay rulers. Legend has it that the raja of the Moluccas won after keeping the ball aloft for 200 body bounces. These days, *sepak takraw* is played at all major regional sports meets.

Bird-singing competitions between the *merbuk* (Peaceful Dove) are not only a popular pastime in Kelantan but have also caught on all over the country. In a major competition, about 300 birds compete against each other while suspended from eight-metre (26-foot) -high poles. *Merbuk* are apparently most relaxed singing at this height. The song is a rolling whistled 'coo', usually repeated six to eight times. Each bird creates its own tune and no *merbuk* can be trained to imitate the song of another. Champion singers change hands for thousands of Malaysian dollars. Contests are held throughout Malaysia and early on Friday mornings on the outskirts of Kota Baru, and as part of public holiday celebrations.

The *rebana*, or **Kelantanese drum,** is made from a hollowed-out log 60 centimetres (two feet) in diameter. Once the rice-planting season is over, villagers often assemble in the paddy-fields to challenge each other in the art of drum beating. Judges come from an independent village and award points on tone, rhythm and timing. The Giant Drum Festival, when villagers pit their rhythmic skills against one another, is held on the first day of May each year.

Wielding a weapon used in Bersilat — Malay self-defence

Marang, 15 kilometres (nine miles) south of Kuala Terengganu, is one of the prettiest fishing villages on the coast. Located just before Marang on the north side of the river is Kampung Patah Malam, a fishing village which can be reached only by a long wooden footbridge. A shallow lagoon full of boats runs along the back of the village, creating an island-like effect. Through the break in the sand bar, which separates the sea from the lagoon, the crescent-shaped, typically Terengganu boats ply to and from the offshore fishing grounds. Along the palm-draped coastline men sit in the shade mending nets beside barriers of woven palms which protect their homes from the monsoon's wrath. Their boats are beached nearby under little thatched garages of palm leaves. Along the shorefront, amongst the villagers' homes, are chalets and bungalows for rent.

Pulau Kapas, a jewel-like isle, lies just off shore from Marang. The island is only a 30-minute boat ride away and has the requisite white sandy beaches and coral-filled waters. Some of the chalets and guesthouses at Marang have speedboats and provide a day's outing complete with picnic lunch and fishing along the way.

Rantau Abang, 60 kilometres (37 miles) south of Kuala Terengganu, is where the giant turtles return every year to lay their eggs. Although five different species of turtles make the annual pilgrimage, the leatherback is the most well known. The largest of all sea turtles, an average nesting female can have a shell length of 1.5 metres (five feet) and weigh over 350 kilograms (771 pounds). The months from June to September are the peak nesting season and the best time for viewing is at night on a high tide. Chalet accommodation is available at the beach, but you probably won't get much sleep; drink plenty of strong coffee to keep awake for the grand event, for it is certainly worthwhile. In the past, people posed for snapshots on the turtles' backs and collected eggs indiscriminately, but these days the nesting is carefully controlled. People also used to listen to radios and build fires while waiting for the turtles, but all these activities scared the turtles away from the beach. It is advisable to let the turtle commence laying her eggs before approaching. The Department of Fisheries keeps close tabs on the turtles' migrations and the collecting of eggs; it even collects the newly-hatched turtles and releases them into the sea, as in the past sea-birds picked off many baby turtles before they reached the sea. An educated public is the best safeguard to ensure that the turtles return every year to Rantau Abang.

Tanjung Jara, 13 kilometres (eight miles) north of Kuala Dungun, is the site of the best-known resort on the east coast. The unique Malay-inspired architecture of this five-star resort blends in with the surrounding seascape. A natural swimming lagoon, cycling, tennis, squash and a variety of water sports is enough to keep even the most hyperactive tourist happy.

Kuala Dungun is another sleepy port on the road south where the goats and cows often outnumber the cars. Most of the 1,500 inhabitants depend on the sea for their livelihood, either by fishing, curing salt fish, or boat building. Outside many of the wooden homes built on stilts are platforms where the salted fish are left to dry in the sun. The coconut palms overhead rustle in the offshore breeze, waves gently lap the golden beach and life goes on in a timeless rhythm. During the fruit season this stretch of coast is lined with wooden stalls selling *kuini*, a delicious local mango. Further south at **Kerteh** is the new petroleum complex, which comes as a culture shock on this laid-back coast. Fishing boats give way to oil tankers, and a giant steel complex of tanks, huge serpentine pipelines and sophisticated suburbs appear. The off-shore petroleum and natural gas fields along this coast have brought new wealth to the state of Terengganu and to the nation. Petroleum is the success story of Malaysia's export economy and its number one foreign exchange earner.

Cherating, just over the border into Pahang state, brings you back into the timeless reality of the east coast; the petroleum and gas complex to the north seems almost like a dream. Here is the Club Med resort with its three private beaches for those who crave luxury and everything laid on and organized. But if you are looking for something at a more grass-roots level, there are plenty of marvellous Malay-style chalets and bungalows along the beach beside the village. Off shore is a small islet called Pulau Ular (Snake Island), which is readily accessible from the village.

Sungai Ular, just down the coast, is a photographer's dream. From the bridge just before the village is a marvellous view of the river choked with fishing boats and wooden houses on a sandy spit beside the sea.

Kuantan, the capital of **Pahang** state, lies 219 kilometres (136 miles) south of Kuala Terengganu. It is easily accessible to Kuala Lumpur, which lies 274 kilometres (170 miles) to the west along a fast new highway. Kuantan is not as classically east coast as the towns further north, but is still quiet and slow-paced compared with the west coast. Along the esplanade by the river are food stalls specializing in Malay food and plenty of good picnic spots. Adjacent to the river is the town centre, with some interesting neo-colonial government buildings set amongst spacious parkland.

Teluk Cempedak, to the north of town, is Kuantan's favourite beach. The swimming is good and the rocky jungle-clad shores to the north are fun for those who like to explore an untouched coastline within a short distance from their hotel. Teluk Cempedak abounds with accommodation — from first-class luxury resorts to smaller Chinese-run hotels for budget-minded travellers. If you are planning a night in Kuantan, this is the best place to stay — not only for the beach, but also because the small village of Teluk Cempedak has many of the best seafood restaurants in the region. There is also a government-run handicrafts shop beside the beach which specializes in locally produced batik and *kain songkit* (silk brocade).

Beserah, a scenic and traditional fishing village, is just a little further out

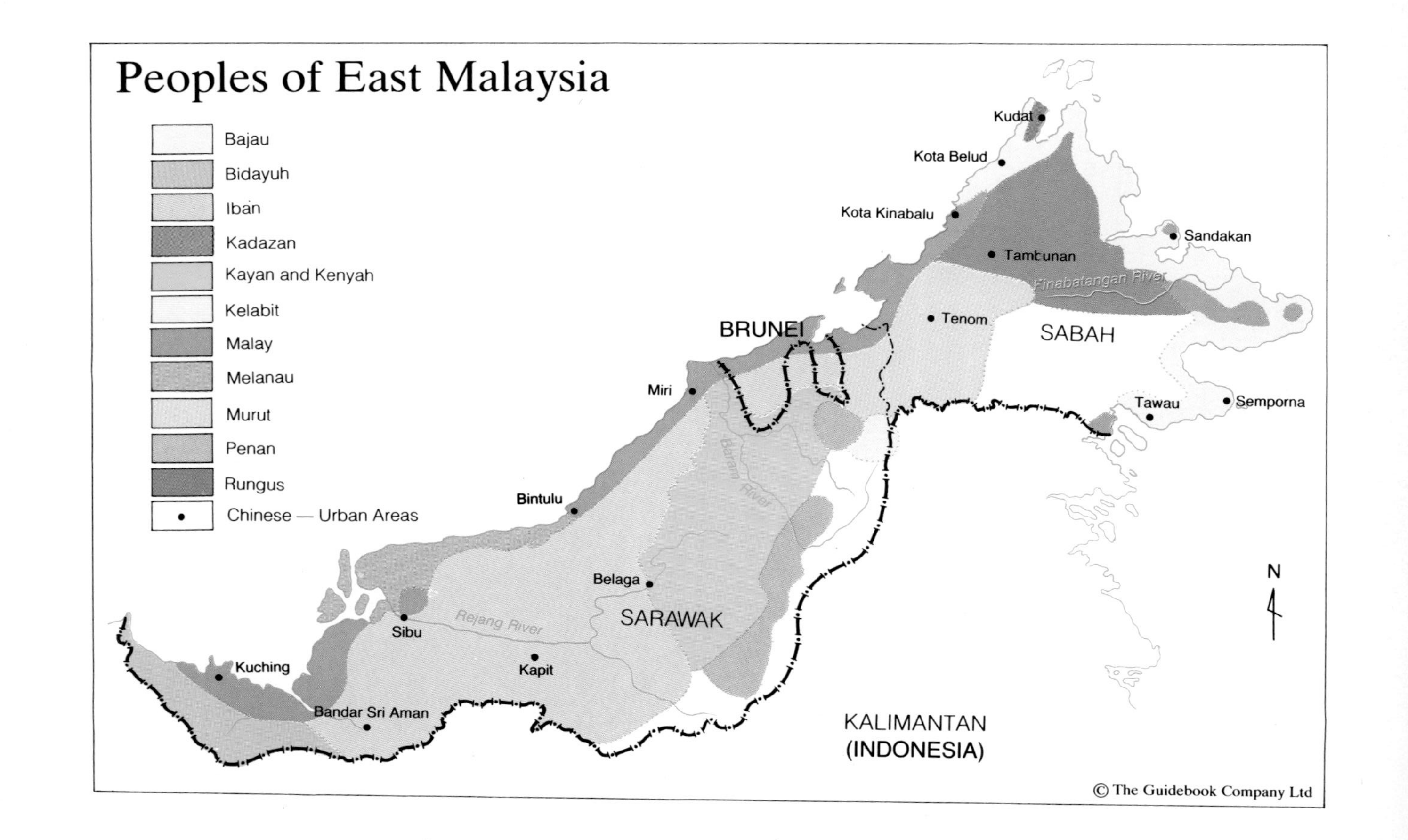
Peoples of East Malaysia
Bajau
Bidayuh
Iban
Kadazan
Kayan and Kenyah
Kelabit
Malay
Melanau
Murut
Penan
Rungus
Chinese — Urban Areas
Kudat
Kota Belud
Kota Kinabalu
Sandakan
Tambunan
Kinabatangan River
Tenom
SABAH
BRUNEI
Miri
Tawau
Semporna
Baram River
Bintulu
Belaga
SARAWAK
Sibu
Rejang River
Kapit
Kuching
Bandar Sri Aman
KALIMANTAN
(INDONESIA)
N
© The Guidebook Company Ltd

of town to the north. A winding one-lane road leads through the waterfront village shaded by a forest of coconut palms. Some of the older homes still have beautiful tiled roofs and in the east coast tradition they are oiled rather than painted. Here, where the relentless trade winds blow the salty air on shore, the houses take on a look of bleached driftwood. Around mid-morning, when the fishing fleet returns, Beserah is witness to a unique scene, possibly the only place in Malaysia where this is a regular occurrence: turban-clad villagers hitch water-buffalo up to wooden carts, and then urge them across a shallow lagoon and on to the beach where they load the day's catch from the fishing boats into baskets on the back of the buffalo carts. The laden carts return to the village further down the beach or to the *ikan bilis* (anchovy) factory on the beach. At the old and dilapidated shed propped up with sandbags, the tiny fish are unloaded, then boiled in vats of sea water and left to dry in the sun. Salted fish is one of Beserah's main occupations and when the fish are running and the catch is good the wooden drying racks are full of rows of silvery fish. Beserah also has its own batik factory out on the main road north, beside the bridge. Here Yusof Deraman, the proprietor, stamps the longer lengths of batik or paints smaller pieces. When he has large orders, the village women help him to wash the batiks in the creek that flows past his workshop.

Pekan, the royal capital of Pahang, is 45 kilometres (28 miles) south of Kuantan. The town sits just upstream from the estuary of the Pahang River, peninsular Malaysia's longest waterway. In this old town is the *istana* or palace of the Sultan of Pahang, fronted by the sweeping lawns of the royal polo grounds. The sultanate traces its line back to the 15th-century Malaccan Sultanate. Here, too, are two white marble mosques which flank the royal mausoleum and the State Museum. Pekan comes to life once a year on the sultan's birthday, when traditional performing arts are staged.

Pulau Tioman — An Idyllic Isle

This island, off the coast of Pahang, is undoubtedly the state's greatest tourist attraction and the most beautiful island off Malaysia's coastline. Although the island falls under Pahang state, it is approached from the port of **Mersing** in Johor, 141 kilometres (88 miles) from Pekan. It is the same distance from Johor Baru in the south. From the jetty at Mersing, ferries and a hovercraft make daily trips to the island. By the wooden ferries, known as 'slow boats', the trip takes about four hours and costs M$15 each way. The hovercraft is faster and about double the cost. For those who want to savour the slow journey out through some of the 64 offshore islands, the ferries offer the more leisurely approach. The ferries leave in the late morning, as after lunch the port's entrance is too shallow. Travellers arriving later may have to put up in Mersing for the night. There are ample hotels and an excellent Government

Rest House right on the edge of the South China Sea. Tioman also has its own airport and daily flights operate from Singapore and Kuala Lumpur. There is one resort hotel on the island, the Tioman Island Resort, which fronts an excellent swimming beach and has the requisite water sports, pool, restaurant and bar. Guests disembark at the main jetty in **Tekek** village where the hovercraft puts in and a hotel jeep plies between the resort hotel, the airport and the jetty. Tekek village has other smaller beachside guesthouses and chalets. For those wanting to get away from it all, the beach further north from Tekek, along a walking trail, has more private thatched A-line cabins right at the water's edge. Nazri's is the original and best-known of these and the ferry will take you direct to his beach. Try to avoid coming to Tioman on public holiday weekends when the island becomes almost over-run by Singaporean holiday-makers; at all other times it is very peaceful.

On a clear day Pulau Tioman can be seen from Mersing as a mountainous blue backdrop to the lesser islands. One hour later, as the boat chugs through the glassy sea past the smaller islands, Tioman emerges in all its splendour. To the south, twin granite peaks soar 914 metres (3,000 feet) above the sea. Ribbons of white coral beaches flanked by coconut palms and surmounted by an interior of virgin rain forest complete the scene. These twin peaks were a well-known navigational beacon for the South China Sea's early mariners and are mentioned in Arab and Chinese sailing charts of 1,000 years ago. In the sheltered coves behind the hills, the sailing ships of old found safe anchorage even during the fierce monsoon. In the towering rain forests of the interior, which are much the same today, those early mariners found timbers to mend their boats, aromatic sandalwood and fresh water, and game with which to stock their larders. At the village of **Juara**, a three-hour walk across the island from Tekek, pottery has been discovered dating back to the 12th-century Song Dynasty of China.

In the late 1950s, Tioman was discovered by Hollywood and many of the scenes of the musical *South Pacific* were shot on the island. At **Mukut**, the most southerly village, is a waterfall which figured in the 'Happy Talk' sequence of the film and the island's resort apparently sits where the film crew made its base.

It is easy to see why they picked this site, for the scenery is absolutely stunning. Many tropical islands have pretty beaches and coconut groves but lack the mountainous interior and the lush vegetation that on Tioman comes right to the water's edge. The waters are crystal clear and excellent for snorkelling. Coral can be found off the resort beach and off Nazri's, but the best is at **Pulau Tulai**, a small islet off the northwest of Tioman. Day trips are organized from the chalets at an average cost of M$10 per person. Scuba diving gear can be hired from the Tioman Island Resort and good diving can be had directly opposite at the neighbouring rocky isle of **Pulau Rengis**. Most of the beachside chalets have small restaurants where fairly basic food

can be had, but don't expect to get the variety of the mainland. Tekek has more food stalls and the resort has an overpriced restaurant. Stock up in Mersing on fresh fruit and other supplies, for the island is still uncommercialized and not much is available at the little stores. If you don't want to pay inflated prices for liquor at the resort bar bring your own supplies from the mainland. Some chalets still operate even in the monsoon season when it is possible to fly in, but the boat service at this time of year is highly irregular and the water is rather murky due to the high seas.

Other Offshore Islands

Other offshore islands abound in the waters southwest and east of Pulau Tioman. Some of these are mere rocky outcrops, others are deserted 'Robinson Crusoe'-type isles, and still others boast of resorts and fishing villages. All are reached from the port of Mersing.

Pulau Rawa is the best-known and longest-running resort island in the region. It is an hour's journey from the port and has bungalow and chalet accommodation, a house restaurant and bar, and a beautiful white sandy beach and clear waters. It is best for a short stay as the island is small and can become a little claustrophobic on crowded weekends. Bookings can be made at the island's office at the jetty in Mersing.

Pulau Besar, a little to the south, has three resorts, a small fishing village and clean beaches, but the sandflies can sometimes become a nuisance.

Pulau Sibu, about two hours from Mersing to the southeast, has two resorts with restaurants and bars. Sibu has one of the most traditional fishing villages on these islands. Off shore from Sibu are many *kelong*, unique fishing platforms on stilts where anchovies are driven into nets with the aid of strong lights. The *ikan bilis*, as they are known, are cooked on the actual fishing platforms. A visit to a *kelong*, especially when the fish are running at night, is a memorable experience. Sibu has golden sand beaches where the swimming is excellent. The corals are good, but the water is not as clear as at Tioman as it is closer to the freshwater streams of the coast.

Pulau Aur, the most distant of the offshore islands, is a six-hour boat ride from Mersing. The island is renowned for its clear waters and there is a sharp dropoff between the two twin islands which lures the scuba divers of the region. *Kampung* houses provide accommodation and basic food. Ask at the jetty for boats to Aur as it is possible to take a local boat ferrying villagers back from town. If you really want somewhere remote, Pulau Aur is perfect.

There are many smaller islands where it is possible to camp. Boats can be organized for a cruise around the many varied islands off Mersing port. They can deposit you on an island and pick you up again or can be chartered for the day or for as long as you wish.

Peninsular Hill Resorts and Jungle Treks

In the rugged mountainous interior of Malaysia are some of the oldest jungles in the world; in comparison, the equatorial forests of the Amazon and the Congo are relative youngsters. The jungle is not only the heartlands of the *orang asli*, literally Malaysia's 'original people', but is also home to a vast array of animals, birds, insects and a staggering cornucopia of botanical life. Jungle exotica such as sandalwood, camphor, resins, rhinoceros horn and bezoars (monkeys' gallstones, prized as powerful magical talismans) were highly sought-after by the adventurous merchants of the East who established trading links with the early peoples 1,500 years ago. The perfect symmetry of the great rain forests makes it difficult for a jungle novice to isolate one tree from another, but an *orang asli* can often identify hundreds of varieties from his own district, a skill vital to the trade in jungle products. Stands of a single species — a common sight in temperate forests — are unusual in the jungle where trees grow more haphazardly and are found only in certain areas and in limited numbers.

Although this blanket of jungle still covers two-thirds of peninsular Malaysia, it continues to be regarded by many as a place of dangers and malevolent spirits. Spencer Chapman, a British Army Officer who spent the Japanese Occupation hiding out in the jungle, described his initial reaction to this green heart in his book *The Jungle is Neutral*. 'In every direction there were tree-clad hills, peak after peak, and ridge after ridge, purple at first, then violet and blue, fading at last into the paler blue of the distance. There was no clearing of any sort to be seen. For the first time I realized the terrifying vastness of the Malayan jungle.'

For those travellers whose heartbeat quickens at the very thought of an adventure in these realms and who don't mind the obvious discomforts, the jungle is a most mystical, rewarding experience. Taman Negara — the National Park — and the more inaccessible Endau Rompin area are two places where you can enter the undisturbed rain forest. But for travellers who like their jungle at a distance, the colonial hill resort of Cameron Highlands is an excellent compromise.

Taman Negara — The National Park

Spread out over the interior of three states — Kelantan, Terengganu and Pahang — Taman Negara occupies a vast 4,343 square kilometres (1,676 square miles) of northern peninsular Malaysia. Within this verdant expanse are dense rain forests, fast-flowing jungle rivers, an abundance of game and the peninsula's highest mountain, Gunung Tahan. For lovers of the outdoors, it is a place for hiking, fishing, swimming, shooting the rapids, mountain climbing, photography and animal watching. Although tigers, leopards, elephants and tapir still roam the isolated hinterlands of the National Park, big game is elusive and difficult to see owing to the dense undergrowth. Monkeys and gibbons are often heard but seldom seen, for they move about in the jungle canopy — often as high as 45 metres (150 feet) above the ground. Observation hides have been built in the park at salt licks, where deer, wild pig and tapir can be observed. At two of these licks, Jenut Kumbang and Jenut Belau, there are high hides where visitors can spend the night.

The headquarters of the National Park are at Kuala Tahan, accessible only by boat from **Kuala Tembeling**. The river journey takes from two-and-a-half to three-and-a-half hours, depending on the river depth. Between Kuala Tahan and Kuala Tembeling are several rapids which are easily negotiated when the river is full; in dry times, however, passengers must walk along the riverbank while the boatmen push the boat upriver.

The National Park is reached from Kuala Lumpur by private car or taxi, bus or train. The first leg is to **Jerantut** in Pahang, about a three- to four-hour journey. Travellers can take either the Raub road or the Kuala Lumpur–Kuantan highway. Share taxis leave for Jerantut from Puduraya Bus Station. Bus services leave from the bus station at Jalan Tun Razak to **Temerloh** and from here you have to continue to Jerantut by taxi. There is a direct bus service from Kuantan to Jerantut. From Jerantut, take a taxi or bus a further 16 kilometres (ten miles) along a steep narrow road to Kuala Tembeling, the start of the river journey. From Singapore, a train leaves at 10 pm and arrives at Tembeling Halt at 8 am the following morning. From here it is a half-hour walk to the jetty. From Kota Baru, a south-bound train leaves from Tumpat at 10 am and reaches Jerantut at 7.30 pm.

At the park itself there are chalets, a rest house and a hostel, complete with bathrooms, piped water, electricity and full catering facilities. There are additional visitors' and fishing lodges, complete with cooking facilities, further into the park. Tents, camp beds and lamps are available at headquarters and tinned food can be purchased at the Rest House shop. Bring along canvas jungle boots or, if you prefer (as many old jungle hands do), a pair of well-worn-in running shoes. Calico leech socks are a plus in the wet season, but don't expect to come out altogether unscathed — leeches have a way of wriggling into even the most solidly laced-up boots.

Taman Negara has some fine angling in the fast-flowing jungle rivers, in which it is estimated there are 300 varieties of freshwater fish. The *kelah*, otherwise known as the Indian Mahseer, is frequently encountered and can weigh up to nine kilograms (20 pounds). Another, the *kelasa*, will give the angler plenty of excitement, for they leap high and run fast. Of course, the further upcountry the angler goes, the better the fishing.

An interesting five-day side trip includes a trip to some painted limestone

caves once used by aborigines and elephants. It is also possible to climb the 2,187-metre (7,175-foot) **Gunung Tahan**. From headquarters to the top takes five days and the return journey four. Guides must be hired and considerable planning and expense are involved, but for those wanting a real adventure into Malaysia's jungle heartland it is time and money well spent.

Tasek Cini — Malaysia's Mystery Lake

Situated in the hinterland of Pahang state is **Tasek Cini**, a series of 13 freshwater lakes known to the *orang asli* as *laut*. Jungle-covered hills surround the lake, pandanus pines grow in the shallows, and during the flowering season from June to September the lake is covered by a carpet of red and white lotus blossoms. Legends tell of a walled Khmer city, surrounded by lotus ponds, that once existed hereabouts. Apparently when an enemy tribe attacked, the inhabitants used a system of aqueducts to submerge the city in water, thus forming Lake Cini. The lake and its lotuses have been there ever since. Aerial photographs indicate that a city may have existed, and linguists point to language and cultural similarities between the Khmer of Cambodia and the *orang asli* of Pahang, but the jungle is adept at concealing secrets. The elder *orang asli* tell of a local fisherman who is believed to have visited the underwater city back in the 1940s. A Loch Ness-type monster said to guard the depths has been glimpsed by locals and even by some British visitors in the colonial days. Apparently the serpent-like monster has two horns, a head 'as big as a tiger's' and blazing red eyes. Archaeologists and scientists have investigated the legend but, like her elusive cousin in Scotland, the *naga* of Tasek Cini remains an enigma.

There are two ways to get to Tasek Cini: if you have your own transportation you can drive to the Cini Resort on the lakeside. Take the Segamat–Kuantan highway and at the 141-kilometre (88-mile) sign from **Segamat** turn into the new oil-palm town of Cini. From here, the road deteriorates into a track which passes Kampung Gumum, an *orang asli* settlement. The resort is just at the end of the road. The thatched-roof resort is well camouflaged in the jungle. Giant trees with trunks as straight as pencils loom above the hideaway resort, and across the lake connected by a boardwalk is a floating restaurant on a jetty. Boats can be hired here for trips around the lakes.

The alternative — and classic — way to arrive at Lake Cini is to take the Kuantan–Kuala Lumpur highway. At the 74-kilometre (50-mile) marker from Kuantan, turn off to Kampung Belimbing, 27 kilometres (17 miles) further down on the Pahang River. From here, motorized wooden longboats take travellers up the Sungai Cini (Cini River) to the lake. The channel-like smaller stream is cool and shaded after the glare out on the wide Pahang River. Shafts of sunlight pierce the gloom, turning the river into a liquid bronze which laps the roots of sunken trees. Snakelike lianas drape to the water's edge and brilliant blossoming vines swathe the towering trees anchored with massive buttress roots. About 15 minutes from the Pahang River the boatman points out a large hole, said once to have housed a 1.6-kilometre (one-mile) -long snake. Villagers believe that British troops killed the snake with a cannon. When the boat emerges out on to the lake, the sunlight is dazzling after the twilit gloom of the tunnel-like river. Clouds and mountains are reflected on the waters of the lotus-filled lake, which is home to *ikan toman* and other delicious fish.

Since the dawn of time, the *orang asli* have lived beside the lake. Their settlement, shaded with fruit trees, is situated on the edge of the jungle. **Kampung Gumum** is usually on the boatman's itinerary, for here visitors can watch a blowpipe demonstration and see the *orang asli* homes which are made of split bamboo.

Tasek Cini would be an interesting place for a scuba diving expedition as boatmen talk of stones under the lake which are perhaps remnants of the legendary city. For those of an adventurous bent, **Gunung Cini**, the neighbouring peak at 823 metres (2,700 feet), waits to be climbed. The peak is said to be the home and breeding ground of the *naga,* and the serrated ridges are said to resemble the scales of the serpent's back.

Endau Rompin Wilderness

The area known as Endau Rompin, which straddles the borders of Johor and Pahang states, is one of the more accessible tracts of virgin rain forest on the peninsula. During 1984–5, this area was the subject of an expedition by the Malayan Nature Society and as a result is to be gazetted as a national or state park.

Endau Rompin is only accessible by boat up the **Endau River** from the port of **Endau**, 37 kilometres (23 miles) north of Mersing in Johor state. Buses to Mersing leave from both Johor Baru and **Kluang**, which are connected to Kuala Lumpur by bus or rail. Share taxis also ply the route from Johor Baru and Kluang. If you have access to a four-wheel-drive vehicle, however, there is an alternative route. From Kahang, on the Kluang–Mersing road, turn off to Ladang Bukit Cantek. After a one-hour drive through oil-palm plantations over fairly smooth laterite, the road deteriorates into a track which winds for another hour to the *orang asli* village of Kampung Peta, on the banks of the Endau River. This brings you within a 40-minute boat ride of the junction of the Endau and Jasin rivers and the location of the expedition's base camp. This meeting point of the rivers is an excellent spot from which to trek and the fishing here is also excellent. Guides can be hired from the *orang asli* village, but there are no stores here and everything you are likely to need will have to be brought upriver on the boat. The cost of chartering a boat may

Kelantanese Arts and Crafts

Traditional arts and crafts still flourish in the northeast state of Kelantan. Until comparatively recently, forbidding terrain to the south and west isolated this pocket of the peninsula, and the state was spared the homogenizing immigrations of the west coast. Today, Kelantan, with its uninterrupted traditions, is considered the cultural heartland of Malaysia. Batik, although a popular cottage craft in Kelantan, is not included below as it is only of comparatively recent origin compared to other traditional crafts.

Silverwork originally came from Perak (the Silver State), but it is only in Kelantan, where devotion to traditional Malay arts burns strongest, that it has survived. Up to the early 20th century, silversmiths worked exclusively in the courtyards of royalty, crafting betel nut sets, tobacco boxes, pillow-end plates and belt buckles. In 1930 a society was set up to rescue this dying craft, for all these objects were relics of a past feudal age, and silversmiths began to make jewellery, spoons and even butter dishes for the colonials. However, the methods used are the same as two centuries ago. In Islamic tradition, design is limited to floral and flowing decorative designs excluding human and animal forms. This has created an indigenous Malay style which is unique amongst the more heavily decorated Thai and Chinese styles. Today, Kelantanese silverwork is much in demand and the future of the craft is assured.

Silk-weaving has changed little over the centuries. The loom, built of the hardest Malay timber and often 90 years old, sits under the veranda of Kelantanese and Terengganu homes; and the weaver, always a woman, works there between her domestic chores. The more ambitious weavers produce the famed *kain songket*, characterized by gold and silver thread, the traditional cloth of royalty. Much of the weaver's work still centres around making traditional, ceremonial Malay dresses, which consume nine metres (ten yards) of this expensive cloth. Others produce sarong lengths characterized by an elaborate centre panel known as a *kepala*. The most gifted weave the *kain songket penuh*, which is covered from end to end in gold thread utilizing designs passed down through generations of weavers.

Wood-carving is another ancient Kelantanese craft which formerly depended on royal commissions. The wooden palaces of the nobility were lavishly decorated with carvings both inside and out. Skilled wood-carvers of the past lived and worked under royal patronage and often stayed at the same court for a lifetime. For centuries, the acme of a Malay wood-carver's art was the decorative wall panel above doors and windows, which provided a frieze around the room. This was cut out for light and ventilation and was adorned with flowers, leafy branches, or extracts from the *Koran* in arabic script. Wood-carving was a dying craft three decades ago, but today it is enjoying a revival and decorative panels adorn the walls of corporation boardrooms and government buildings across the nation.

Shadow-puppet making was traditionally the work of the puppeteer, or *To' Dalang*. *Wayang kulit*, the shadow-puppet play, literally means 'shadows made from skin', the puppets traditionally being crafted from sun-dried cowhide.

Traditional Malay shadow puppets

Hides were purchased from the butcher, then scraped and dried until translucent before being cut out. Figures are cut from the hide and their decorative dress is finely chiselled. An elaborate and delicate puppet can take nine hours to complete. A bamboo spine is inserted and the puppet is then lavishly painted. The 2,000-year-old Indian epic *The Ramayana* is the favourite Kelantanese puppet play. Prince Rama is still the hero, but his two Malay followers, Pa' Dogol and Wak Long, provide the comedy; they were invented by a Malay puppeteer over 100 years ago. In Kelantan, *wayang kulit* is still performed in the villages, but elsewhere it is performed only on special festive occasions.

be prohibitive for a lone traveller, but is reasonable if shared between a group. This trip is inadvisable, if not impossible, during the monsoon season — November to March — as the rivers are too high and the jungle is uncomfortably wet.

Early morning on the Endau River is the best time to travel for the air is still cool and fresh. Timber mist rises from the rain forest which looms beside the banks. The roar of the river as the rapids are skilfully negotiated makes conversation difficult. Where the sunlight penetrates to the riverbanks, flowering lianas, with clusters of yellow blossoms, light up the evergreen of the jungle. White-faced monkeys rattle the tree-tops and, frightened by the noise of the boat's engine, flee chattering into the gloom of the jungle. At the junction of the Jasin and Endau rivers, tracks lead off into the jungle.

Once inside the forest, the noise of the river dies down and the jungle sounds take over: an orchestra of buzzing cicadas, burping frogs and a chorus of bird and monkey calls which produce a weird hypnotic effect. Up in the tree-tops, where the great trunks suddenly burst into branches, are huge hanging fern gardens. Close by the old base camp is a stand of luminescent bamboo, which glows in the dark. It is impossible to walk along the overgrown tracks without a *parang* — the long curved bush knife — to hack the rattans and ferns from the path. Inside the virgin forest, untouched by loggers, it is dark and cool. The ground here is covered with a thick carpet of dead leaves. Palms with fronds the size of umbrellas hide the buttress roots of giant trees, and out of this wavy green sea tree trunks rise straight upwards to the roof of the jungle 50 metres (160 feet) high.

In the vicinity of the old base camp is a 31-metre (103-foot) -high tree tower, which gives an excellent view of the surrounding jungle. There is also a trail to the top of Gunung Janing where a rare *Livistona* fan-palm forest can be found. On the **Jasin River**, upstream from base, is a scenic waterfall, and downstream a little island called Pulau Jasin which contains unique flora.

Wildlife is abundant in this region: troops of gibbons are heard in most of the valleys, banded leaf monkeys can be spotted, and if you are lucky you may glimpse a leopard or even a tiger, as their tracks are quite plentiful here. The local *orang asli* know of two who live in the vicinity. The tracks of elephants, pigs, *rusa* (deer) and tapir can also be seen. Rhinoceros hornbills, with their characteristic bulbous bills, are frequently seen at dusk.

Although Endau Rompin is not as easily accessible as the National Park, it is definitely worth the time and trouble taken for this is a chance to see the region in its natural state. When eventually it becomes a state or national park, access will obviously be improved, but with the arrival of more visitors the big game will move further away into the more inaccessible hinterland.

Cameron Highlands

The 'queen of Malaysia's hill resorts', Cameron Highlands — in the northwest corner of Pahang state — is 1,524 metres (5,000 feet) above sea level. At this altitude the air is cool and fresh and the nights can even become quite chilly. For travellers who want a respite from the hot, humid lowlands, the highlands are an interesting diversion; it is even possible to sit beside a roaring log fire in the evenings. Jungle trails abound in the surrounding hills, and tea plantations, terraced vegetable and flower farms, golf courses, tennis courts and colonial-style bungalows can be found hidden amongst the winding resort roads.

Cameron Highlands is easily accessible. From Kuala Lumpur take the bus or train to **Tapah** in Perak state, a journey of 158 kilometres (98 miles). Buses and taxis regularly ply the route from Tapah to Cameron Highlands — a distance of 60 kilometres (37 miles). The climb from Tapah to the highlands is along a winding, scenic road built during colonial times. The road winds serpentine-like through the hills, overhung with lush tropical forest. Giant bamboo stands, jungle palms and tree ferns grow in profusion along the ascent route. *Orang asli* can often be seen wandering along the road returning from hunting trips armed with blowpipes. Children gather at the side of the road to sell freshly-cut bamboo shoots from the jungle.

Ringlet, the first township of the highlands, is an agricultural centre. In the rich soil and cool air, cabbages, lettuce, tomatoes and other temperate vegetables thrive. **Tanah Rata**, the principal township, lies less than 13 kilometres (eight miles) away and another 304 metres (1,000 feet) up. Chalets, cottages and first-class hotels abound in this highland centre, which still has an English colonial atmosphere about it. Many of the stores and restaurants are run by Indians who first ventured to the highlands to work on the tea plantations. **Boh Tea Estate**, the largest and best-known, was set up during the Depression when J.A. Russell, an Englishman, took a gamble and applied for a land grant to start a tea plantation at Cameron Highlands, which was just then being opened up. The estate was carved from the jungle by *orang asli*, who cut the forest with axes and hand saws, but when the crops were to be planted, Indians, who were experienced with tea, were imported. Boh Tea Estate, set amongst rolling hills of manicured tea bushes, can be reached by taking the turnoff at the Habu Power Station ten kilometres (six miles) back along the main road from Tanah Rata.

In 1885, a government surveyor on an expedition into the main range reported finding 'a fine plateau with gentle slopes shut in by loftier mountains.' The plateau was named after the surveyor, William Cameron. Three years later the Resident of Perak expressed the opinion that a good sanatorium and a resort for health, pleasure, gardening or farming purposes could be built, but nothing much eventuated until 1925 when it was decided

to develop Cameron as a hill resort. Tea planters and Chinese vegetable growers arrived and wealthy planters and government officials built houses for weekend retreats. The Japanese Occupation, and then the Emergency when communist terrorists roamed the highlands, saw Cameron in decline, but today the area is developing rapidly.

Ye Olde Smokehouse, a 50-year-old Tudor-style hotel opposite the golf course, is the ultimate colonial hideaway. Its stone walls are covered in ivy, and dahlias and poinsettias grow in profusion around the flagstoned garden restaurant. Inside are intimate bars with cosy fireplaces, overstuffed chintz lounges and a reading room full of English *Country Life* magazines. On the wall beside the 'Rules of the Bar' is a framed newspaper clipping from 1925 about the first Englishwoman to trek in the highlands. Rooms here are expensive, but if you want to experience the life of a colonialist in the tropics there is nowhere quite like this hotel, except perhaps its sister establishment, Foster's Lakehouse. The next best thing to taking a room for the night is to have a Devonshire tea, complete with scones and home-made strawberry jam, in the garden restaurant outside.

The cool highlands offer numerous jungle paths to explore. Close by Tanah Rata township are trails leading to **Robinson Falls** and **Parit Falls**, both about an hour's easy walk. Near the falls, brilliantly coloured butterflies are abundant. Butterfly-collecting nets can be purchased in the town stores. Trails also lead to the well-known hilltops of **Gunung Beremban**, 1,841 metres (6,040 feet), and **Gunung Jasar**, 1,696 metres (5,564 feet). On clear days a panoramic view of Ipoh, the Straits of Malacca and other towns can be seen from most peaks.

For the sports-minded there is an 18-hole golf course with undulating fairways, a meandering stream and tricky greens. There are also tennis and badminton courts and, at Parit Falls, a natural jungle pool for swimming.

Further on from **Brincang**, the town north of Tanah Rata, are valleys of intricately terraced market gardens. Mountain springs are tapped and gravity-fed down through the terraces full of spring onions, cabbages and other vegetables that cannot grow on the lowlands. Set on the peaks of these hills, amongst the terraces, are narrow-laned colonies of Chinese houses where the farmers and their families live. At the roadside markets, strawberries, tangerine oranges and passionfruit are available when in season.

The other well-known hill resorts of Fraser's Hill and Genting Highlands have been covered under 'Out-of-town Drives' in the Kuala Lumpur section, Penang Hill in the section on Penang, and Maxwell's Hill (Bukit Larut) in 'The Drive North to Penang'.

East Malaysia (Borneo) — The Last Frontier

A traveller in the tropics last century remarked, 'it is a humbling experience, and surely a healthy one, to enter a landscape that man has not been able to alter, to dominate, to twist to his own purposes.' And although the great jungled island of Borneo has seen its forests dwindle and its traditional lifestyles disappear in the wake of progress, it is still one of the world's last wild horizons.

East Malaysia, as the states of Sarawak and Sabah have been coined, spreads across approximately 198,000 square kilometres (76,428 square miles) of the northern reaches of Borneo; Indonesian Kalimantan takes up the remainder. Distances are vast: Kota Kinabalu, the capital of Sabah, is 864 kilometres (537 miles) from Kuching (Sarawak's capital). Roads link a few of the major centres, but even the highways often deteriorate into dirt roads which lengthen the travelling time considerably. Traditionally, rivers were the only means of access and this is still the case in much of East Malaysia, particularly in Sarawak where motorized longboats and steel-bottomed express boats have cut travelling time from days to hours. Flying has reduced travelling time even more drastically. Month-long overland journeys to remote longhouses, cut off even from riverine traffic, have been reduced to a flight of a few hours.

Borneo's jungles are legion and cover most of East Malaysia, culminating in the soaring peak of Mount Kinabalu which at 4,101 metres (13,698 feet) is the highest mountain not only in Malaysia but also between New Guinea and the Himalayas. East Malaysia's rivers are also longer than those on the peninsula, with the Rejang of Sarawak flowing 563 kilometres (350 miles) from source to sea. Much of the wildlife of Borneo is similar to that of peninsular Malaysia, but a number of animals are unique to the island. The most famous of these is undoubtedly the orang-utan, known as *mias*, which was once prevalent but is now considered an endangered species.

Man has lived in Borneo since the dawn of time. Around 40,000 years ago, stone-age families dwelled in the Niah Caves. Perhaps the nomadic Penan, who still hunt with blowpipes in the great forests, are their descendants. Later migrations of the Kenyah and Kayan peoples, and the Iban, the bloodthirstiest of the head-hunters, settled along the waterways, building their longhouses and introducing shifting agriculture. The coastal Malays followed, along with Chinese merchants, and the ethnic pot-pourri that today is East Malaysia emerged.

Kingdoms arose along the South China Sea coast known to the Chinese as P'o-ni, probably the forerunner of Brunei. Chinese reports mention the Sarawak delta as a gold-smelting centre from the seventh century, and by the 15th century P'o-ni exchanged envoys with China and was one of only four kingdoms to receive an imperial inscription. But while all the activity concentrated on the coast, the interior — cut off by the tremendous obstacles of jungle and mountains — remained in isolation. During the Brooke family's reign as the 'White Rajas' of the 19th and 20th centuries, change was still gradual, possibly helped by the original White Raja James Brooke's notion of the 'noble savage', but after the Second World War Borneo emerged from her soporific era and entered the modern age.

Out of sight of the boom oil towns and the logging camps, though, it is not too difficult to find the old Borneo, where tattooed elders still reminisce of head-hunting days, where the rice-wine still flows freely at the harvest festival, and where the oldest rain forests on earth are to be found.

Sarawak — Land of the Hornbills

Seen from above, at the point where the pale blue of the South China Sea stops, an ochre-coloured river resembling an old Chinese dragon coils through a deep-green carpet of trees which spreads as far as the eye can see. This serpentine river maze constitutes the delta of the Sarawak River, the nucleus of Malaysia's largest state of the same name. Kuching, the capital, is another 32 kilometres (19 miles) upstream. Indonesian Kalimantan borders the state to the south and east, Sabah her sister state borders to the north, and part of the northwest coast belongs to the Sultanate of Brunei.

Travellers can fly direct to Kuching from Kuala Lumpur, Penang, Kota Kinabalu and Singapore on daily flights with Malaysia Airlines. There are also less-frequent flights from Bangkok and Jakarta. Feri Malaysia runs the cruise ship *Muhibbah* between Singapore, Kuantan, Kuching and Kota Kinabalu. It departs Singapore at 8.30 pm Friday, leaves Kuantan at 2 pm Saturday and arrives at Kuching at 9 pm on Sunday. Rates for the Singapore–Kuching return trip range from M$400 for a berth in a standard cabin to $710 for a suite.

Sarawak's emergence as a separate political entity began in 1841 when James Brooke, an Indian-born Englishman looking for adventure, sailed in his schooner *The Royalist* into Borneo at the height of a rebellion. After helping the Raja Muda of Brunei to suppress the uprising he was rewarded with huge land grants in what is today Sarawak. Brooke set up his capital at Kuching and established a dynasty of 'White Rajas' which ruled Sarawak until the Second World War. Brooke shared Raffles' dream of a benevolent English administration which would protect the trader while fostering native welfare. The self-styled 'White Raja' quickly won over the local Land Dayaks or Bidayuhs, a peaceful people who had suffered under the Sultan of Brunei's rule, and Brooke pardoned the Malays and gave them administrative positions. With the Sea Dayaks, or Iban, he faced greater resistance, for their love of travel, warfare and head-hunting went contrary to the grain of

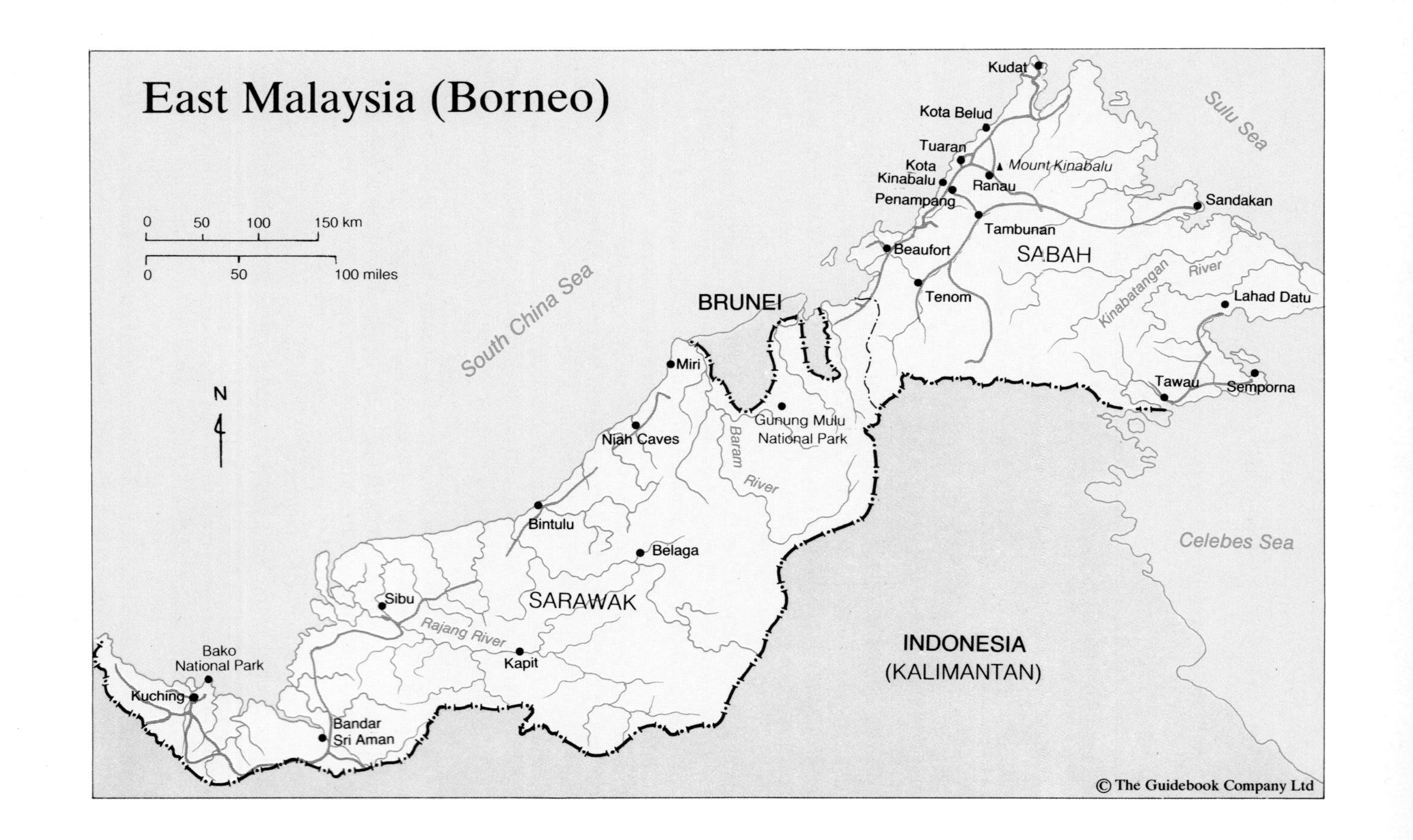

East Malaysia (Borneo)
0
50
100
150 km
0
50
100 miles
N
South China Sea
Sulu Sea
Celebes Sea
BRUNEI
SABAH
SARAWAK
INDONESIA
(KALIMANTAN)
Kudat
Kota Belud
Tuaran
Kota Kinabalu
Mount Kinabalu
Ranau
Penampang
Sandakan
Tambunan
Beaufort
Tenom
Kinabatangan River
Lahad Datu
Tawau
Semporna
Miri
Gunung Mulu National Park
Baram River
Niah Caves
Bintulu
Belaga
Sibu
Rajang River
Kapit
Bako National Park
Kuching
Bandar Sri Aman
© The Guidebook Company Ltd

Brooke's notions of government, but ultimately the 'White Raja' won them over. Although London refused to grant James Brooke a formal protectorate, in 1863 a consul was appointed to Kuching. This association between Britain and Sarawak helped to reinforce the connection with the Malay peninsula. The Brooke style of government, which included consultations with native chiefs and the personal relationship that Charles — James' successor — fostered with the Iban, together with their opposition to Western commerce which they feared would undermine the indigenous way of life, helped to establish a unique identity for Sarawak. In 1963 Sarawak joined the Federation of Malaysia.

Sarawak today is a multicultural, multiracial land. The upriver Ibans make up 30 percent of the population; the Chinese, who dwell mainly in the towns, comprise 29 percent; the Malays from the coastal regions make up 20 percent; and the remaining 21 percent consists of Bidayuh, Melanau, Kayan, Kenyah, Kelabit, Murut, Penan and others.

Gawai, the harvest festival held around the beginning of June, is the best time to visit upcountry, for the longhouses throw 'open house', the *tuak* (rice-wine) flows freely and the partying goes on for days.

Kuching — Capital of the 'White Rajas'

According to local lore, when James Brooke — the first 'White Raja' — was conferring with Malay chiefs a cat ran through the room. When asked what it was, they replied, 'kuching', meaning 'cat'. Apparently Brooke was rather taken with the name, and adopted it for the capital of his fief.

Although the rule of the 'White Rajas' ended over three decades ago and Kuching is now firmly entrenched in the progressive age, the town still has an aura of those earlier, romantic days. In the bustling downtown area, Kuching's Chinatown sits on one side of the river, while on the other is the serene Astana, once the Brooke residence, and further upriver the white, battlemented Fort Margherita. The river, as it has always done, dominates the town. In the chocolate-hued waters, logs float down from the timber camps upstream and colourful covered *sampan*, known as *tambang*, criss-cross the river from the market to the Malay *kampung* homes along the riverbank. Steel-bottomed express boats roar past in a plume of spray, tubby fishing trawlers head downstream, a wooden boat full of bananas floats along with the current, and boys pole along the foreshore, flinging nets into the river to bag their evening meal. The rivers are the real thoroughfares of the land; the loggers use the new roads, but real life revolves around the rivers.

Kuching is the stepping-off place for the rest of Sarawak. From the airport, flights connect with all the major towns, express boats run to Sibu where connecting boats will take you as far upriver as you wish, and buses and taxis ply the road which links the coastal towns. Be warned, the road distance may

Peoples of East Malaysia

Dozens of different tribes and dialect groups make up the diverse population of Sarawak and Sabah. Below is an alphabetical listing of the major groups:

Bajaus, a Muslim seafaring people sometimes known as 'Sea Gypsies', live in Sabah's coastal region. A fearless colourful people, they are renowned as expert horsemen and cattle breeders and comprise 13 percent of Sabah's population.

Bidayuh, or Land Dyaks, a rice-growing tribe from the Kuching area of Sarawak, were the first people to come under the influence of Sarawak's 'White Rajas'. Formerly the womenfolk wore characteristic brass rings around their legs.

The **Chinese** predominate in urban areas, forming a sizeable minority in both Sabah and Sarawak. Centuries ago, the Chinese traded porcelain and beads for Borneo's gold, rhinoceros horn, hornbill ivory and birds' nests, but the ancestors of today's Chinese immigrated here during the English colonial rule.

Iban form the majority in Sarawak, living beside all the major rivers in their communal longhouses. Fond of travelling and warfare, the Iban were immortalized as Borneo's fearless head-hunters. Today they grow hill rice and pepper and many work in Kuching.

Kadazan, or Dusun, are Sabah's largest tribe and live in the hill country near Mount Kinabalu. Although many still practise traditional terrace-farming, they are equally at ease in urban areas. Sabah's first Chief Minister was a Kadazan. Their traditional black attire is trimmed with silver braid and they are artisans with bamboo.

Kayan and **Kenyah** are related tribes from the upper reaches of the Baram and Rejang rivers. Physically they are the largest of the indigenous peoples and are expert boatmen. They excel at beadwork, wood-carving and basketry and are renowned for their music and dance.

Kelabit live in the high Bario plateau and are skilful agriculturists, growing vegetables and the best hill rice in Malaysia. Kelabits treasure old Chinese 'dragon' jars and buffaloes and, like other Borneo peoples, they enjoy rice-wine, especially at harvest time.

Malays were politically the most important people in Borneo even before the coming of the English. These dignified, sensitive Muslim people dwell mainly in the coastal regions of both Sabah and Sarawak where they constitute a large minority.

Melanau are the original coastal inhabitants of Sarawak. Predominantly Muslim, they resemble the Malays and traditionally were known for their sago farming in the swampy coastal region. They are excellent boatmen and fishermen.

Murut, known as 'hill people', live in the hilly border regions of Sabah/ Sarawak. They are shifting cultivators and excel at hunting and gathering jungle produce. Last of the Borneo peoples to give up head-hunting, they still hunt with the blowpipe.

Penan or **Punan** are East Malaysia's only true nomadic people. Some are now settled, but most prefer to live off the jungle. They inhabit the more remote upper Baram and Rejang river region. Penan are skilful sword, *parang* and blowpipe makers, and weave the best mats and baskets in Borneo.

Rungus are a Kadazan group who dwell in the Kudat region of Sabah. The women wear distinctive knee-length black sarongs, brass bracelets and beaded necklaces. They are rice-farmers and own coconut plantations.

See also the map on page 126.

Dayaks in the interior still retain many of their traditional customs

not look far, but only a couple of hours outside Kuching the gravel begins. If you are pressed for time it is better to fly to the nearest downriver town and then to go by boat upstream. Many tour operators specialize in upriver trips, with overnight stays in longhouses, but for the more adventurous traveller it is not difficult, and a lot more rewarding, to venture off on your own. Sarawak folk are renowned for their hospitality — there is always a spare mat on the longhouse floor and a bowl of rice for the visitor, no matter how humble the home.

Kuching has a range of accommodation, from the luxurious Holiday Inn that soars over the Sarawak River providing a panoramic vista, to the moderately-priced Chinese hotels. East Malaysia is slightly more expensive than peninsular Malaysia, so expect to pay a little more for accommodation, food and drink.

City Sights

Most of the town sights are within easy walking distance of the downtown area on the southern bank of the river. *Tambang*, the small ferry boats, provide a unique look at the city from the river and are the best way to visit the sights on the northern side of the river.

Sarawak Museum was built in 1888 during the reign of the Second Raja, Charles Brooke, together with Alfred Russell Wallace, the scientist who co-authored Darwin's theory of evolution. Although the museum has been expanded with modern extensions, the original building — apparently designed by Brooke's French valet to resemble a Normandy townhouse — is still the focal point of the complex. The museum, probably the best in Southeast Asia, offers the visitor a vivid introduction to the country's diverse cultures and is the best preparation for an upriver journey. A Kenyah artisan has decorated one wall with a traditional 'Tree of Life' design reproduced from a longhouse wall. Dolls carved from palm pith, known as *dakan*, were used by the Melinau to take away evil spirits which caused sickness. There is an Iban longhouse, complete with skulls hanging from the ceiling, carved totem poles for ensuring luck with the hunt, head-dresses made of hornbill feathers, 1,200-year-old funeral boats from the Niah Caves, and a myriad of insect life that so entranced Wallace that he spent 15 months near Kuching and collected over 2,000 species.

Fort Margherita, built in 1841, was named after Charles Brooke's wife, the Ranee Margaret. During the raja's reign sentries would announce 'all's well' every hour on the hour throughout the night, for the fort was the guardian of the town of Kuching. Today it houses the Police Museum and its collection of antique weapons. Situated on the northern bank of the Sarawak River, the fort is easily reached by ferry from the town wharf. In one of the towers is the 'Chamber of the Laughing Skulls', containing some 200-year-old skulls apparently sold to the museum by an Iban who swore that the skulls laughed. Also in the museum is the only cannon ever cast in Sarawak, which was used in Brooke's 'anti-piracy' campaign when he warred against Rentrap, the famous rebel Iban chief.

Astana, situated downstream from Fort Margherita, was the home of the 'White Rajas' and is the current residence of the Governor of Sarawak. Set amidst rolling green lawns, the palace — built in 1870 — is an elegant reminder of an earlier era. Charles, the Second Raja, apparently cultivated a betel-nut plantation behind the Astana so that he could offer the fresh nut to tribal chiefs when they visited.

Masjid Besar (The Main Mosque) is situated opposite Jalan Mosque, near the Kuching bus station. When James Brooke first arrived at the little Malay fishing village which was to become the capital, there was already a small wooden mosque on the riverside where the present mosque stands. The first Masjid Besar was built of wood in 1852; it was renovated in 1880 and in 1932 the roof was replaced with a dome. The present gilt-domed mosque still incorporates part of its historic predecessor.

Pasar Dayak (The Dyak Market), just opposite the Main Mosque, is where the Bidayuh or Land Dyaks gather to sell their produce from their out-of-town smallholdings. During the fruit season this is a good spot to stock up on durian, *langsat*, mangosteen and sweet little bananas.

Tua Pek Kong, Kuching's oldest Chinese temple (built in 1876), is situated on Jalan Padungan. Winged dragons and lotus blossoms entwine the heavy carved roof beams above the main altar where a golden Buddha presides. Frescos of Buddha's life, and symbolic panels featuring cranes (symbols of immortality), adorn the exterior walls.

At **Pandungan** is the temple of **Tien Hou**, the Goddess of Seamen, where the fishermen come to pray for good catches. Opposite the little hillside temple is a bustling fishing village on stilts, and on the muddy foreshores are colourful fishing boats with eyes painted on the prows.

Downriver Trips

Santubong is Kuching's most popular seaside picnic spot. Located 32 kilometres (20 miles) downstream from the capital, where the Sarawak River empties into the South China Sea, it is only an hour's ride by express boat. Santubong is an excellent swimming beach, and fishing trips or cruises can be organized with the local Malay fishermen. At Sungai Jaong, 1.5 kilometres (one mile) upriver from Santubong village, Buddhist- and Hindu-influenced rock carvings have been discovered. This river delta region was an important trading centre during the Tang and Sung Chinese dynasties which spanned the seventh to the 13th centuries. Government chalets provide accommodation, but these must be booked in advance through the District

Office in Kuching. At nearby **Damai Beach** there is a luxury five-star resort.

Bako National Park, Sarawak's most accessible wilderness area, is only two hours by speedboat from Kuching at the mouth of the Sarawak River. White sandy bays intersected with steep cliffs border the heath forest which is unique to Sarawak. In the heathland scrub are found carnivorous pitcher plants, unique 'ant plants' which live in association with ant colonies, and ferns which drape over the stunted bonsai-like trees. Large monitor lizards, wild pigs, long-tailed macaques and sambar deer are commonly seen in the park. The long-nosed monkey, known as *Orang Blanda* (Dutchman), characterized by its long bulbous nose, is sometimes seen along the coast and is found only in Borneo. Sunbirds, kingfishers and reef egrets are amongst the more commonly seen birds of the park. Mid and high tide is the best time for swimming; there are good beaches at Telok Assam near the hostel, and at Telok Paku, a 45-minute walk, and Telok Pandan Kechil, a 90-minute walk, from here.

Rest house and hostel accommodation is available at the park, with cooking facilities. The rest house provides bed linen and cooking utensils, but at the hostel you have to bring your own. Prices vary accordingly. All food must be brought in. Tents are available for hire for M$1 per night. Commercial tour operators organize trips to the park, but it is easily accessible to those who like to make their own arrangements. Boats leave the Long Wharf, Jalan Gambier, Kuching between 7 and 8 am and between 1 and 2 pm, arriving at Kampung Bako two-and-a-half hours later. The fare is M$2 each way. Boats return at 7.30 am and noon. Another popular way to reach Bako is to take the bus from Kuching Bus Station to Bako Fishing Village and go from there by longboat to the park. The bus fare is M$2.10 one way and the boat ride is $6 per boatload. Accommodation must be booked through the National Parks and Wildlife Office, Jalan Gartak, Kuching, tel. 082–24474. Permits to stay at Bako National Park will be issued once the accommodation charges have been paid. As the sea can be rough from October to March it may not be possible to get to the park, but check first at the Park Office in Kuching.

Upriver Safaris

Skrang River, a journey of four hours by road and another hour upriver from Kuching, is an Iban stronghold where whole communities live side by side in traditional longhouses beside the river. It is a popular safari, and a number of tour operators organize the entire trip, including the drive, meals and overnight accommodation at a longhouse. One company even has its own guest longhouse. However, trips are relatively easy to organize if you like to organize things yourself. Buses and taxis ply between Kuching and Sibu, though the road is dirt from just outside Bandar Sri Aman. From this latter

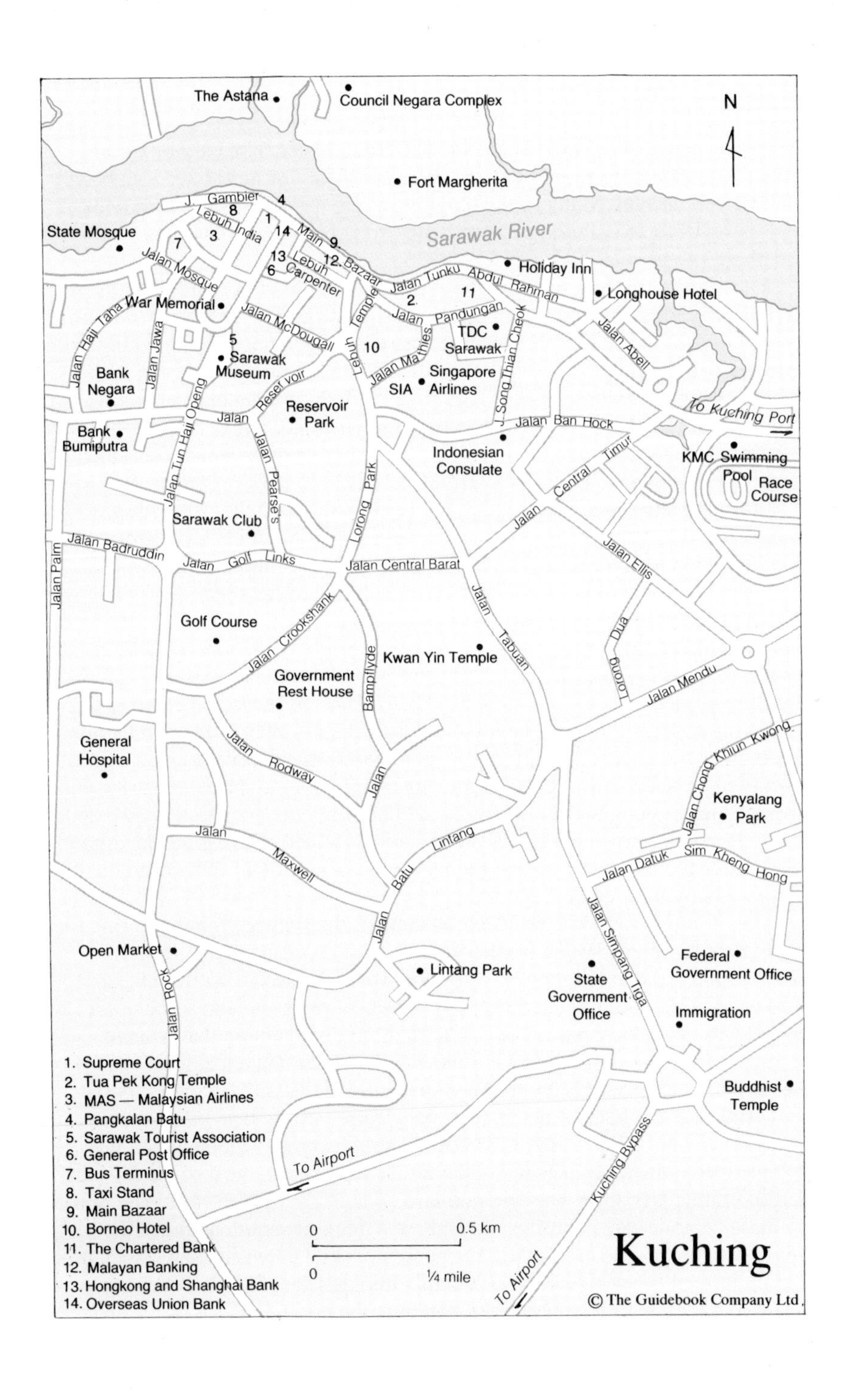
The Astana
Council Negara Complex
N
Fort Margherita
Sarawak River
State Mosque
J. Gambier
Lebuh India
Main Bazaar
Lebuh Carpenter
Jalan Mosque
Holiday Inn
Longhouse Hotel
Jalan Tunku Abdul Rahman
War Memorial
Jalan McDougall
Lebuh Temple
Jalan Pandungan
TDC Sarawak
Jalan Haji Taha
Jalan Jawa
Sarawak Museum
Jalan Mathies
Singapore Airlines
SIA
J. Song Thian Cheok
Jalan Abell
Bank Negara
Reservoir
Reservoir Park
Jalan Tun Haji Openg
To Kuching Port
Jalan Ban Hock
Bank Bumiputra
Jalan Pearse's
Indonesian Consulate
KMC Swimming Pool
Race Course
Lorong Park
Jalan Central Timur
Sarawak Club
Jalan Badruddin
Jalan Golf Links
Jalan Central Barat
Jalan Ellis
Jalan Palm
Jalan Crookshank
Golf Course
Jalan Tabuan
Lorong Dua
Kwan Yin Temple
Government Rest House
Bampflyde
Jalan Mendu
General Hospital
Jalan Rodway
Jalan Chong Khiun Kwong
Kenyalang Park
Jalan Maxwell
Jalan Batu Lintang
Jalan Datuk Sim Kheng Hong
Jalan Simpang Tiga
Open Market
Lintang Park
State Government Office
Federal Government Office
Immigration
Jalan Rock
Buddhist Temple
Kuching Bypass
To Airport
1. Supreme Court
2. Tua Pek Kong Temple
3. MAS — Malaysian Airlines
4. Pangkalan Batu
5. Sarawak Tourist Association
6. General Post Office
7. Bus Terminus
8. Taxi Stand
9. Main Bazaar
10. Borneo Hotel
11. The Chartered Bank
12. Malayan Banking
13. Hongkong and Shanghai Bank
14. Overseas Union Bank
0
0.5 km
0
¼ mile
Kuching
© The Guidebook Company Ltd

town you can also organize transport to Skrang River. The jetty on Skrang River is just near the main road and there are plenty of motorized longboats to take you upriver. Many of the longhouses are used to putting up paying guests, so if you have time on your hands you could move from one longhouse to another upriver.

The road north from Kuching bisects pepper plantations, and the hills of Indonesian Kalimantan loom to the east. At **Bandar Sri Aman**, 197 kilometres (122 miles) from Kuching, there is an old wooden fort dating from Brooke's time. **Fort Alice** was built in 1864 and has small turrets and a medieval-type drawbridge. Fort Alice was built on the Batang Lupar River to deter the Skrang River Iban from making downstream raids. The Batang Lupar is also the home of the huge man-eating crocodiles which occasionally make the headlines with their nefarious doings.

From the jetty on the Skrang River, where you board the pencil-thin longboats, the journey upriver through the occasional rapids is a memorable one. Wooden longhouses on stilts with thatched roofs appear on the banks, men fling out fishing nets, and women — some bare-breasted — wash clothing in the shallows. An average Skrang longhouse contains about 26 *bilik*, or apartments, where separate families reside. Each *bilik* has a living room, loft, gallery and an open platform. In the loft the family stores its rice, farming implements, tools for handicrafts and sacred seeds and charms. Off the living room is the *ruai*, the long gallery which is open to the community. Here domestic chores are carried out and guests entertained. Another large unroofed veranda is where the pepper and *padi* (unhusked rice) are dried and the washing is hung out. Longhouses are built high off the ground and extend along the river terrace for 20–50 metres (65–165 feet). During the day, most of the men are out in the rice or pepper fields and the older folk spend their time weaving mats and other crafts.

The Skrang River was the scene of some of the fiercest fighting during the early Brooke years. Skulls, blackened and grimy with age, hang from the upright poles in one longhouse. A tribal elder says that the skulls date back 150 years. Head-hunting died out only about 40 years ago and some of the oldest tribesmen have a head or two to their credit, claiming that women wouldn't have anything to do with them if they hadn't taken at least one head. Many of the elders are tattooed in the old style, with decorated throats and arms and elongated holes in their ears from wearing heavy brass ornaments. In one longhouse is a weighty antique brass cannon which was pillaged from the rajas of Brunei on a piracy raid. Inside most of the *bilik* are large ceramic jars, known as 'dragon jars', which are used to store rice. Some of these ceramics are centuries old and are a mark of wealth amongst the Iban. Although some *bilik* now have generators and television sets, much of the traditional life still lingers, especially amongst the old folk. An evening spent in the flickering lantern light watching the hornbill dance by a tribal elder is still a magical experience. The Iban are renowned for their hospitality and even in the longhouses which are being constantly visited by tourists they are still just as warm and friendly as ever.

The **Rejang River**, Sarawak's longest waterway, reaches into the heart of the country. From **Sibu**, a town rich in timber, rubber and pepper, the mighty river flows past old forts, *kampung* scenes and longhouse life to **Kapit**, 160 kilometres (100 miles) upstream. Between Kapit and **Belaga** the river becomes more tortuous, and it is here that the notorious Pelagus rapids are encountered. Upstream are the Kenyah and Kayan people, and downstream the Iban.

The Kayan and Kenyah people were once the great rivals of the Iban and occupied the whole interior of Sarawak from the Pelagus rapids to the Baram River in the north. In 1863 Charles Brooke led an expedition of 15,000 Ibans against the Kayan and Kenyah people in retaliation for the killing of two of his officers. They thought they were safe behind the great rapids, but the 'great Kayan expedition' pushed them way up beyond Belaga. Today they have filtered down again and are found around their former hunting grounds. The Kayan and Kenyah people are entirely different from the Iban, with different languages, traditions and social systems. Formerly they were a very superstitious people and their lives were regulated by omens. If an 'unlucky' bird flew across their path they would abandon a journey and sometimes not even leave the longhouse. They are artisans at beadwork, wood-carving and palm-leaf weaving, and their songs, music and dance are the most highly developed of all the Borneo peoples. The Kayans are the originators of the stylized war dance and the hornbill dance, in which hornbill feathers are tied to the ends of their fingers to accentuate their slow and graceful movements.

Kayan and Kenyah men are the most skilful boatmen in Sarawak, probably because they live in the upper reaches of the rivers where rapids are an everyday occurrence. Just before Belaga town on the Rejang are the famed **Pelagus rapids**. There are seven rapids over a 2.5-kilometre (1.5-mile) stretch of the river and each has a name: Rapoh (a grave), Mawang (a fruit), Sukat (to survey), Pantu (wild sago), Lunggak (a knife), Nabau (python) and Bidai (big mat). The rapids are caused by the sudden drop of the riverbed in an area surrounded by rocks. The river drops with such force that sprays of water result. It is beautiful to see but dangerous to venture through if you are inexperienced at rapid navigation; the Pelagus rapids have taken their toll of victims.

To get to the upper Rejang, first take an express boat up to Kapit, a journey of four hours. Permission to go further upriver should be sought from the Resident, 7th Division, Kapit. From Kapit, smaller boats run to Belaga and beyond. Life here revolves around the river and there is always traffic, for the upriver folk use boats like landlocked folk use cars.

Caves of the North

Some of the world's longest, largest and most spectacular cave systems are situated in the north of Sarawak. At Niah National Park is the Great Cave, where archaeologists in the 1950s discovered 40,000-year-old human remains and the Painted Cave, where stone-age man decorated the walls 1,200 years ago. A day's journey upriver on the Baram leads to Sarawak's latest and most remote wilderness region, Gunung Mulu National Park, where limestone hills have eroded into the most awe-inspiring cave system in the world.

Miri, an oil- and gas-rich town in the northwest, is the stepping-off place for both Niah and Mulu. At least five daily flights connect Kuching with Miri, and other flights ply from Labuan and Kota Kinabalu in Sabah. In Miri town there is an interesting waterfront, an old Chinese temple and an open-air food centre at the beach with excellent seafood.

Niah National Park

Niah National Park is located 96 kilometres (60 miles) south of Miri, outside the town of **Batu Niah** which is easily accessible by bus and taxi. The taxi fare from Miri to Batu Niah is M$15. Once in Batu Niah you can follow the footpath down the Niah River to the Visitors Bungalow at Pangkalan Lobang. Across the river is the start of the plankwalk to the caves. Longboats can be hired for the short river journey. The trip from Miri, through the caves and back again can be done in one day if you are on an organized tour, but if you plan to take local transportation it is advisable to stay overnight at the Visitors' Bungalow. Hostel accommodation is available, with bedding and cooking facilities. Bookings for the bungalow are made through the National Parks and Wildlife Office in Miri, tel. 36637. However, there is usually ample room at the bungalow if you just arrive without prior arrangement. An overnight stay costs M$2.50 per person. Guides are highly recommended if you plan to explore inside the Great Cave as there are some gaping dropoffs and it is easy to get lost amongst the myriad cave passages. Remember to bring a strong torch.

According to legend there was once a village on a hill called Bukit Terayeng. A new longhouse was to be built, so a child was sacrificed — as was the custom — to ensure that the gods were satisfied. But the child's grandmother cursed the villagers and for five days she beat gongs and danced until the sky became black and a stony rain fell, turning all the inhabitants to rock and all the houses into caves. Bukit Terayeng is found deep within the Great Cave of Niah.

Longboats ferry visitors to the caves across the Niah River to the start of the boardwalk through the jungle. An old-fashioned shop here sells provisions and a sign in Chinese says 'Swifts and Bats Excreta Collectors'

Association', for these caves are home to millions of swifts and bats and the hills inside the cave are formed from their guano. Raised 1.5 metres (five feet) from the rain forest floor, the boardwalk winds past huge buttress-rooted trees draped with lianas and up to the limestone massif that contains the **Great Cave**. A short climb up some wooden stairs brings you to the **Trader's Cave** and the remains of an old longhouse once used by birds' nest collectors. These intrepid gatherers still shimmy up poles hundreds of feet high in the death-defying business of collecting swifts' nests to satisfy Chinese gourmands' taste for the glutinous delicacy, birds' nest soup. If you visit the caves during April/May or September/October it is possible to watch the collectors working high up under the roof of the yawning caverns. Another set of steps leads to the Moon Cave, commonly known as the Great Cave. Up on the roof of the mammoth cavern hang the fragile infrastructures of the nest collectors; the small black spots on the ceiling are the nests, made from swifts' saliva, which fetch M$650 a kilo on the market. To the left are the archaeological digs, dating from the late 1950s when the Sarawak Museum carried out excavation work. Five metres (16 feet) down in the guano, the curator discovered a human skull dating back to 40 millennia ago. At that time it was the most exciting discovery since Java Man.

In the gloom of the Great Cave the smell of guano is almost overpowering, the humidity is easily 100 percent and clothing quickly becomes saturated. Above, the clicking echo-locators of swifts sound like an electronic orchestra as they probe the inky recesses of the caves. Torchlights pick out crickets with long antennae, scorpions, and baby bats which hang suspended from crevices in the ceiling. The trail climbs up and down almost vertical staircases and around mountains of guano until daylight appears at the end of a long tunnel. From here there is another boardwalk to the **Painted Cave**. Discovered in 1958, this cave contains the only red haematite rock paintings in Borneo. Alongside are some small canoes, known as 'ships of the dead', which were used by the Niah cave people as coffins. The wall paintings were made with *sireh* and lime, the same red staining as on betel-nut chewers' teeth. These murals and the symbolic death ships were crafted around 1,200 years ago. Apparently in around AD 700 the Niah people were trading birds' nests and hornbill ivory with Chinese traders for porcelain and beads, but in around 1400 they deserted the caves and vanished from history. Some scholars believe that the nomadic Penan may be descended from these early cave-dwellers.

From the Painted Cave the trail joins up with the main plankway. A trail to the right leads to Rumah Chang, an Iban longhouse, while other trails lead around the limestone massif of **Gunung Subis**, which dominates the surrounding countryside. Back at Pangkalan Lobang, directly beside the bungalow, is the Park Information Centre with displays on the history, geology, flora and fauna of the park.

Gunung Mulu National Park

Gunung Mulu National Park, Malaysia's least known and most spectacular national park, is also the most remote. Gunung Mulu, a sandstone mountain, rises 2,376 metres (7,795 feet) in the midst of the park. Rivers originating on the mountain rush down through cliff-lined gorges which dissect a strip of jagged limestone cliffs. Huge 50-metre (164-foot) -high trees hide their flanks, and piercing this green canopy are whole mountainsides of jagged limestone pinnacles described by an early expeditioner as 'the world's most nightmarish surface to travel over'. Inside these limestone peaks are huge caverns, including the Deer Cave, the Clearwater Cave, which winds for 52 kilometres (32 miles) through the hills and is probably the largest cave passage in the world, and the recently discovered Sarawak Chamber (not yet open to the public), which is thought to be the largest cave chamber in the world, around the size of 16 football fields. The park is vast, covering about 52,866 hectares (130,631 acres), and is located along the Sungai Melinau, an offshoot of the Tutuh River in Sarawak's far north.

It is possible for budget-minded and resourceful travellers to get to Mulu on their own, but permits are required to visit anywhere north of Marudi on the Baram River. These are available from the Resident's Office in Miri. From Kuala Baram at the mouth of the **Baram River**, express boats head upriver for three hours to **Marudi,** the last town on the Baram. From here, another express boat goes to **Long Panai**, a further three-hour trip. From here, motorized longboats ply another three-hour journey to the park. Until recently, the journey took as many days as it now does hours. Near Park Headquarters are three basic resorts run by Kenyah people. To enter the caves you must have a guide and report first to the Park Officer in the headquarters. This is one trip when it is preferable to have all the organizing done for you, and of all the different tour operators Borneo Adventure Travel Service of Miri, run by Kenyahs from the Ulu Baram district, is by far the best. For M$500 each they provide a five-day expedition to Mulu which includes all meals, accommodation, informative English-speaking guides, boat fares and transfer from your hotel in Miri. They also organize permits, which are sometimes hard to get owing to troubles upriver between tribal groups and the logging companies.

Like an armoured longboat, the steel-plated Marudi Express cleaves through the milk-chocolate waters of the Baram. On-board videos screen wrestling matches for a rapt crowd of Kenyah loggers returning to camp and old Penan tribesmen with basin-cut hair-dos and elongated ears. Primeval sago palms, wooden homes on stilts and frontier-type timber camps appear sporadically until you reach Marudi. From here to Long Panai, where you change to a longboat for the final leg branching off to the **Tutuh River**, longhouses start appearing beside the riverbank. In the distance loom the

佛

jagged peaks of **Gunung Mulu** flanked by smaller, rounded white-topped hills. Limestone cliffs appear at the turnoff to the **Melinau River** where the water is a greeny-black, for this is the start of the national park and there is no logging here. The Melinau is still a wild river.

At dusk you arrive at the Mulu Hot Springs Resort, where on the veranda over hot tea and biscuits the magnificent vista of the park is revealed. Two wispy grey spirals, like smoke signals, drift across the sky from the caves. These are actually hundreds of thousands of bats exiting the mighty Deer Cave for their nightly forage in the jungle.

At dawn you move further on down the Melinau into the virgin rain forest where the clear green water is overhung with limestone cliffs. At the base of one of these, the river stops abruptly. Spenser St John, the first European explorer to reach here (in 1856), recalled the same experience. He thought that the river stopped, but it actually goes underground through the longest cave system in Southeast Asia, the **Clearwater Cave**. Up to this point, anyone — from the old and feeble to a toddler — can accomplish the trip, but once you enter the awesome entrance, the trip becomes an adventure suitable only for the fit and reasonably fearless. If you suffer from claustrophobia, turn back now. After an hour or two of caving, it is readily understood why guides are a necessity and why only two of Mulu's caves are open to the public. In the half-light of the entrance a unique one-leafed plant clings to the limestone walls — the first of many strange cave dwellers which include blind white snakes, translucent crabs, and crickets with feelers six times the length of their bodies. Further into the inky-black recesses of this giant cave is a rushing chest-high river which must be forded while clinging to a rope. Boulders covered with guano, slippery from the constant dripping water, make every step eventful. In the more constricted passageways, torchlight shows up delicate stalactites and stalagmites. Three hours into the cave, sunlight bursts through a hole in the roof through which vegetation cascades. To this point it is about 1.5 kilometres (one mile) and it is staggering to contemplate that the cave winds on for a further 50 kilometres (31 miles) into the gloomy realms of white cockroaches and blind spiders. The Royal Geographic Society Expedition of 1978 explored 26 kilometres (16 miles) and was inside the cave for a week. Apparently this hole in the roof provides the last natural light; it is dark from here on.

Deer Cave, the following day's trek, defies description. Nowhere in its two-kilometre (1.2-mile) length is it ever less than 100 metres (328 feet) high. At the cavernous entrance hall three spectacular waterfalls cascade to the floor from 190 metres (623 feet) up. Light penetrates into almost all of this cave so it doesn't seem as eerie as Clearwater Cave with its inky black dropoffs and cold rushing river. Even so, it is no child's play getting about this vast cavern. Mountains of evil-smelling guano have to be traversed and a rope-ladder descent negotiated before reaching the **Garden of Eden** framed by the mouth of the Deer Cave. This verdant hidden valley drains into Deer Cave and the prodigious rainfall is constantly enlarging the cavern.

In Mulu not all the limestone features are in caves, for 900 metres (2,952 feet) up on Gunung Api are limestone needles — known as **The Pinnacles** — which rise 45 metres (148 feet) above the tree-tops. Expeditions can be organized to view this unique formation. Two nights are spent at a small camp in the rain forest and as this climb is steep and physically gruelling it is recommended only for the very fit. Six-day expeditions to the summit of Gunung Mulu can also be organized. For all Mulu trips, contact Borneo Adventure Travel Service, Fatimah Hotel, 49 Brooke Road, Miri, Sarawak, tel. 085–30255, telex MA 74254.

Good comfortable running shoes are recommended for cave trekking, preferably the canvas type which dries easily. A strong torch is a must and long pants should be worn as protection against sharp limestone outcrops. River travel can be cool in the early morning and late afternoon so a sweatshirt is also useful. It is best to leave most of your luggage in Miri and just bring a small daypack to Mulu with a change of clothes.

Sabah — Land below the Wind

About the size of Ireland, and Malaysia's second largest state, Sabah is situated in the far north of Borneo, below the typhoon belt. While her sister state, Sarawak, is riddled with rivers, Sabah is dominated by mountains. Mount Kinabalu, Malaysia's loftiest peak, seems impossibly high for this part of the world, and from its ramparts on a clear day most of the state can be seen. The mountain not only dominates the scenery, it also invariably dominates the traveller's agenda. But there is more to Sabah than mountain-climbing. In the surrounding hill country — peopled by Sabah's largest ethnic group, the Kadazan — are picturesque rice-growing villages; along the seaboard are water villages where the Bajau, or Sea Gypsies, live; at Sandakan is the world's largest orang-utan sanctuary; and off shore are dozens of idyllic coral reef islands.

Before the coming of the Europeans, Sabah was a collection of scattered autonomous communities under a vague allegiance to the Sultan of Brunei. In the 18th and 19th centuries, when few lands remained unexplored, British merchants and adventurers turned their sights to Borneo. The isolation of this great island from the Western world, its mysterious head-hunting inhabitants and the seemingly endless jungle gave rise to tales which had armchair travellers in Europe imagining that gold and diamonds lay on the ground just waiting to be picked up. Chinese and Arab traders, however, had been voyaging here for centuries before the Europeans arrived. In 1521, Ferdinand Magellan's companions put in at Brunei, and the Spanish, the Dutch and the odd Englishman visited these shores, but nothing much happened until an American trader named Moses obtained a lease from the Sultan of Brunei. This lease passed on to an Austrian Baron and then into the hands of Alfred Dent, an Englishman. After signing treaties with Brunei and the Sultanate of Sulu, who controlled some of the northeast of Sabah, Dent established the British North Borneo Company in 1881. Unfortunately, these merchants lacked the charisma of Sarawak's 'White Rajas' and so encountered recurring resistance, the most famous being the Mat Salleh Rebellion of 1895–1905. Mat Salleh commanded the supernatural powers of legendary Malay warriors; his *parang* or cleaver could produce lightning and his mouth flames. Today Mat Salleh is regarded as a hero of Malay nationalism. In 1963, when the Federation of Malaysia was announced, the Philippines and Indonesia immediately severed diplomatic relations, alleging that some of the territories claimed by Malaysia were theirs. But in 1966 when Sukarno was ousted, the new army-dominated government of Indonesia made peace and the Philippines dropped active pursuit of its claims.

Malaysia Airlines has daily flights to Kota Kinabalu — Sabah's capital — from Penang, Kuala Lumpur and Singapore. From Jakarta, travellers can fly to Sabah via Kuala Lumpur four times a week, and from Hong Kong direct flights ply the route twice weekly. Cathay Pacific Airways provides twice-weekly services from Hong Kong to Kota Kinabalu via Brunei.

From a map of Sabah it looks easy enough to drive from one side of the country to the other, but what appears as a main road is in fact often nothing more than a rocky, pot-holed track through the jungle. The road north to Kudat, south to Beaufort, and the two roads west to Tambunan and Ranau are sealed, but from there on the surface is gravel all the way to the east coast. Hire cars are a great way to see the south and northwest, for much of the beauty of Sabah is in the landscape and it is easier to stop for snacks, to take photographs or to go for a swim if you have your own car. Without a four-wheel drive (you can hire one, but they are exhorbitantly expensive) and weeks to spare, it is easier to fly to the east coast towns of Sandakan, Semporna, Tawau and Lahad Datu from Kota Kinabalu.

Kota Kinabalu — Sights and Offshore Islands

Sabah's capital, formerly known as Jesselton, is quite a new city, having been built on the ruins of the original town which was razed to the ground during the Second World War. What the city lacks in historic buildings, it makes up for in its superb geographical setting. Jungle-clad hills rise as a backdrop and just off shore lie a string of coral islands.

The **State Mosque**, a splendid example of contemporary Islamic architecture situated at the junction of Jalan Tunku Abdul Rahman and Jalan Penampang is worth a visit. A large golden dome surmounts the main prayer hall, which is supported by massive pillars topped with smaller golden domes. The mosque is open to visitors every day except Friday.

The **Sabah State Museum**, located opposite the mosque on a hilltop, commands an excellent view of the town and the offshore islands. This impressive modern building is a stylized version of a traditional longhouse. The museum houses arts and crafts of the Kadazan, Bajau, Murut and Runggus peoples, including their beautifully woven conical hats and basketware.

Tanjung Aru is an excellent white-sand beach just five kilometres (three miles) from the town centre. Although there is plenty of accommodation in Kota Kinabalu, the luxury resort at Tanjung Aru is a favoured place to stay because of the beach and its close proximity to town. Even if you don't plan to stay at the resort, the beach lined with casuarina trees is a great place in which to stay cool, for Kota Kinabalu is a hot and steamy town.

The **offshore islands** of the **Tunku Abdul Rahman National Park** are undoubtedly Kota Kinabalu's greatest tourist attraction. These five idyllic islands close to the town have excellent swimming beaches, clear water, plenty of live coral for the snorkeller and scuba diver, and even jungle trails.

Boats leave from the island jetty near the fish market. The return trip to Pulau Sapi is M$8 and to Police Beach on Pulau Gaya, M$9.

Pulau Gaya is the biggest island in the group and the site of the National Park Headquarters. Police Beach, enclosed by a bay, has crystal-clear waters and shady trees and is the best beach on the island. Along the southern shore are undamaged coral reefs with rich marine life. If you are not a snorkeller the park has a glass-bottom boat for hire. Around the island are 20 kilometres (13 miles) of nature trails. Part of the southwestern trail from Headquarters is a raised boardwalk above a mangrove swamp. Pied Hornbills, noted for their huge beaks, nest here in hollow tree trunks. Hornbill ivory was much sought after by the early Chinese merchants for making delicate carvings. Monkeys, squirrels and the odd wild pig still frequent the island.

Pulau Sapi, near Pulau Gaya, is about 25 minutes by boat from town and the most popular and developed of all the group. There are day shelters, public toilets and barbecue stands here and camping is permitted. A small coral reef runs close to the jetty and then parallel to the beach. Here are found Staghorn and *Seriatopora* corals which abound with damselfish, anemone fish and wrasse. Pulau Sapi is home to a troop of crab-eating monkeys who sometimes swim at the beach, and also resident here are the magnificent White-Bellied Sea Eagles, which soar high above in the wind currents over the beach.

Pulau Mamutik is a relatively unspoilt island rich in corals, particularly off the northeastern tip. There is a house on the island which can be rented through National Park Head Office in Kota Kinabalu.

Pulau Sulang is the furthest island from Kota Kinabalu and the least frequented by day-trippers. The best coral reefs in the park are found here, together with a rich diversity of marine life, the best sign of a healthy reef. On the southern end of the island, stretching in a wide arc across the bay, is a dense reef with the most rewarding diving of the island group. Travellers intending to stay overnight must bring everything with them as this island is still undeveloped. Permission must be obtained from the park office in Kota Kinabalu.

Kinabalu National Park

This world-famous park contains not only the granite massif of **Mount Kinabalu,** at 4,101 metres (13,454 feet), but also a range of climatic zones from lowland tropical rain forest up through montane oak forests and mossy 'cloud' forests to the alpine realms. Covering an area of 754 square kilometres (291 square miles), the park is bordered by the terraced fields of the Kadazan people who have always dwelt within the shadow of the great peak. Mount Kinabalu's name derives from the Kadazan words *aki* and *nabalu*, meaning 'the revered place of the dead'. For them the mountain is sacred and the resting place of spirits. However, these beliefs don't stop the local people from guiding travellers up the summit trail.

Kinabalu Park is a welcome relief from the somewhat stifling temperature at sea level, for the mercury rarely climbs above 20°C (68°F). The nights are considerably cooler, and at Panar Laban — the overnight stop on the summit trail — the temperature range is a mere 2°–10°C (36°–50°F). There is plenty to do at the park even if you don't intend to scale the peak, which is a demanding climb even for the very fit. Trails wind around the headquarters region, through the montane forest and alongside clear mountain streams. The visitor may be lucky enough to see barking deer or tree shrews, and many of Kinabalu's orchids bloom in these lower realms.

Accommodation at the park varies from simple hostel-type facilities at M$10 each to twin-bed cabins at $80 per cabin on weekends and $50 on weekdays. Two- and three-bedroom chalets are also available for families or groups. Each cabin has a fireplace, kitchen, shower, gas-cooker, refrigerator and cooking utensils. There is an excellent canteen at Headquarters, serving Malaysian and Western food. All accommodation must be booked and paid for in advance at the Sabah Parks Office in Jalan Tun Fuad Stephens, opposite the Central Market in Kota Kinabalu. Those intending to climb the mountain must also make arrangements at this office for accommodation at the overnight huts at 3,344 metres (10,971 feet). Panar Laban huts are basic at M$4 per person a night, though cooking utensils and a gas stove are provided. Sleeping bags can be hired here for $2. At the new Laban Rata Resthouse, complete with hot water, electricity and a canteen, the rate is $25 per person. Authorized guides must accompany climbers on the two-day climb and cost $50 regardless of the number of people in the party. Porters, who are optional, are paid $50 for carrying a ten-kilogram (22-pound) load and are worth every cent. The rarified air makes even carrying a camera a chore. A permit ($10) is needed to make the ascent.

Buses to the park run from the bus station in Kota Kinabalu, just near the old clock tower. Tickets are available from the Tuaran United Transport Office for either the 7.30 am or noon bus. The journey takes about two hours and costs M$8. The minibus stops for ten minutes in **Tamparuli**, a main street full of weatherboard two-storey Chinese shophouses and a market square shaded by a scarlet 'flame of the forest' tree. From here the road climbs the lesser hills. If you take the morning bus the mountain is revealed in all its majesty, whereas on the afternoon bus the mountain is obscured by cloud. Vegetable stalls with highland lettuces, cabbages and other temperate vegetables fringe the steep-sided route. At a roadside stream, where water pours out of the hillside along a bamboo aqueduct, the bus driver often stops for a refreshing washup and then, with a grinding of gears, climbs the heights to the Park Headquarters.

Climbing Mount Kinabalu

To ascend this lofty granite peak on the 'Summit Trail' is the goal of most travellers who make their way to this part of the world. And for those who make the gruelling climb and stand on the summit to watch the sun come up over Sabah, it is indeed a memorable — even a spiritual — experience. The Kadazan's reverence for the mountain is not difficult to understand.

Climbers should be warned, however, that it is no easy stroll; much of the climb is up steep staircases made of tree roots, and nowhere is the incline moderate. Those suffering from high blood pressure, heart trouble or asthma are advised not to attempt the climb. Even physically fit climbers may find trouble with the rarified air and it is not uncommon for climbers to suffer from altitude sickness after 3,050 metres (10,000 feet). Sir Hugh Low, a British Colonial Officer who made the first recorded climb in 1851, called it 'the most tiresome walk I have ever experienced'. Travellers today have it easy; Low had to walk from the coast before he even started the ascent.

Bring along plenty of warm, waterproof clothing (the mercury can drop to freezing at night), some chocolate, a torch and a waterbottle.

To reach the start of the 'Summit Trail', climbers can walk or take a jeep four kilometres (2.5 miles) to the Power Station at 1,800 metres (6,000 feet). It is best to start at around 7 am when the air is cool and fresh. Around here

Flora of Mount Kinabalu

From the great tropical lowland rain forest, through the montane oak, rhododendron and conifer forests, to the alpine meadow plants and stunted bushes of the summit zone, the plantlife of Mount Kinabalu is diverse, complex and often unique. Over half the plants growing above 912 metres (2,992 feet) are found nowhere else in the world.

Rafflesia, the world's largest flower, is found near Poring Hot Springs in dense rain forest. Named after Singapore's founder, Stamford Raffles, who first discovered it in Sumatra (its only home besides Malaysia), this fleshy parasitic plant produces a single bloom 45 centimetres (18 inches) across. After taking months to reach maturity, the flower blossoms and then wilts within four days.

Pitcher Plants, carnivorous oddities of the plant world, thrive in the cloud forest. Shaped as 'pitchers' full of liquid, these plants live on the nutrients of drowned, dissolved insects. This ingenious system allows them to thrive in poor soil.

Low's Pitcher Plant (*Nepenthes lowii*) is named after Sir Hugh Low, who made the first recorded ascent of Kinabalu in 1851. This species has a graceful, flared pitcher 20 or so centimetres (eight inches) in length and is found at around 2,134 metres (7,000 feet).

Mossy Pitcher Plant (*Nepenthes villosa*), up to 25 centimetres (ten inches) in length, often grows half-buried among roots in moss and leaf litter. This large and ornate pitcher is found beside the trail at around 2,743 metres (9,000 feet).

Rhododendrons, with their showy blooms, grow in abundance. A large variety of species spans the climb from the lowland forest to the alpine realms, where bonsai trees can be found clinging to cracks in the granite summit region.

Slender-leafed Rhododendron (*Rhododendron stenophyllum*), with its characteristic long, thin leaves and red tubular blooms, is the lowest-growing of the rhododendrons. It is found near Carson's Falls at the beginning of the summit trail at 1,981 metres (6,500 feet).

Low's Rhododendron (*Rhododendron lowii*) is first glimpsed at around 2,438 metres (8,000 feet). Its showy heads of large peach-yellow blooms grow up to 30 centimetres (12 inches) across. The Golden Rhododendron (*Rhododendron retivenium*) is sometimes mistaken for Low's, but its leaves are smaller and narrower. The main flowering season is November to January, but some can be seen flowering year round.

Heath Rhododendron (*Rhododendron ericoides*) with its small red tubular flowers and tiny leaves, is found only on Kinabalu. It first appears at around 2,896 metres (9,500 feet) and is one of few plants to grow on the summit plateau. In rock crevices, the stunted rhododendron matures, flowers and fruits when only a few inches high.

Box-leafed Rhododendron (*Rhododendron buxifolium*) is in full bloom from February to April and its crimson flowers can be seen dotting the stunted vegetation around the huts at Panar Laban. It grows from 2,896 metres (9,500 feet) to the edge of the tree line at 3,353 metres (11,000 feet).

Tea-tree (*Leptospermum*), known locally as '*sayat sayat*', is a shrubby tree with small greyish leaves and starry white flowers. It begins at around 2,743 metres (9,000 feet) and continues right to the summit plateau where it grows in rock crevices. Sayat-sayat, the highest huts on the mountain, are named after the tree, which grows there in abundance.

Mountain Necklace Orchid (*Coelogyne papillosa*), a lovely white-flowered orchid, grows around Sayat-Sayat at 3,810 metres (12,500 feet). During the flowering season in November this orchid covers the rock crevices like drifts of snow. Kinabalu Park has over 1,500 varieties of orchids, but many are difficult to spot as they grow high up in the tree canopy.

Kinabalu Buttercup (*Ranunculus lowii*), a small alpine meadow flower, grows in open ground below the granite slopes. This bright yellow flower is found on wet ground around the Panar Laban huts at 3,353 metres (11,000 feet).

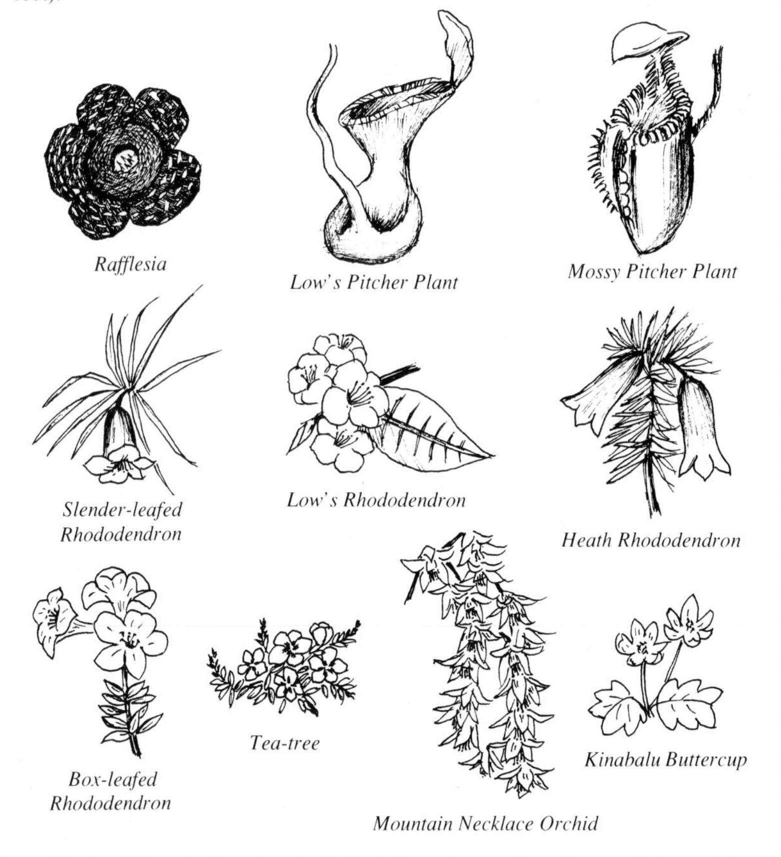

Rafflesia

Low's Pitcher Plant

Mossy Pitcher Plant

Slender-leafed Rhododendron

Low's Rhododendron

Heath Rhododendron

Box-leafed Rhododendron

Tea-tree

Kinabalu Buttercup

Mountain Necklace Orchid

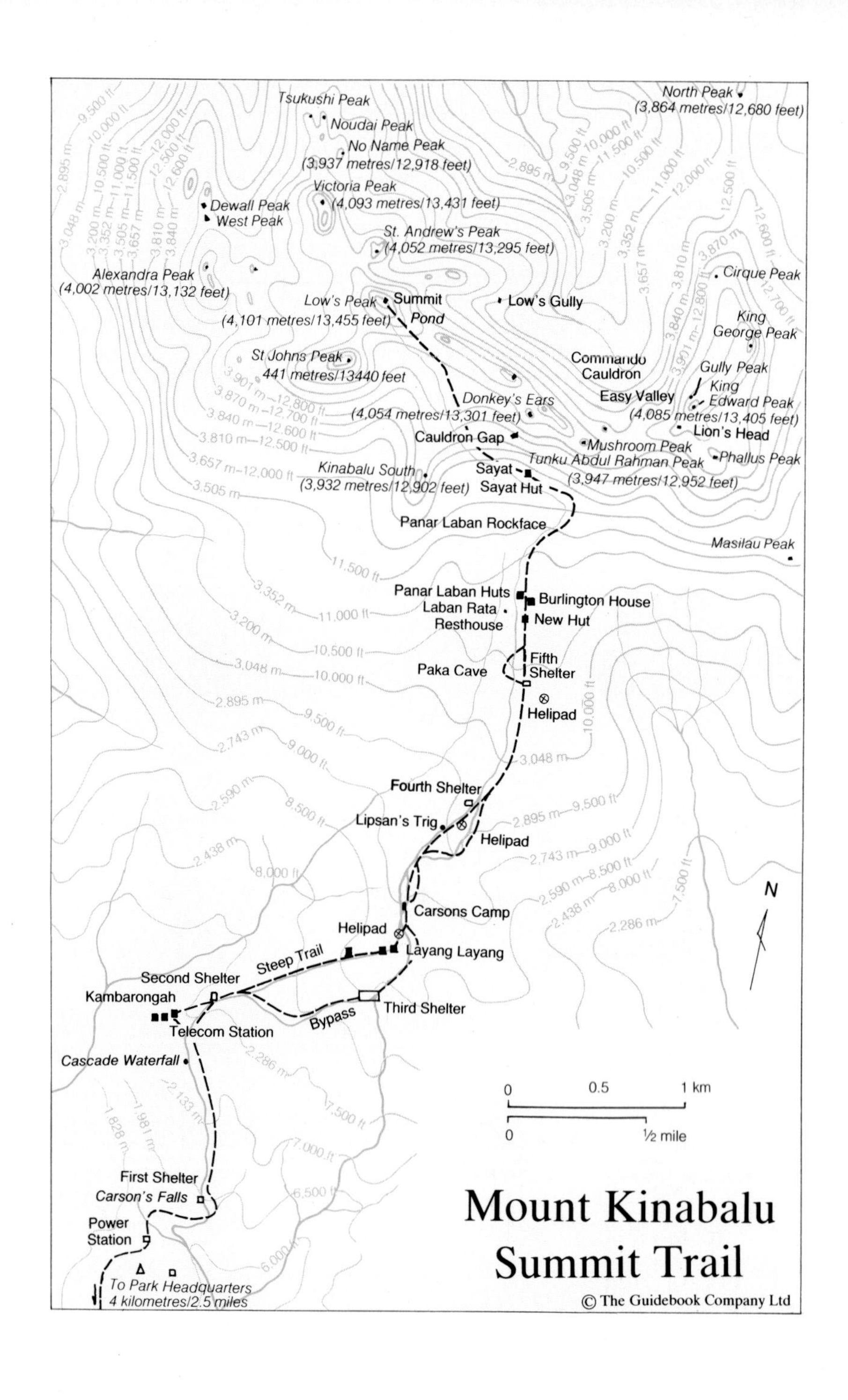
Tsukushi Peak
Noudai Peak
No Name Peak
(3,937 metres/12,918 feet)
Victoria Peak
(4,093 metres/13,431 feet)
North Peak
(3,864 metres/12,680 feet)
Dewall Peak
West Peak
St. Andrew's Peak
(4,052 metres/13,295 feet)
Alexandra Peak
(4,002 metres/13,132 feet)
Cirque Peak
Low's Peak
(4,101 metres/13,455 feet)
Summit
Pond
Low's Gully
King George Peak
St Johns Peak
441 metres/13440 feet
Commando Cauldron
Gully Peak
Easy Valley
King Edward Peak
(4,085 metres/13,405 feet)
Donkey's Ears
(4,054 metres/13,301 feet)
Lion's Head
Cauldron Gap
Mushroom Peak
Phallus Peak
Tunku Abdul Rahman Peak
(3,947 metres/12,952 feet)
Kinabalu South
(3,932 metres/12,902 feet)
Sayat
Sayat Hut
Panar Laban Rockface
Masilau Peak
Panar Laban Huts
Burlington House
Laban Rata Resthouse
New Hut
Fifth Shelter
Paka Cave
Helipad
Fourth Shelter
Lipsan's Trig
Helipad
Carsons Camp
Helipad
Layang Layang
Steep Trail
Second Shelter
Kambarongah
Telecom Station
Bypass
Third Shelter
Cascade Waterfall
First Shelter
Carson's Falls
Power Station
To Park Headquarters
4 kilometres/2.5 miles
N
0
0.5
1 km
0
½ mile
Mount Kinabalu
Summit Trail
© The Guidebook Company Ltd

are some of the 40 varieties of oak trees found on Kinabalu. Beyond **Carson's Falls** the trail climbs steeply up a tree-root staircase to the 1,951-metre (6,400-foot) First Trail Shelter. Rhododendrons can be seen here where the Mossy (or Cloud) Forest starts. Gnarled pine trees covered in moss, and dripping with orchids and other epiphytes, grow here in this zone of almost permanent cloud.

At around 2,134 metres (7,000 feet) — at the Second Shelter — carnivorous pitcher plants cling to the moss on the side of the trail. The trail continues through a bamboo forest where Miss Gibbs Bamboo, a delicate climber named after the first woman to make the ascent in 1910, drapes the trees like moss. Species of warblers can be seen flitting through the tree ferns. At **Carson's Camp**, at 2,651 metres (8,700 feet), Low's Rhododendron, with peachy-yellow blooms, can be seen. The trail winds up over a rocky ridge and through a cloudland of tea-tree, with delicate white flowers and trunks like gnarled driftwood. The mist swirls and chills and the air grows cold and thin as the new **Laban Rata Resthouse** appears out of the gloom. Footsteps quicken towards the canteen and a most welcome cup of tea. The old Panar Laban Hostel is a little further on, at 3,353 metres (11,000 feet). The name **Panar Laban** is derived from the Kadazan word meaning 'place of sacrifice'; it was here that early explorers had to sacrifice a white cockerel and seven eggs in order to appease the resident spirits. This tradition is still performed once a year.

After the tropical lowlands, the nights up here are positively chilly and everyone retires early for the 3 am start, which is necessary if the summit is to be reached in time to see the sunrise. Torchlight illuminates a series of climbs up rockfaces, loose easy-to-stumble-on rockfalls, and above **Sayat Sayat** — the highest hostel — looms the great granite Summit Plateau itself. Striated by glaciers from the last Ice Age, the rocky plateau becomes one huge waterfall in the rainy season. In the thin air the stellar constellations seem near at hand, glimpsed in a navy-blue sky through the twin peaks known as Donkey's Ears. Low's Peak — the summit — is reached just as a pink sunset breaks over Sabah. From the peak, the view is breathtaking. The Crocker Range floats in an ocean of cloud, and far to the northeast some Philippine islands can be seen. Low's Gully, a dark gloomy chasm directly beside the peak, falls almost vertically for 1,000 metres (3,280 feet).

After signing the visitor's book (kept in a metal box), the descent begins. The scenery can be appreciated more on the way down, but it is even tougher on the legs. Almost as common a malady as 'mountain sickness' is 'knee-jam', when the climber is forced to descend like a crab. Those who make the triumphant ascent are issued a certificate by the Park Headquarters.

Poring Hot Springs are a must for those suffering from aching muscles after a Kinabalu descent. Situated 43 kilometres (27 miles) to the east of the park, the hot mineral baths are temperature-graduated from pool to pool.

Poring Hot Springs is surrounded by lush rain forest, where the Rafflesia — the world's largest flower — is found. Giant bamboos grow in abundance here, for *poring* is the Kadazan word for 'bamboo shoot'.

There is cabin and hostel accommodation at Poring, but overnight visitors must bring their own food as there is no canteen. Bookings can be made through the Sabah Parks Office in Kota Kinabalu.

The Drive North

Many Kota Kinabalu-based tour operators specialize in organized trips to many of the following places of interest, but it is easy enough to explore on your own, particularly if you hire a car for a couple of days. The 180-kilometre (111-mile) trip from Kota Kinabalu to Kudat in the north is an easy two-day return drive.

Mengkabong Water Village is a half-hour drive north from Kota Kinabalu. Turn off at Jalan Mengkabong, just south of **Tuaran**. Here the Bajaus, a Muslim people known as 'The Sea Gypsies', dwell in a village built high above the water. Wooden boardwalks link the village to the shore, but much of the activity centres around the water. Housewives paddle *sampan* to and from their neighbours; a group of men stand in the shallows, cleaning out a fishing *perahu*; and children somersault into the water. In this village, children can swim as soon as they can walk.

Kota Belud, 77 kilometres (48 miles) north of Kota Kinabalu, is the hub of Bajau country and home to the best *tamu*— Sunday market — in Sabah. Held every Sunday between 7 am and noon, the *tamu* is where the local Bajau and Kadazan people come to sell and barter a vast array of fresh fruit and vegetables, handicrafts, and weird and wonderful jungle products. From Kota Belud town, turn right at the gold-domed mosque in the direction of **Ranau**. At the next roundabout follow the '*tamu*' sign and the crowds. Under the shade of huge tropical trees a water-buffalo auction is in full swing. The lumbering beasts with their crescent-curved horns are unloaded off pickup trucks or simply ridden there bareback, for the Bajau are Sabah's best horsemen and are equally at home astride a water-buffalo. Under canvas awnings and gay umbrellas the colourful women vendors sell everything from giant clams and salt fish to wild durians from the jungle, blocks of salt, rattan straps for bamboo backpacks and the cheapest basketware and local handicrafts in Sabah. There are whole lanes of cheap t-shirts; an Indonesian medicine seller extols the virtues of traditional medicines; and old batik-clad women chew betel nut amidst many other scenes which make this Sunday *tamu* so special.

Even if you miss the *tamu*, the surrounding countryside is a panorama of terraced rice fields set amongst the hills crowned by the soaring ramparts of Mount Kinabalu. Water-buffalo wander across the road and boys ride horses

AH CHAW LO·DGING HOUSE
亞洲大旅店

招待週到
雅潔房舍
AH CHOW GENERAL GOODS DEALERS.

CHOP ASIA
亞洲商行
Oliver
Lido
AAP7302

Mulu and the Penan

In the dappled twilight of the oldest jungles on earth, deep inside the remote interior of Sarawak, live the Penan, Malaysia's last nomadic people. In the shadows of Mount Mulu — the pivot of the newly-formed Gunung Mulu National Park — lie the traditional homelands of these jungle folk, and because they are so dependent on the jungle for their livelihood they are the only tribe still allowed to hunt within the park boundaries. Although some Penan have lived in settlements for years, they do not adapt well to the sedentary life and many prefer the free nomadic life in the jungle, on which their livelihood still depends. A few are part-time farmers but most, after a brief rest in the settlement, disappear once again into the jungle.

We had just emerged from the mouth of a cave in the Gunung Mulu National Park, and were trekking back to the river when out of the gloom of the rain forest emerged a Penan and his wife. They had killed a wild boar and she carried the head portion and he the rear. The pig had already been gutted in the jungle and its belly sewn up with rattan, and they had constructed clever backpacks from what was available in the forest — their hardware store and supermarket combined. No one knows the jungle as the Penan do — even our Kenyah guide attested to that. The Kenyah and Kayan peoples, who dwell in the upper reaches of the great river systems, have for centuries acted as middlemen in the trade of jungle exotica between the Penan and the Chinese merchants. Eastern apothecaries sought rhinoceros horn, monkeys' gallstones and the dried bladders of honey bears, and the Penan were the suppliers. Today, with many of these animals facing extinction, the nomadic people collect mainly rattans, resins, medicinal herbs and weave fine mats for their livelihood. At Long Imam, a Penan settlement on the upper Tutuh River, womenfolk sit on the wooden verandas weaving baskets and mats of black and white designs from split rattan. First they must walk a day's journey deep into the jungle where the best rattan grows, then they dry, split and finally colour it with a dye made of jungle leaves.

Penghulu Nyaluk, the Penan chief of Long Imam, dresses in traditional fashion, with basin-cut hair-do, indigo-coloured loincloth, bone earplugs and armloads of tusk and rattan bangles. He lives in the settlement but has his own room — constructed like the traditional temporary jungle shelter — out the back, close by his pet monkey. His powerful physique belies his age and he is still a mean shot with the blowpipe. The Kenyah say that when the Penan shoot with the blowpipe they can send the dart further than any of Sarawak's hunting tribes. Their blowpipes, made of *belian* (Borneo ironwood), are highly sought-after. To make a blowpipe requires skill and infinite patience. Often the craftsman has to sit in a tree so that the pipe can hang straight down while the hole is bored with hot steel, half an inch at a time. The finished bore must be absolutely straight or the trajectory of the dart will be put off. Darts are made of bamboo slivers fitted with a plug of light wood at one end. If the plug fits the blowpipe tightly, the dart will go further, but if the plug is not such a snug fit the dart will have a shorter range. The sap of the *tajem* tree, a powerful nerve poison which causes paralysis and death within minutes, is used to coat the dart. Some Penan own shotguns, but they can break down and bullets are expensive — the blowpipe is more reliable.

The true jungle Penan are very pale-skinned from generations of living in the shade of the great forests. Even today, some of the older people won't venture into the settled cleared areas for they are fearful of the sun which they believe will make them sick. Since the Penan have no calendar system they have evolved a unique system of marking the time from knots in rattan. For future meetings they knot a length of rattan with the same number of knots as there are days to go until the meeting. Each day they untie a knot until the appointed day arrives.

Although the Mulu Caves are a recently discovered wonder of the world, the Penan have always known of them. They have always hunted the wild boar and deer that take refuge in the mouths of the yawning caverns, but they never ventured inside what they believed to be the realm of the spirits.

Like all nomadic peoples the world over, their livelihood is in jeopardy as the great rain forests of the world diminish every year. Government agricultural projects provide a bridge from the old world to the new and some nomads prefer the more settled life. But it is in the jungle that most of the Penan are really at home. At least the loggers cannot damage Gunung Mulu National Park, the Penan's traditional home and spiritual source.

bareback across fields dotted with bamboo houses.

Kudat, 180 kilometres (112 miles) north and the end of the West Coast Highway, is the home of one of Sabah's most interesting ethnic minorities, the Rungus. In Kudat market-place you may be lucky and catch a glimpse of shy Rungus girls dressed in knee-length black sarongs, heavy brass bracelets and beaded necklaces. Traditional longhouses are found ten kilometres (six miles) from town. In May and December — the Rungus festival times — the famous *Mongigol* dance is performed. According to Rungus belief, the earth cannot be dug except to bury the dead. When the British told them to plant coconuts they refused because the coconut closely resembles a human skull with two 'eyes' and a 'husk' of hair. But today many Rungus own coconut plantations.

Along the coast are excellent swimming beaches, particularly **Bak Bak Beach** where the South China Sea meets the Sulu Sea. Not far away, across the sapphire-blue Straits of Balabac, is the Philippines.

Tamu are held on Sunday mornings at **Sequati**, about 23 kilometres (14 miles) from Kudat. Brass gongs and *parang*, the Malay machete, can be found here. Rungus longhouses are also found at Kampung Tinangol, 46 kilometres (29 miles), and at Kampung Nangkaran, some 61 kilometres (38 miles), from Kudat.

Across the Crocker Range

Apart from the road to Kinabalu National Park, there is another highway into the interior that skirts the top of the Crocker Range, then dips down into the picturesque terraced valley of Tambunan, home of the Kadazans, and through the interior to Tenom, home of the Muruts. Hire cars are ideal for this trip, but minibuses run from Kota Kinabalu to Tambunan, Keningau and Tenom. From Tenom, Sabah's only railway runs through a spectacular gorge to Beaufort on the coast.

Penampang, a Kadazan centre, is just 13 kilometres (eight miles) from Kota Kinabalu and the start of the highway across the Crocker Range. Here in the village of Monosopiad is a house nicknamed 'The House of Skulls'. Hanging from the ceiling are 42 skulls said to have been acquired in battle over 100 years ago by Monosopiad, whose descendants own the house. Kadazan priestesses occasionally perform ceremonies to appease the spirits of the skulls.

From here the road to Tambunan climbs up through the hills, alongside villages set on ridges above boulder-strewn mountain rivers. Higher up, the air freshens and cools, and clouds roll in from the humid lowlands and billow across the road. From the pale blue of the coast the sky deepens by degrees until at the top of the **Crocker Range** it is a bright cornflower blue. Sometimes the clouds part, revealing a vista of violet hills sweeping down to

BOB.

the coast where islets hover in the glittering waters of the South China Sea. At sunset this view is spectacular. Along the top of the divide, orchids and other epiphytes adorn the trees and moss carpets the ground. From the top of the range the road drops through some towering rain forest and bamboo groves until, at a bend in the road, a picturesque highland valley appears.

Tambunan, surrounded by terraced rice paddies and hills of russet-coloured bamboo groves, must be one of Sabah's prettiest sights. Tambunan looks its best during the rice-growing season, when the paddy-fields are irrigated, but it is after the rice harvest that the valley comes to life. At the Pesta Kaamatan, the Kadazan's Harvest Festival held during mid-May, the festivities include buffalo races, rafting and *tapai*-drinking contests. Age-old traditions, centred around the rice spirit, Bambarayan, are re-enacted. Seven ears of ripe *padi* are picked from the best field and offered as a gift to the rice spirit. The field is then harvested, but the seven ears are kept in a special place of honour in the home.

Bamboo dominates Tambunan: the houses are made of split bamboo traditionally set on stone foundations, fences are constructed from split giant bamboo, and backpacks for carrying firewood are woven from bamboo, apart from a myriad of other uses. Streams bubble out of the surrounding hills and are cunningly diverted to water the crescent-shaped rice fields. Mid-stream in the Sunsuron River, lorry drivers park their vehicles for a convenient clean-up. In pools in the boulder-strewn creeks, village children cavort and swim while their mothers slap their washing on smooth river pebbles.

On a small hillock in the valley is the grave of Sabah's most famous son, Mat Salleh, who led an uprising against the British colonial system. This charismatic Bajau prince was a *pangeran*, a warrior imbued with magical powers. It is recounted that, as a youth, Mat Salleh could throw a buffalo by its horns and that rice scattered by him turned into wasps. The warrior chief would launch his raids from stone-walled forts surrounded by bamboo-spike barriers before retreating into the jungle. The English expeditions sent into the wilds to pursue Mat Salleh were kept on the run until he was finally killed during the seige of his Tambunan fort. It took a further five years after his death for the English to quell the rebellion. Tambunan, with its bamboo houses and rice paddies, is a fitting resting place for Sabah's favourite native son. Overnight accommodation is available at the Government Rest House on a hill above the town.

Tenom, at the end of the Interior Highway, is home to the Murut people, Sabah's traditional hunters and gatherers and the last tribe to give up head-hunting. These days, many work on cocoa and rubber plantations, but life for most still centres around the longhouse and their traditional shifting agriculture. Occasionally they still foray into the jungle to hunt wild boar with blowpipes and to collect rattans, medicinal herbs, beeswax and edible birds' nests which they trade with the Chinese merchants in town. Tenom, like most Sabah towns, is lined with Chinese shophouses, for the Muruts live out of town. **Kemabong**, a Murut and Chinese area close to town, is a picturesque garden village approached from a hanging bridge over the Padas River. Longhouses are found at Kampung Marais and at Kampung Kalibatang, where blowpipes are still made.

Tour companies operating from the Tanjung Aru Beach Hotel and Kota Kinabalu run trips to Tenom which include a visit to a Murut longhouse and a return trip to Kota Kinabalu via the railway. There is a Government Rest House and a couple of Chinese hotels in town for overnight stays.

A **jungle railway** operates daily, linking highland Tenom to lowland Beaufort. Rail passengers can board the train at Tanjung Aru, close to Kota Kinabalu, and travel down the coast past small towns and rice fields to Beaufort, or vice-versa. **Beaufort** is a steamy town of wooden shophouses set on stilts beside a wide brown river where loggers pole rafts of giant timbers downstream. From here the railway climbs up through the Crocker Range, skirts the banks of the Padas River, burrows through stone tunnels and winds above the churning rapids of the wild **Padas Gorge**. A ride on the Tenom/ Beaufort railway is a good alternative to a jungle trek, for you can travel through virgin rain forest in the comfort of your railcar. From Beaufort, minibuses and taxis run to Kota Kinabalu.

East along the Sulu Sea

On Sabah's East Coast, frontier-style timber towns and bustling fishing ports are scattered along the Sulu Sea, Malaysia's most remote coastline. Most travellers take a day flight to Sandakan to visit the Orang-utan Sanctuary, the area's most obvious tourist attraction. For more adventurous travellers with time to explore there are idyllic offshore islands with possibly Malaysia's best scuba diving and traditional fishing villages still virtually untouched by tourism.

Sandakan, 386 kilometres (240 miles) from Kota Kinabalu, was once the capital of North Borneo. This bustling harbourside town is best known for the **Sepilok Orang-utan Sanctuary**, which is 24 kilometres (15 miles) from town. Sandakan can be reached easily by daily flights from Kota Kinabalu or, for the stout-hearted, minibuses ply the gruelling East West Highway — a bone-rattling ten-hour journey. The Sepilok Forest Reserve provides a sanctuary for the world's largest collection of orang-utan, immortalized in Victorian times as the 'wild men of Borneo'. The reserve was originally set up in 1964 as a rehabilitation centre for injured and illegally captured orang-utans. Since then, over 100 apes have been released back into the forest and many of the present population in the surrounding jungle are their descendants. On the ground, with their stooping gait and dangling arms, the apes look ungainly, but up in the trees they are an impressive sight as they

On the Trail of a Great Writer — Somerset Maugham

Anthony Burgess, Joseph Conrad, Paul Theroux, Han Suyin, Noel Barber and many other well-known authors have written of their travels and experiences in Malaysia, but it is Somerset Maugham, the celebrated English novelist, who immortalized the Malay archipelago in his renowned short stories.

Maugham first journeyed to the East while doing espionage work for the British during the First World War and he returned countless times until his last visit in 1959. Stalking his trail, the one fact that is immediately apparent is that most of the life he wrote about no longer exists. But although the players have long since departed, the settings for many of his short stories still remain. The colonial white planters and government officials and their wives were his main material, for when a European visited Malaya in the 1920s and '30s the only locals he was likely to meet were coolies on the rubber estates, houseboys, barmen and other servants. Many of the Europeans Maugham wrote of lived incredibly isolated lives, often not seeing other white folk for weeks on end. The women, alone at home with only their servants for company and dying of boredom, were perfect prey for illicit affairs and ripe material for some of Maugham's more tragic tales. Many of Maugham's Malaysian stories are about the very people he stayed, dined and chatted with — often very thinly disguised. His habit of including in his stories characters he met caused quite a lot of resentment and he was often in danger of libel action, although he was never taken to court.

'The Letter', his most famous short story, later made into a movie starring Bette Davis, was based on one of Malaysia's most celebrated scandals and, according to rumour, Maugham's version was very close to the truth. In 1911 Mrs Ethel Proudlock, wife of the headmaster of Kuala Lumpur's prestigious Victoria Institute, shot and killed a white engineer whom she maintained had attempted to rape her. The prosecution implied that he was her lover and she was convicted of murder and sentenced to be hanged. Believing her to be innocent, the stunned European community pressured the sultan; he granted her a pardon and she was bustled back to England. In Maugham's version of the story, she is acquitted and 'The Letter', which proved that the murdered man was indeed her lover, was destroyed.

On his earlier visits, Maugham was accompanied by an American, Gerald Haxton, his 'travelling companion-secretary', and it was through him that he gleaned much of the material for his short stories. Haxton was an adventurous extrovert, a great socializer, drinker, gambler and a good bridge player (a necessity when travelling with the celebrated novelist). Maugham recalled an instance when Gerald gave him the low-down on a tale. 'I set a time to dine at the white man's club, but Gerald, as usual, became involved with some friends in the bar. I was very hungry, and became finally very provoked waiting for Gerald, knowing his addiction to drinking and gambling. I was nearly through dinner when he staggered in. I was thoroughly out of sorts, and about to raise a stink about his inconsideration, when he said: "I'm sorry, I know I'm drunk, but as an apology I've got a corking good story for you." ... What he told me became one of my best stories, "Footprints in the Jungle", a true murder story of a wife and her lover who killed her husband.'

Tanah Merah — the setting for the story — is Malacca, for where else could be 'the old Raad Huis that the Dutch built . . . . and on the hill stand the grey ruins of the fort by aid of which the Portuguese maintained their hold over the unruly natives.' He talks of 'vast labyrinthine houses of the Chinese merchants, backing on the sea.' These are the ancestral Straits Chinese homes on Malacca's Jalan Tun Tan Cheng Lock, but these days reclaimed land separates the sea from the 'loggias' where the merchants used to 'enjoy the salt breeze'.

The club where Gerald drank at the bar and Maugham sat impatiently dining alone was the Malacca Club, known as the Town House. The two-storey, twin-domed building still stands, but today, ironically enough, it is a monument to Malaysia's independence struggle. The Malacca Club is now in Taman Melaka Jaya and this quote from Maugham still hangs on the wall in the conference room. 'The club faces the sea; it is a spacious but shabby building; it has an air of neglect and when you enter you feel that you intrude. It gives you the impression that it is closed really, for alterations and repairs, and that you have taken indiscreet advantage of an open door to go where you are not wanted. In the morning you may find there a couple of planters who have come in from their estates on business and are drinking a gin-sling before starting back again; and latish in the afternoon a lady or two may perhaps be seen looking with a furtive air through old numbers of the "Illustrated London News". At nightfall a few men saunter in and sit about the billiard-room watching the play and drinking sukas. But on Wednesdays there is a little more animation. On that day the gramophone is set going in the large room upstairs and people come in from the surrounding country to dance. There are sometimes no less than a dozen couples and it is even possible to make up two tables of bridge.'

In 1929 Maugham cruised the ports of Borneo, staying with local government officials and planters and collecting the material for several more of his short stories, including 'Neil MacAdam'. The hero of this tale is a young assistant curator who comes to work in a Borneo museum. It is obviously Kuching's Sarawak Museum thinly disguised, for where else in the region is 'a handsome stone building' a notable museum. He steams up what must be the Sarawak River, for 'on the bank grew thickly nipah palm and the tortured mangrove; beyond stretched the dense green of the virgin forest. In the distance, darkly silhouetted against the blue sky, was the rugged outline of a mountain . . . . Here and there on the banks, were Malay houses with thatched roofs, and they nestled cosily among fruit trees . . . . Kuala Solor straggled along the left bank of the river, a white, neat and trim little town, and on the right on a hill were the fort and the Sultan's palace.' Kuala Solor is none other than Kuching and if you steam up the river today, despite modern encroachments, the mangroves, Malay houses and the fort and '*istana*' (palace) are all still there.

swing from tree to tree. The rehabilitation process is long and complex, for young orang-utans can only learn to climb by watching others. Once they have acquired certain skills and are mature enough they are taken out to feeding platforms deep in the jungle where they gradually gain confidence in their natural environment. In 1983 a rehabilitated female gave birth to twins after mating with a completely wild male — one of the sanctuary's success stories. Orang-utans have a life span of 30 years and give birth to only three or four young in that time, which is one reason why they have come so close to extinction. The orang-utan Rehabilitation Centre can be visited between 9 am and noon and from 2 to 4 pm daily. Special programmes, films, talks and slide shows can be arranged with prior notice. There are three nature trails into the primary jungle. The shortest of these takes 15 minutes to walk, while the main trail is 4.8 kilometres (three miles) in length.

The **Gomantong Caves**, about 32 kilometres (20 miles) south of Sandakan, are famous for their edible birds' nests. Swiftlets nest in the caves found in a sheer limestone cliff-face that rises 240 metres (787 feet) from the forest floor. During nest-harvesting time, skilled collectors of the Orang Sungei tribe climb the awesome heights to gather the prized nests. This dangerous occupation is governed by the superstitions and folklore of the Orang Sungei and their age-old trade with the Chinese merchants. Permission to visit the caves can be obtained from the Sandakan Forest Department and boats run from the Sandakan Fish Market at 9 am. The journey from Sandakan to the Buang Sayang jetty on the Suanlamba River takes two hours, and from here it is an additional three kilometres (1.8 miles) by pickup to the sanctuary. There is a good camping ground outside the caves and fresh water is available.

Turtle Island Park, consisting of three islands and their surrounding coral reefs, is a two- to three-hour journey by boat north from Sandakan, close by the Philippines border. Green and Hawksbill turtles come here to lay their eggs. Because the egg-laden females come in with the night or early morning tide, there are chalets in which travellers can stay overnight. The rate at the chalets on Pulau Selingan is M$20 each for an overnight stay. There are also hatcheries, where baby turtles can be seen scrambling back into the sea. The peak season is between June and September and boat transfers and accommodation can be arranged through the Sabah Parks Office or through tour operators.

Semporna, in the southeast, is the stepping-off place for the best diving islands in Malaysia. Travellers can get to Semporna by air via Sandakan and **Tomanggong** or fly direct from Kota Kinabalu to **Tawau**; the rest of the way is by road. A colourful and lively Bajau town, Semporna is renowned for its seafood, and at the waterfront fish market lobsters, prawns, crabs and fish of every description abound. Off shore are some idyllic coral-fringed islands which are the remnants of an ancient volcanic crater. On these islands live the Bajau Laut, the most maritime of all the Bajau-speaking groups in Sabah. They live either in traditional boats called *lipa-lipa* or in pilehouses at the water's edge.

Semporna's offshore islands are infrequently visited and are just being discovered by the diving fraternity. This is real divers' territory, for at **Pulau Sipadan** the turquoise waters give way to the dark depths of the ocean floor. Along the coral reefs that fringe the 600-metre (1,968-foot) dropoff, the diving is superb. Turtles also come to the islands to nest and are a common sight swimming off the reef. Apart from the prolific coral, large game fish are plentiful and there is even a jetty on the island for night dives when turtles can be seen journeying up the sand to the beach. Borneo Divers — the only professional diving operation in Sabah — organizes special dive packages, including flights from Kota Kinabalu, tent accommodation, meals and tanks. Divers bring their own gear (except weights and belts) or it can be hired. Contact Borneo Divers, tel. (088) 53074 or telex MA 81644 BDIVER for all details.

If you prefer just to explore the island or to snorkel, there are plenty of fishing boats available for hire in Semporna. At Bohey Dulang Island there is an oyster farm which produces Borneo half-round pearls.

M
4182
P

Practical Information

Basic Malay Vocabulary

Bahasa Malaysia, or Malay as it is commonly known, is relatively easy to pick up as it is written in the Latin alphabet and is not a tonal language. In Malay there are no articles: *kupu* means 'a butterfly' or 'the butterfly'. Plurals are made by doubling the noun: *kupu-kupu* (butterflies). Adverbs are used to denote tense: *sudah,* 'already', indicates the past, and *belum*, 'not yet', indicates the future.

Even if a traveller learns only a few basic words and phrases, it is good public relations. After hearing you speak a few phrases, Malays will often exclaim, 'pandai cekap Bahasa Malaysia', meaning that you are clever to know their language.

Numbers

one	*satu*
two	*dua*
three	*tiga*
four	*empat*
five	*lima*
six	*enam*
seven	*tujuh*
eight	*lapan*
nine	*sembilan*
ten	*sepuluh*
eleven	*sebelas*
twelve	*dua belas*
thirteen	*tiga belas*
twenty	*dua puluh*
twenty-one	*dua puluh satu*
thirty	*tiga puluh*
fifty	*lima puluh*
hundred	*ratus*
one hundred	*seratus*
two hundred	*dua ratus*
thousand	*ribu*
one thousand	*seribu*
million	*juta*

Useful Phrases

how are you?	*apa khabar*? (the most common greeting)
I'm fine	*khabar baik* (the only reply)
never mind	*tak apa*
thank you	*terima kasih*
you're welcome	*sama sama*
yes	*ya*
no	*tidak* (more commonly tak)

good morning	*selamat pagi*
goodnight	*selamat malam*
have a good trip	*selamat jalan*
(in reply to above)	*selamat tinggal* (goodbye from those who stay behind)
excuse me	*maafkan saya*

Questions and Directions

how much is this?	*berapa harga?*
what is your name?	*siapa nama awak?*
my name is...	*nama saya...*
I come from...	*saya datang dari*
where is...	*di mana...?*
what?	*apa?*
why?	*kenapa?*
I want to go to...	*saya mahu pergi ke...*
turn left	*beluk kiri*
turn right	*beluk kanan*
go straight	*terus*
stop here	*berhenti di sini*
in front	*depan*
behind	*belakang*

Places

island	*pulau*
village	*kampung*
mountain	*gunung*
hill	*bukit*
river	*sungai*
beach	*pantai*
town	*bandar*
road	*jalan*
street	*lebuh*
lane	*lorong*
post office	*pejabat pos*
bathroom	*bilik air*
toilet	*tandas*
market	*pasar*
coffee shop	*kedai kopi*
lake	*tasek*
estuary	*kuala*
museum	*musium*
mosque	*masjid*

Useful Words

today	*hari ini*
yesterday	*semalam*

tomorrow	*esok*
day	*hari*
week	*minggu*
month	*bulan*
year	*tahun*
hungry	*lapar*
sleep	*tidur*
bathe	*mandi*
buy	*beli*
sell	*jual*
I	*saya*
you	*awak*
he, she	*dia*
good	*baik*
okay	*baiklah*
can	*boleh*
bus	*bas*
police	*polis*
expensive	*mahal*
cheap	*murah*
south	*selatan*
north	*utara*
west	*barat*
east	*timor*

Food and Drink

to eat	*makan*
to drink	*minum*
water or drinks	*air*
rice	*nasi*
fried rice	*nasi goreng*
rice and curries	*nasi padang*
eggs	*telur*
meat	*daging*
chicken	*ayam*
fish	*ikan*
vegetables	*sayur*
salt	*garam*
sugar	*gula*
hot (temperature)	*panas*
hot (chilli hot)	*pedas*
cold	*sejuk*
coffee	*kopi*
tea	*teh*
bread	*roti*

Glossary

Atap A roof thatch made from *nipah* or *rumbia* (sago) palm fronds and sewn with rattan.

Baba and nonya The menfolk (*baba*) and the women (*nonya*) of the Straits Chinese, a unique minority group of Malaysianized Chinese.

Baju melayu Traditional dress of Malay men, comprising loose trousers, a long-sleeved collarless shirt (*baju*) and a short sarong, known as *samping*, which is worn over the trousers.

Belacan A paste of dried prawns or fish used as an ingredient for making sambal relish.

Bersanding A ceremony at a Malay wedding when the bride and groom are seated next to each other on a bridal dais and given traditional offerings.

Bomoh A traditional medicine practitioner who is believed to possess special healing powers. He also performs religious rites in villages and is often hired for special ceremonies to keep away rain.

Bugis People who originated from Sulawesi (Celebes) and who first immigrated to the Malay peninsula in the 15th century.

Bumiputra Literally means 'sons of the soil' and is the term used to describe the aborigines, Malays and related groups whose cultural affinities are indigenous to the region.

Halal From the Arabic meaning 'permissible according to divine law', it is generally used to describe food specially prepared for Muslims.

Hari Raya The Muslim festival at the end of Ramadan, the fasting month.

Kain songket A type of woven silk brocade, shot with gold and silver threads, made on the east coast of the peninsula.

Kampung A cluster of houses which comprise the Malaysian village.

Kavadi Wooden frame decorated with peacock feathers and long, thin spikes attached to the carrier's body. Used by Hindu penitents at the Thaipusam festival.

Kelong A marine fish trap resembling a house on stilts set high above the water.

Kenduri A Malay feast held for weddings and other special occasions when the entire village, friends and relatives are invited.

Kompang A small tambourine-type drum traditionally played at Malay wedding ceremonies.

Kris The wavy-bladed Malay dagger sometimes believed to possess magical properties.

Langgiang A shrimp net on the end of two 'V'-shaped poles which is pushed through shallow water. Said to have originated with the 16th-century Portuguese.

Minangkabau A matriarchal society originally from Sumatra who settled extensively in Negri Sembilan state.

Orang asli The aboriginal tribes of the peninsula, comprising the Negritos (Batek, Jahai, Kensiu, Kintak, Lanoh, Mendrik); the Senoi (Che Wong, Jah Hut, Mah Meri, Semai, Semok Beri, Temiar); and the Proto Malay groups (Jakun, Kanak, Orang Laut, Orang Selitar, Semelai and Temuan).

Orang laut An aboriginal tribe known as 'the sea peoples', who comprised the navy of the Malaccan Sultanate. Hang Tuah, the legendary warrior, was said to be an *orang laut*.

Pantun Traditional Malay poetry in quatrain style; the first line rhymes with the third and the second with the fourth.

Parang The general-purpose heavy-bladed Malay machete.

Pasar malam An open-air night market which rotates locations. The favourite night entertainment of Malaysia.

Perahu A boat or ship, but commonly used for Indonesian wooden sailing vessels.

Potong jambul A traditional Malay ceremony when the baby's hair is first cut, generally at around one year of age.

Ramadan or **Bulan Puasa** The month-long Muslim fast which is one of the essential rules of Islam.

Santan The milk or cream obtained by grating and squeezing coconut flesh.

Semangat A vital force, or the soul of life, which many Malays believe exists in both man and things.

Sepak takraw A Malay sport played with a small rattan ball described as 'aerial football over a net'.

Sireh Betel leaves which are chewed with areca nut. Once a popular pastime but now only common amongst the elderly.

Silat The traditional Malay art of self-defence.

Songkok The velvet fez-like cap worn by Malay men. *Songkok haji* is the small white circular cap traditionally worn by those who have made the pilgrimage to Mecca.

Sunat The circumcision ceremony for Malay boys.

Warung A roadside eating stall.

Wayang kulit The traditional Malay shadow-puppet play performed in the northern states of Kelantan, Kedah and Terengganu.

Useful Addresses

Telephone Information

Local directory assistance	tel. 103
Domestic long distance information and booking	tel. 101
International directory assistance and booking	tel. 108
Police/Ambulance/Fire	tel. 999
Hospital Besar (Kuala Lumpur)	tel. 292–1044
Rail information (Kuala Lumpur)	tel. 274–9422

Airline Offices

Kuala Lumpur (tel. code 03)

Subang Airport:	
Telephone Check-in Service and DCA Information Counter	tel. 746–1014/ 1235
Malaysia Airlines, Bangunan MAS, Jalan Sultan Ismail, Kuala Lumpur 50250:	
Administration	tel. 261–0555
Reservations (24 hour)	tel. 746–3000
Airport	tel. 746–4555
Airlines landing at Subang Airport:	
AI — Air India	tel. 242–0166
BA — British Airways	tel. 242–6177
CI — China Airlines	tel. 242–2383
CX — Cathay Pacific	tel. 238–3377/ 3355
GA — Garuda	tel. 248–4072
JL — Japan Airlines	tel. 261–1722
KE — Korean Airlines	tel. 242–8311
KL — KLM Royal Dutch Airlines	tel. 242–7011

LH —	Lufthansa	tel. 261–4666
PK —	Pakistan International Airlines	tel. 242–5444
PR —	Philippine Airlines	tel. 242–9040
QF —	Qantas Airways	tel. 238–9133
SU —	Aeroflot Soviet Airways	tel. 261–3231
SN —	Sabena	tel. 242–5244
SQ —	Singapore Airlines	tel. 292–3122
TG —	Thai Airways International	tel. 293–7100

Penang (tel. code 04)

Malaysia Airlines, Reservations and Ticketing		tel. 620–011
Airport		tel. 830–811
BA —	British Airways	tel. 616–342
CI —	China Airlines	tel. 627–091
CX —	Cathay Pacific	tel. 620–411
GA —	Garuda	tel. 365–257
JL —	Japan Airlines	tel. 378–046
LH —	Lufthansa	tel. 362–545
SU —	Aeroflot Soviet Airways	tel. 615–170
SQ —	Singapore Airlines	tel. 362–621
TG —	Thai Airways International	tel. 366–233

Commonwealth Embassies

Australia — tel. 242–3122
6 Jalan Yap Kwan Seng

Canada — tel. 261–2000
7th floor, MBF Plaza

India — tel. 456–2570
United Asian Bank Building, Jalan Tun Perak

New Zealand — tel. 248–6422
193 Jalan Tun Razak

Singapore — tel. 261–6277
209 Jalan Tun Razak

United Kingdom — tel. 248–7122
13th floor, Wisma Damansara, Jalan Semantan

Burma — tel. 242–3863
No 5 Taman U Thant 1

China — tel. 242–8495
229 Jalan Ampang

Denmark tel. 241–6088
123 Jalan Ampang

East Germany tel. 456–2894
29 Jalan Ampang Hilir

France tel. 248–4318
218 C–F, Lorong Damai 13, off Jalan Ampang

Indonesia tel. 984–2011
233 Jalan Tun Razak

Italy tel. 456–5122
99 Jalan U Thant

Japan tel. 243–8044
11 Persiaran Stoner, off Jalan Tun Razak

The Netherlands tel. 243–1143
4 Jalan Mesra, off Jalan Damai

Norway tel. 243–0144
11th floor, Bangunan Angkasaraya, Jalang Ampang

Pakistan tel. 248–3822
132 Jalan Ampang

The Philippines tel. 248–4233
1 Changkat Kia Peng

Spain tel. 248–4868
200 Jalan Ampang

Sweden tel. 248–5981
6th floor, Bangunan Angkasa Raya, Jalan Ampang

Switzerland tel. 248–0622
16 Persiaran Madge

Thailand tel. 248–8222
206 Jalan Ampang

United States tel. 248–9011
376 Jalan Tun Razak

USSR tel. 456–7252
263 Jalan Ampang

West Germany 3 Jalan U Thant	tel. 242–9665

Rental Car Agencies

Avis	tel. 241–7144
Hertz	tel. 243–3433
Sintat	tel. 248–2388

Tourist Development Corporation Offices

Kuala Lumpur 26th floor, Menara Dato Onn, Putra World Trade Centre, Jalan Tun Ismail	tel. 293–5188 (Area Code 03)
TDC Southern Region Suite 215, 2nd floor, Orchid Plaza, 2 Jalan Wong Ah Fook, Johor Baru	tel. 223–590 (Area Code 07)
TDC Northern Region 10 Jalan Tun Syed Sheh Barakbah, Penang	tel. 620–066 (Area Code 04)
TDC East Coast Region 2243 Ground floor, Wisma MCIS, Jalan Sultan Zainal Abidin, Kuala Terengganu	tel. 621–893 (Area Code 09)
TDC Sarawak 2nd floor, AIA Building, Jalan Song Thian Cheok, Kuching	tel. 246–575 (Area Code 082)
TDC Sabah Block L, Lot 4, Bandaran Sinsuran, Kota Kinabalu	tel. 211–698 (Area Code 088)

Hotels

Malaysia has accommodation to suit every budget — from simple local lodging houses to international-class hotels. Many of the island resorts offer luxury hotels or the more simple *kampung*-style chalets for the budget-conscious or those who like their resorts at a more grass-roots level. Government Rest Houses provide simple, and clean rooms and are often situated in more rustic surroundings on the outskirts of towns.

Every town has at least one hotel offering standard accommodation, and the larger urban centres invariably host an international-standard hotel. Most first-class and luxury hotels listed have a bar, restaurant and swimming pool. Prices fluctuate according to seasonal trends (public holidays, school holidays, wet season). A 5 percent government tax is levied on all hotels, and for luxury hotels there is an additional 10 percent tax.

Cameron Highlands

Luxury and First Class

Strawberry Park Resort

PO Box 81, Lot 195, 39007 Tanah Rata, Pahang. Tel. (05)941166. M$140–170. 130 rooms.

Favourite Singaporean resort hotel, offering tennis, squash and horse-riding. Great views over the highlands.

Ye Olde Smokehouse Hotel

By the Golf Course, 39000 Tanah Rata, Pahang. Tel. (05)941214/5. M$85–380. 16 rooms.

Tudor-style English country house. Relive the colonial days in the antique-filled rooms with fireplaces and dine on Devonshire teas in the garden restaurant.

Merlin Hotel

39000 Tanah Rata, Pahang. Tel. (05)941211/313. M$80–135. 64 rooms.

Popular with golfers as hotel fronts an excellent 18-hole course.

Foster's Lakehouse Hotel

Lubok Taman, Milestone 30, 39200 Ringlet, Pahang. Tel. (05)996152. M$130–300. 12 rooms.

A colonial, Tudor-style retreat, with beautiful gardens overlooking a lake.

Standard

Kowloon Hotel

34–35, 39100 Brinchang, Pahang. Tel. (05)941366. M$35–45. 24 rooms.

Good value and clean, with hot water and central location.

Cherating

Luxury and First Class

Club Mediterranee

26080 Cherating, Kuantan, Pahang. Tel. (09)591131. M$165–220. 300 rooms.

Two private beaches, all water sports, tennis, archery and batik painting. Packages include all meals, activities and disco.

Standard

Cherating Mini Motel

26080 Kampung Cherating, Pahang. Tel. (09)592527. M$25–40. 12 rooms.

Malay-style chalets right on the beach with basic facilities.

Budget

Kampung Inn

Jalan Cherating Lama, 26080 Cherating, Pahang. No telephone. M$8–28. 12 rooms.

Seaboard thatch-roofed huts popular with young budget travellers.

Bukit Fraser (Fraser's Hill)

Fraser's Hill Merlin
49000 Bukit Fraser, Pahang. Tel. (09)382279. M$80–300. 109 rooms.
Favourite weekend retreat for city folk. Opposite golf course and near jungle.

Holiday Bungalows
Fraser's Hill Development Corporation, 49000 Bukit Fraser, Pahang. Tel. (09)382201. M$25–55. 65 rooms.
Bungalows and chalets have full catering facilities and fireplaces. Set amidst rolling jungle-clad hills. Excellent for families.

Genting Highlands

Genting Highlands Resort
69000 Genting Highlands, Pahang. Tel. (03)2111118. M$125–1,000. 700 rooms.
Malaysia's only hotel with a casino. Regional gamblers' favourite retreat.

Ipoh

Royal Casuarina Hotel
24 Jalan Gopeng, 30250 Ipoh, Perak. Tel. (05)505555. M$130–330. 217 rooms.
Out-of-town luxury overlooking the racecourse.

Station Hotel
Jalan Kelab, 30000, Ipoh, Perak. Tel. (05)512588. M$50–60. 34 rooms.
Colonial-style, located right at the railway station. Perfect for nostalgia-seekers.

Johor Baru

Holiday Inn
Jalan Dato Sulaiman, Century Garden, 80250 Johor Baru, Johor. Tel. (07)323800. M$110–250. 200 rooms.
Just minutes to Singapore. Excellent coffee shop and popular disco.

Tropical Inn
15 Jalan Gereja, 80100 Johor Baru, Johor. Tel. (07)221888. M$100–350.
Downtown location with good local hire-car agency.

Standard

Merlin Tower Hotel
Jalan Meldrum, 80000 Johor Baru, Johor. Tel. (07)325811. M$55–160. 100 rooms.
Good value and centrally located. Minutes to Singapore.

Budget

Rumah Rehat (Government Rest House)
Jalan Sungai Chat, 80100 Johor Baru, Johor. Tel. (07)222081. M$30 double. 18 rooms.
Set on a rise overlooking the Straits of Johor. Breezy and spacious.

Kapit

Kapit Long House Hotel
Berjaya Road, Kapit, Sarawak. Tel. (082)96415. M$27–60. 21 rooms.
Best accommodation available in town. Good spot to clean up after upriver treks.

Kota Baru

Luxury and First Class

Hotel Perdana
Jalan Mahmud, 15720 Kota Baru, Kelantan. Tel. (09)785000. M$75–320. 136 rooms.
Best hotel in Kota Baru. Good central location and excellent service.

Standard

Resort Pantai Cinta Berahi
Pantai Cinta Berahi, P.O. Box 157, 15710 Kota Baru, Kelantan. Tel. (09)781307. From M$50. 21 rooms.
Excellent swimming beach and close to Kota Baru.

Long House Beach Motel
Pantai Cinta Berahi, Kota Baru, Kelantan. Tel. (09)740090. M$31–42.
Excellent value. Rooms front the beach and the restaurant serves Thai-style food.

Budget

Rebana Hostel
Opposite Old Palace (Istana Kota Lama), Jalan Sultanah Zainab, 15050 Kota Baru, Kelantan. No telephone. M$4–9.
Budget travellers' hangout. Interesting, well-travelled proprietor.

Kota Kinabalu

Luxury and First Class

Tanjung Aru Beach Hotel
Tanjung Aru, 88999 Kota Kinabalu, Sabah, East Malaysia. Tel. (088)58711. M$190–250, suites up to M$1,200. 294 rooms.
Excellent luxury resort close to town. Boat trips and diving excursions available to nearby islands.

Hyatt Hotel
Jalan Datuk Salleh Sulong, 88994 Kota Kinabalu, Sabah, East Malaysia. Tel. (088)219888. M$185–260. 315 rooms.
Centrally located, excellent service and sweeping views of the city and offshore islands.

Hotel Shangri-La
Bandaran Berjaya, 88000 Kota Kinabalu, Sabah, East Malaysia. Tel. (088)56100. M$140–155.
Popular with local businessmen. Good value.

Standard

Asia Hotel

68–69 Jalan Bandaran Berjaya, 88000 Kota Kinabalu, Sabah, East Malaysia. Tel. (088)53533. M$30–50.

Airconditioned with in-house videos. Good budget value.

Kuala Lumpur

Luxury and First Class

Shangri-La Hotel

11 Jalan Sultan Ismail, 50250 Kuala Lumpur. Tel. (03)2486536. M$180–255, suites to M$750. 722 rooms.

Ultimate in luxury and service. Repeat winner of regional gold awards. Excellent Chinese restaurant serving dim sum lunch.

The Regent of Kuala Lumpur

Jalan Sultan Ismail, 50250 Kuala Lumpur. Tel. (03)2425588. M$160–180, suites to M$1,700. 375 rooms.

Located in the capital's hotel centre. Tastefully decorated rooms.

Kuala Lumpur Hilton

Jalan Sultan Ismail, 50250 Kuala Lumpur. Tel. (03)2422222. M$178–225, suites to M$1,600. 589 rooms.

Favourite venue for Malaysian royalty. Superb service and decor.

Pan Pacific Hotel

Jalan Chow Kit Baru, 50746 Kuala Lumpur. Tel. (03)4425555. M$140–180. 571 rooms.

Adjacent to the Putra World Trade Centre and opposite 'The Mall', Kuala Lumpur's biggest shopping complex. Selera Coffee Lounge serves an excellent Malay-style buffet lunch.

Holiday Inn City Centre

Jalan Raja Laut, 50750 Kuala Lumpur. Tel. (03)2939233. M$100–140. 250 rooms.

The most centrally located and best value-for-money hotel in the city.

Holiday Inn on the Park

Jalan Pinang, 50732 Kuala Lumpur. Tel. (03)2481066. M$120–165. 200 rooms.

Each room has a superb view of the racecourse and the tree-lined residential area of Ampang.

Hyatt Saujana Hotel and Country Club

Subang International Airport Highway, 46710 Petaling Jaya. Tel. (03)7461188. M$120–180. 223 rooms.

Just minutes from the airport and set amidst 160 hectares (400 acres) of landscaped gardens containing two 18-hole golf courses.

Merlin Hotel
2 Jalan Sultan Ismail, 50250 Kuala Lumpur. Tel. (03)480033. M$125–170. 673 rooms.
Located near airline offices and embassies.

Standard

South East Asia Hotel
69 Jalan Haji Hussein, off Jalan Tunku Abdul Rahman, 50300 Kuala Lumpur. Tel. (03)2926077. M$65–120. 204 rooms.
Quite comfortable and situated in the heart of the market district. Good area for browsing.

Champagne Hotel
141, off Jalan Masjid India, 50100 Kuala Lumpur. Tel. (03)2986333. M$38–52. 35 rooms.
Best value in downtown area. Interesting Indian shops and Muslim restaurants nearby.

Kuala Terengganu

Luxury and First Class

Pantai Primula Hotel
Jalan Persinggahan, 20904 Kuala Terengganu, Terengganu. Tel. (09)622100. M$115–160. 294 rooms.
Only minutes from downtown, situated beside a long sandy beach. The grill beside the waterfall is excellent value for dinner.

Motel Desa
Bukit Pak Apil, 23000 Kuala Terengganu, Terengganu. Tel. (09)623033. M$90–100. 19 rooms.
Located on a hill overlooking the town. Good views and breezes.

Standard

Pulau Kapas View Beach House
Kampung Pantai Rhu Muda, 21600 Marang, Terengganu. Tel. (09)682403. M$10–70. 29 rooms.
19 kilometres (12 miles) south of Kuala Terengganu, situated in an idyllic fishing village beside a long white beach. Boat trips are organized to offshore islands. Malay-style chalets.

Kuantan

Luxury and First Class

Kuantan Hyatt Hotel
Telok Cempedak, 25050 Kuantan, Pahang. Tel. (09)525211. M$130–180. 185 rooms.
Located beside Kuantan's most popular beach and just minutes from downtown.

Unusual aquamarine-coloured pool. Large open veranda-style snack bar overlooks the beach.

Merlin Inn Resort
Telok Cempedak, 25050 Kuantan, Pahang. Tel. (09)522388. M$90–160. 106 rooms. Each room has a beach view.

Standard

Hotel Kuantan
Telok Cempedak, 25050 Kuantan, Pahang. Tel. (09)524744. M$30–60. 25 rooms. Excellent value airconditioned rooms just opposite the Hyatt. The beach is the same whether you stay at a luxury or standard hotel.

Kuching

Luxury and First Class

Holiday Inn Hotel
Jalan Tuanku Abdul Rahman, 93100 Kuching, Sarawak, East Malaysia. Tel. (082)423111. M$134–165. 320 rooms.
Superb views of the bustling Sarawak River from every room. Try their fruit bowl, a marvellous variety of tropical fruits.

Damai Beach Resort
Damai Beach, PO Box 2870, 93756 Kuching, Sarawak, East Malaysia. Tel. (082)423142, 411777. M$180–700. 202 rooms.
Sarawak's only beach resort. Water sports and excursions to nearby Bako National Park.

Standard

Borneo Hotel
Jalan Tabuan, 93100 Kuching, Sarawak, East Malaysia. Tel. (082)24121/4. M$42–56. 37 rooms.
Good value and centrally located.

Kudat

Greenland Hotel
9–10, Block E, 89050 Kudat, Sabah, East Malaysia. Tel. (088)412502. M$50–80.
Spotless, good value, with airconditioning and colour TV.

Malacca

Luxury and First Class

Ramada Renaissance Hotel
Jalan Bendahara, 75100 Melaka. Tel. (06)248888. M$95–160. 295 rooms. Downtown luxury in the heart of the city. Rooftop swimming pool, disco and excellent coffee shop.

Malacca Village Resort
Air Keroh, 75450 Melaka. Tel (06)323600. M$120–300. 146 rooms.
Situated 16 kilometres (ten miles) from Malacca, this striking resort is built like a Malay village. Swimming pools, tennis courts, horse-riding and an authentic Japanese restaurant.

Tanjung Bidara Beach Resort
Tanjung Bidara, 78300 Melaka. Tel. (06)531201. M$70 upwards. 80 rooms.
35 kilometres (28 miles) north of town at best swimming spot on the Straits. Water sports and beachside pool.

Shah's Beach Motel
Tanjung Kling, 76400 Melaka. Tel. (06)511120. M$80 upwards. 49 rooms.
Favourite seaside resort for expatriates from Singapore and Kuala Lumpur. Ten kilometres (six miles) from town.

Standard

Westernhay Hotel
4th Milestone, Klebang Besar, 75200 Melaka. Tel. (06)223196. M$16–24. Ten rooms.
An old Chinese mansion by the sea. Basic and clean, said to be haunted.

Majestic Hotel
188 Jalan Bungah Raya, 75100 Melaka. Tel. (06)222367. M$16–32. 20 rooms.
Downtown colonial hotel, somewhat rundown but good for nostalgia buffs. Has ceiling fans and wooden swing doors on the rooms. Restaurant and bar.

Budget

Chong Hoe Hotel
26 Tukang Emas, 75200 Melaka. Tel. (06)226102. M$9–20. Ten rooms.
Cleanest and best value in town. Situated right in the heart of old Chinatown. Very popular, sometimes hard to get rooms.

Mersing

Mersing Merlin Inn
1st Milestone, Endau Road, 86800 Mersing, Johor. Tel. (072)791312. M$70–90. 34 rooms.
Situated in a quiet, out-of-town location. Perfect as a base for offshore island tripping.

Resthouse Mersing
490 Jalan Ismail, 86800 Mersing, Johor. Tel. (07)791101. M$29–33. 18 rooms.
Excellent value. Located on the seafront with a vista of offshore islands. Restaurant and bar. Popular with expatriate families from Singapore.

Miri

Ria Fatimah Hotel
49 Brooke Road, 98009 Miri, Sarawak. Tel. (085)30255. M$64–125. 54 rooms.
Good base for upriver trips to Mulu National Park. Excellent Malay-style buffet lunch. Best local travel operator on premises.

Penang (Pulau Pinang)

Luxury and First Class

Eastern and Oriental Hotel
10 Lebuh Farquhar, 10200 Pulau Pinang. Tel. (04)375322. M$125–165. 100 rooms.
The 'Raffles' of Penang, luxurious colonial atmosphere. The city's best-known hotel.

Casuarina Beach Hotel
Batu Ferringhi, 11100 Pulau Pinang. Tel. (04)811711. M$140–190. 175 rooms.
Situated beachside on Penang's favourite beach. Landscaped grounds with shady casuarina trees and coconut palms.

Rasa Sayang Hotel
Batu Ferringhi, 11100 Pulau Pinang. Tel. (04)811811. M$130–200, suites to $2,200.
One of the many luxury beachside hotels. Water sports, tennis and bicycle hire.

Golden Sands Hotel
Batu Ferringhi, 11100 Pulau Pinang. Tel. (04)811911. M$140–200.
Another beachside luxury hotel; you can take your pick along this coast. All have excellent service and a host of activities.

Shangri-La Inn
Jalan Magazine, 10300 Pulau Pinang. Tel. (04)622622. M$115–155. 442 rooms.
Located in the Komtar complex beside Penang's only skyscraper. Central location close to commercial and business district.

The Merlin Penang
3 Jalan Larut, 10050 Pulau Pinang. Tel. (04)376166. M$95–135. 279 rooms. Situated in the heart of the historic area of town. Close to good bazaar shopping.

Palm Beach Hotel
11100 Pulau Pinang, Batu Ferringhi. Tel. (04)811621. M$90–140. 145 rooms.
Slightly cheaper than other beachside resort hotels. All hotels regardless of price share the same beach.

Standard

Bellevue Park Hill Hotel
Pulau Pinang 11300, Penang Hill. Tel. (04)892256. M$60–80. 12 rooms.
A cool hilltop colonial retreat. Enjoy lunch in the garden overlooking Penang. Great views and good walking trails.

Lone Pine Hotel
97 Batu Ferringhi, 11100 Pulau Pinang. Tel. (04)811511. M$35–75. 54 rooms.
Best value in Batu Ferringhi, just down the beach from the luxury hotels. Open-air beachfront restaurant shaded by huge casuarina trees.

Budget

Chung King Hotel
398A Lebuh Chulia, 10200 Pulau Pinang. Tel. (04)377607. M$10–12. 13 rooms.
One of literally dozens of cheap hotels which abound in the old downtown area. These hotels haven't changed since the 'Hippie Trail' days of the '60s.

Pulau Besar

Hillside Chalets
Pulau Besar, 86800 Mersing, Johor. Tel. (07)221855 (Johor Baru Office). M$40 per chalet.
Malay-style thatched-roof bungalows on a tropical island, one hour from Mersing.

Pulau Besar Village Resort
c/o Tourist Centre, 86800 Mersing, Johor. Tel. (07)791204. M$23–34.50.
Thatched-roof chalets overlooking beach. Bar and restaurant.

Pulau Langkawi

Luxury and First Class

Langkawi Island Resort
Pantai Dato Syed Omar, 07000 Pulau Langkawi, Kedah. Tel. (04)788209. M$95–150. 220 rooms.
The island's most luxurious resort, with stunning views of a bay studded with islands. The beach here is not good for swimming. Trips can be made to outer islands from the jetty.

Standard

Semarak Langkawi Beach Resort
Pantai Cenang, 07000 Pulau Langkawi, Kedah. Tel. (04)7173650. M$55 upwards. 32 rooms.
Malay-style resort on the island's best beach.

Sandy Beach Motel
Pantai Cenang, 07000 Pulau Langkawi, Kedah. M$15–25. 20 rooms.
Popular spot for local holidaymakers. Very good value on a beautiful white-sand beach.

Asia Hotel
1a Jalan Persiaran Putra, Kuah, 07000 Pulau Langkawi, Kedah. Tel. (04)788216. M$30–48. 16 rooms.
Chinese-style hotel in central location in the duty-free town of Kuah. Close to excellent eating stalls.

Pulau Pangkor

Pan Pacific Resort Pangkor
Teluk Belanga, 32300 Pulau Pangkor, Perak. Tel. (05)939091. M$170–280. 161 rooms.
Luxury resort on an excellent white-sand beach. Reached easily from Ipoh.

PanSea Pangkor Laut
c/o Lumut Post Office, 32300 Pulau Pangkor, Perak. Tel. (05)951320. M$98–153. 94 rooms.
Malay-style architecture blends in with the picturesque surroundings. An idyllic beach.

Pulau Rawa

Rawa Safaris
c/o Tourist Centre, 86800 Mersing, Johor. Tel. (07)791204. M$30–36. 33 rooms.
Most established private island resort offshore from Mersing. Malay-style chalets and an open-sided restaurant and bar. Beautiful white sand beach. Popular with Singaporeans on weekends.

Pulau Tioman

Luxury and First Class

Tioman Island Resort
86800 Pulau Tioman, Pahang. Tel. (07)275444. M$85–175. 68 rooms.
Well-designed beachside resort backed with virgin jungle. Water sports facilities available. Tennis, swimming, restaurant and bar. The only luxury hotel on the island.

Budget

Nazri's
86800 Pulau Tioman, Pahang. M$10 for a hut for two; bungalows with own bathroom (sleep four) are M$35.
The forerunner and still the best of the many Malay-style chalets that abound on the island. Thatched A-line huts on clean white sand. Basic facilities and a family restaurant.

Ranau

Hotel Perkasa Mount Kinabalu
W.B.T. 11, 89307 Ranau, Sabah, East Malaysia. Tel. (088)89307. M$75–200. 74 rooms.
Only luxury hotel with a view of Mount Kinabalu. Refreshingly cool atmosphere. Hotel bus links with Kinabalu National Park.

Rantau Abang

Rantau Abang Visitor's Centre
13th Milestone off Dungun, 23009 Dungun, Terengganu. Tel. (09)841533. M$80–90. Ten rooms.

Traditional timber chalets on a sandbar between a lagoon and the sea. The venue for watching the leatherback turtles lay their eggs.

Sandakan

Hotel Ramah

Two kilometres (1.2 miles), Jalan Leila, 90000 Sandakan, Sabah, East Malaysia. Tel. (088)45811. M$110–170.

The town's most luxurious hotel.

Sibu

Premier Hotel

Sarawak House Complex, 96008 Sibu, Sarawak, East Malaysia. Tel. 23222. M$80–150. 120 rooms.

Best hotel for hundreds of kilometres in either direction. Luxury before heading upriver.

Taiping

Rumah Rehat Baru (Government Rest House)

Taman Tasik, 34000 Taiping, Perak. Tel. (04)822044. M$12–32. Suites $48–74. 26 rooms.

Huge breezy rooms with ceiling fans and balconies overlooking the Lake Gardens. Exceptional value.

Tanjung Jara

Tanjung Jara Beach Hotel

8th Milestone off Dungun, 23009 Dungun, Terengganu. Tel. (09)841801. M$67–160. 100 rooms.

Malaysia's best-known beach hotel. The stunning Malay-type architecture, based on 18th-century palace design, blends perfectly with the surroundings.

Tasek Cini

Tasek Cini Resort

Tasek Cini, via Belimbing, 26030 Kuantan, Pahang. Tel. (01)332841. M$20–50. 15 rooms.

Malay-style timber chalets beside the lake in a virgin jungle setting.

Teluk Intan

Rumah Rehat (Government Rest House)

368 Jalan Daly, 36000 Teluk Intan, Perak. Tel. (05)611724. M$16–32.

Basic facilities with overhead fans. Attached restaurant.

Restaurants and Eating-out Spots

Eating-out tops the list of Malaysia's leisure pursuits and, not surprisingly, even the most humble *kampung* boasts at least one food stall. The range is great, from plush luxury hotel restaurants to smaller, more intimate, streetside eating houses and the all-time favourite of Malaysians and visitors alike, the outdoor eating markets. Every town hosts at least one of these markets and diners can order specialities from the various stalls. This is a great place to try a number of different dishes cheaply, for at the airconditioned venues they invariably add sales tax, and at five-star establishments you can expect to pay the same inflated prices as you would back home. In the cities and larger towns, parking areas become open-air eating markets at night and the action goes on until the wee hours.

Below is a small selection of eating-out venues around Malaysia, but there are hundreds of other spots just as good that can easily be sniffed out by the resourceful and adventurous traveller.

Kuala Lumpur

Malay

Kampung Restoran
Jalan Tun Perak. Tel. (03)2437113.
Specializes in home-style traditional Malay food.

Sate Ria
9 Jalan Tuanku Abdul Rahman. Tel. (03)2911648.
A popular chain of restaurants, now worldwide, featuring *satay*, Malaysia's national dish.

Sri Yasmin Restaurant
6 Jalan Kia Peng. Tel. (03)2415655.
A sister establishment housed in a colonial-style bungalow. Buffet lunch on the terrace, dinner on the first floor. Try the Perak and Terengganu cuisine.

Yasmin's
2nd floor, UDA — Ampang Park Shopping Centre, Jalan Ampang. Tel. (03)2487377.
Famed establishment run by a Malaysian princess. Excellent cuisine and traditional dances each evening.

Malay food stalls can be found on Jalan Brickfields, Jalan Bukit Bintang, Jalan Imbi, off Jalan Raja, Jalan Kampung Baru and on the top floor of Central Market.

Chinese

Eden Seafood Village Restaurant
29B Jalan SS 22/23, Damansara Jaya. Tel. (03)7193184.
Select your own live fish, prawns, lobsters, crabs and oysters from aquarium tanks.

Hai-Tien-Lo
Pan Pacific Kuala Lumpur, Jalan Putra, Tel. (03) 2935555.
Offers an impressive menu of 170 dishes from all over China.

Ming Palace
Ming Court Hotel, Jalan Ampang. Tel. (03)2618888.
Specializes in Szechuan cuisine. Try the Savoury Brinjal with traditional Ngan See Kuen (Silver Thread Buns).

Shang Palace
Shangri-La Hotel, Jalan Sultan Ismail. Tel. (03)2322388.
The place to go for *dim sum* lunch in a setting reminiscent of a rich nobleman's mansion.

The Pines
297 Jalan Brickfields. Tel. (03)2741194.
Specializes in Cantonese food in a pleasant garden setting.

Indian

Bilal Restaurant
33 Jalan Ampang. Tel. (03)2320804.
Specializes in fiery coconut-based South Indian cuisine.

Shiraz
Medan Tuanku Abdul Rahman. Tel. (03)2910035.
Famous for its Moghal-inspired rich North Indian cuisine.

For excellent Indian Muslim fare, the area around Jalan Masjid India abounds with small restaurants, and the parking lot at the end of the road converts at night into an outdoor eating market.

Western

Le Coq D'Or
121 Jalan Ampang. Tel. (03)2429732.
Dine in original splendour in the Victorian mansion of a Chinese tin baron who stated in his will that his palatial home could become a restaurant only if nothing inside was changed.

Suassa Brasserie
The Regent of Kuala Lumpur, Jalan Sultan Ismail. Tel. (03)2425588.
The capital's award-winning and most exclusive grillhouse.

The Coliseum
98 Jalan Tuanku Abdul Rahman. Tel. (03) 2926270.
Definitely for nostalgia seekers — Somerset Maugham spent a lot of time here. Basic English fare in an old-world, somewhat seedy, atmosphere.

Japanese

Genji Restaurant

Petaling Jaya Hilton, Jalan Barat, Petaling Jaya. Tel. (03)7559122.

Hearty eaters should try their 'Viking' buffet lunch with *sushi*, *tempura*, *soba*, *shumai*, *sashimi*, and *miso* soup.

Keyaki

Pan Pacific Kuala Lumpur, Jalan Putra. Tel. (03)2935555.

Has three separate counters for *teppanyaki*, *shabu shabu* and *tempura*, with traditional Japanese decor and music.

Thai

Sri Chiengmai

14 Jalan Perak. Tel. (03)2482927.

Specializes in northern Thai cuisine.

Taiwanese

Goldleaf Lontong

44 Jalan Bukit Bintang. Tel. (03)2480803.

Korean

Koryo-Won Korean Restaurant

G-15, Kamplex Antarabangsa, Jalan Sultan Ismail. Tel. 2427655.

Specialities include ginseng chicken soup and Kalbee ribs of beef.

Malacca

Nonya

Ole Sayang Restaurant

192 Taman Melaka Jaya. Tel. (06)231966.

Serves traditional *nonya* food, specializing in home-made *cendol* and fish cooked in tamarind.

Restoran Peranakan

317 Klebang Besar. Tel. (06)236317.

Specializes in authentic *nonya* cuisine. Located in an authentic Baba mansion overlooking the Straits of Malacca.

Portuguese

Restoran De Lisbon

Medan Portugis, Kampung Portugis.

Savour devil curry, baked fish and *sambal* crabs in the delightful seaside Portuguese Square. Best spot for beers, Portuguese music and cultural shows; open until the wee hours.

Chinese

Famed Chinese food stalls in Malacca include the 'chicken rice' shop beside the Chung Kiaw Bank on Jalan Hang Jebat (lunch only), the 'pork *satay*' at the corner coffee shop on Jalan Hang Jebat and Jalan Lekiu (afternoons only), and the Chinese roast pork stall in the covered walkway next to the Kong Wah Hotel in Jalan Bunga Raya.

Malay

Malay food is best enjoyed at the Klebang food stalls right on the beach at Pantai Klebang, eight kilometres (five miles) north of town. Specialities include *ayam percik* (chicken barbecued on a bamboo spike) and baked fish.

Penang: Covered in the 'Eating Out in Penang' section (see pages 103–4).

Ipoh

Cathay Restaurant
90 Jalan Chamberlain. Tel. (05)513322.
One of Ipoh's favourite Chinese restaurants.

Pulau Langkawi

Coffee Terrace
Langkawi Island Resort, 0700 Pulau Langkawi. Tel. (04)788209.
Expensive food, but the view is absolutely stunning — a sweeping vista of a bay filled with islands.

Excellent seafood can be found at the Malay outdoor eating stalls in Kuah town along the seafront.

Kota Baru
Upstairs at the Central Market is recommended for *nasi campur* (rice with curries) at lunch, and the carpark opposite at night, when it becomes a giant eating market. Try the skewered squid and the famous Kelantanese-style *ayam percik* (barbecued chicken smothered in satay sauce).

Kuala Terengganu

Cascade Grill
Pantai Primula Hotel, Jalan Persinggahan. Tel. (09)622100.
Good steaks, in a nice setting beside a waterfall.

At Pantai Buruk, on the coast just south of town, are Malay food stalls specializing in Terengganu-style cuisine. Great fresh fruit juices.

Kuantan

Hugo's Hyatt Kuantan
Teluk Cempedak. Tel. (09)525211.
Kuantan's most sophisticated restaurant for Malay and Western cuisine.

Katong Seafood Restaurant
35 Teluk Cempadak. Tel. (09)529947.
Specializes in claypot curry fishhead and chilli crab. Cheaper and better than the Hyatt.

Cameron Highlands

Ye Old Smokehouse
By-the-Golf-Course, Tanah Rata. Tel. (05)941214.
Marvellous colonial atmosphere; strawberries and cream and Devonshire teas in the garden, and roast beef in the evening beside a cosy fireplace.

Sarawak

Mandarin Room Restaurant
22 Green Hill, Kuching. Tel. (082)25731.
Classic Chinese cuisine and excellent seafood.

Ria Fatimah Hotel
49 Brooke Road, Miri. Tel. (085)30255.
Their coffee shop serves an excellent and moderately-priced Malay lunch buffet.

Serapi Restaurant
Holiday Inn, Jalan Tunku Abdul Rahman, Kuching. Tel. (082)423111.
Western and Malay cuisine in five-star style beside the Sarawak River.

Sabah

Garden Seafood and Steamboat
EG11 Komplex Kuwasa, Karamunsing, Kota Kinabalu. Tel. (088)210662.
Apart from their advertised specialities, they also serve Korean and Japanese food.

Restoran Sri Mela
9 Jalan Laiman Diki, Kampung Air, Kota Kinabalu. Tel. (088)55136.
Specializes in traditional *nonya* and Malay food.

Tivoli House
Shangri-La Hotel, 75 Bandaran Berjaya, Kota Kinabalu. Tel. (088)53533.
Famous for its steaks, seafood and lively nightlife.

Major Malaysian Festivals and Holidays

A multicultural, multi-religious nation, Malaysia has literally dozens of festivals and celebrations scattered liberally through the calendar. Many religious festivals follow the lunar calendar and the dates change from year to year, while others are celebrated on fixed dates. The following are the most important annual events.

January

New Year's Day	1 January is a national public holiday.

February

Thaipusam	Hindu festival in honour of Lord Subramaniam. At Batu Caves, Kuala Lumpur, thousands of penitents, in a trance-like state and carrying *kavadis* attached to their bodies with hooks, climb up to a clifftop shrine.
Chinese New Year	On the first day of the Chinese calendar, families hold reunion dinners; homes and businesses hold open house and are bedecked with red banners; and firecrackers are exploded. The following days are spent visiting families and giving out *angpau* (red packets containing money).
Maha Shiva Rathiri	A national Hindu festival in honour of Lord Shiva, observed with vegetarian feasts and special prayers.
Chap Goh Meh	The 15th day of Chinese New Year is the traditional end of the festivities.

March

Israk and Mikraj	A Muslim festival held in homes and mosques, to celebrate the ascension of Prophet Muhammad.
Cheng Beng	Chinese 'All Soul's Day', when graves are visited and offerings made to ancestors.

April

Kelantan Kite Festival	Colourful, elaborate Kelantanese kites, known as *wau*, often up to two metres (six feet) wide, compete in this annual festival.
Vesakhi	The Sikh New Year is celebrated with the reading of the holy book, the *Granth Sahib*, baptism and blood donation.
Chithirai Vishu	The Hindu New Year is celebrated with prayers and religious ceremonies.

Good Friday	Christians celebrate the resurrection of Christ. In Malacca there is a candlelit procession at St Peter's where a life-sized statue of Christ is borne above the crowd.
Ramadan — Bulan Puasa	The fasting month for Muslims, during which time no food or drink can be consumed between sunrise and sunset. Special prayers called *Tarawih* are performed nightly at mosques.
May	
Tadau Keamatan	The rice-harvest festival of the Kadazan of Sabah is a time for feasting, drinking rice-wine, holding buffalo races and other celebrations.
Vesak Day	A national public holiday commemorating Lord Buddha's birth, the day of his enlightenment and the day he achieved Nirvana.
Hari Raya Puasa	A national holiday celebrating the end of the fasting (Aidil Fitri) month. Special traditional food is prepared, prayers are said at the mosque and, dressed in new clothes, Muslims visit relatives and friends and throw 'open house' for the following month.
June	
Gawai Harvest Festival	Sarawak's indigenous people, particularly the Dyak and Iban, celebrate their rice harvest with much merrymaking, drinking of rice-wine, and other traditional ceremonies and festivities.
Birthday of his Majestey the Yang di Pertuan Agung	Celebrated on 3 June, this national holiday is held to honour the supreme head of state.
Kelantan Giant Drum Festival	At the end of the rice harvest, villagers challenge each other at beating the *rebana*, a drum made of a hollow log.
Feast of San Pedro	Held on 29 June annually to honour St Peter, the patronn saint of fishermen. Malacca's Portuguese-Eurasians celebrate with much merrymaking and their decorated boats are blessed by the priest.
August	
Hari Raya Haji	This national holiday is celebrated by Muslims to honour those pilgrims who have completed the Haji to Mecca. Special prayers are offered, relatives are visited, and those who can afford it sacrifice a goat or cow to give to the poor.

Festival of the Hungry Ghost	During this colourful month-long festival, Chinese operas are held and special offerings made to appease the spirits of the dead.
Maal Hijrah	The Muslim New Year is the first day of the Islamic calendar and a public holiday.
National Day — Hari Merdeka	A public holiday with special processions and celebration to honour the gaining of Independence in 1957.
September	
Awal Muharram	Devout Muslims honour the death of Hussain, the Prophet's favourite grandson, by fasting and performing special prayers.
Mooncake Festival	Celebrates the overthrow of the Mongol warlords in ancient China. Mooncakes are exchanged and eaten, children carry colourful lanterns, and special prayers are said to the Goddess of the Moon.
Feast of Santa Cruz	On 13 September, an annual pilgrimage to the Santa Cruz Chapel in Malacca is made to honour a miracle cross which was reputedly found in the jungle.
Giant Top-Spinning Festival	This annual contest in Kelantan brings together the nation's best top spinners. The *gasing*, or top, weighs 5.5 kilograms (12 pounds) and can often spin for an hour.
October	
Deepavali	A national holiday when the Hindu Festival of Lights is celebrated with prayers in the temples and family feasts.
November	
Prophet Muhammad's Birthday	A national holiday to celebrate the Prophet's birthday in AD 571. Muslims throughout Malaysia gather for processions, religious lectures and to recite holy verses from the *Koran*.
December	
Penang Festival	A month-long carnival when Penang hosts an international film festival, and the Chingay procession which features acrobatics and fantastic costumed figures.
Feast of St Francis Xavier	Catholics in Malacca honour the saint by a special service in the Portuguese church ruins on St Paul's Xavier Hill.
Christmas Day	A public holiday throughout Malaysia and celebrated by the nation's Christians.

Times around the World

When it is 12 noon in Kuala Lumpur (standard time for both peninsular and East Malaysia), the standard time in the following cities is:

Beijing	12 pm
Chicago	10 pm*
Hong Kong	12 pm
Honolulu	6 pm*
London	4 am
Los Angeles	8 pm*
Moscow	7 am
New York	11 pm*
Paris	5 am
San Francisco	8 pm*
Sydney	2 pm
Taipei	12 pm
Tokyo	1 pm

* On the preceding day.

Train Schedules and Fares

Malaysia-Haadyai/Bangkok Travellers

The International Express departs Bangkok at 3.15 pm and arrives at Butterworth at 12.10 pm on the following day. Southbound passengers may continue their journey to Kuala Lumpur by the Express Sinaran (XSP), departing Butterworth at 2.15 pm and arriving at Kuala Lumpur at 8.20 pm. To extend the journey to Singapore, board the night mail (Mel Senandung Malam), departing Kuala Lumpur at 10 pm and arriving at Singapore at 6.40 am.

Passengers originating from Singapore and bound for Bangkok may join the night mail (Mel Senandung Malam), departing at 10 pm to Kuala Lumpur, and therefrom connect with the Express Sinaran (XSP) leaving Kuala Lumpur at 7.30 am to Bukit Mertajam, then on the International Express to Bangkok, arriving at 8.35 am on the following day. The International Express departs daily from Butterworth to Bangkok and vice versa. International Travel documents are required for entry into Thailand. Passengers are also subject to the normal customs procedures at the border.

(*Note*: Malaysia's anti-drug laws are severe and carry the death penalty.)

Single Journey Fare Between Principal Stations

From Kuala Lumpur

	Class 1	Class 2	Class 3
Padang Besar	$65.60	$29.60	$18.20
Alor Setar	$57.10	$25.80	$15.80
Butterworth	$47.40	$21.40	$13.20
Bukit Mertajam	$46.20	$20.80	$12.80
Taiping	$36.50	$16.50	$10.10
Ipoh	$25.50	$11.50	$ 7.10
Tapah Road	$18.90	$ 8.50	$ 5.30
Kuala Lumpur	-	-	-
Seremban	$ 9.00	$ 4.10	$ 2.50
Tampin	$15.20	$ 6.90	$ 4.20
Gemas	$21.90	$ 9.90	$ 6.10
Segamat	$25.50	$11.50	$ 7.10
Kluang	$35.30	$15.90	$ 9.80
Johor Baru	$45.00	$20.30	$12.50
Singapore	$48.60	$21.90	$13.50
Kuala Lipis	$49.80	$22.50	$13.80
Krai	$75.30	$34.00	$20.90
Wakaf Bharu	$83.80	$37.80	$23.30
Tumpat	$87.20	$38.90	$23.90
Haadyai	$69.10	$31.50	-
Bangkok	$128.20	$59.00	-

From Butterworth

	Class 1	Class 2	Class 3
Padang Besar	$20.70	$ 9.30	$ 5.80
Alor Setar	-	-	$ 3.50
Butterworth	-	-	-
Bukit Mertajam	$ 1.50	$ 0.70	$ 0.50
Taiping	$11.70	$ 5.30	$ 3.30
Ipoh	$22.50	$10.20	$ 6.30
Tapah Road	$29.20	$13.20	$ 8.10
Kuala Lumpur	$47.40	$21.40	$13.20
Seremban	$57.10	$25.80	$15.80
Tampin	$62.00	$27.90	$17.20
Gemas	$69.20	$31.20	$19.20
Segamat	$71.70	$32.30	$19.90
Kluang	$82.60	$37.20	$22.90
Johor Baru	$92.30	$41.60	$25.60

Singapore	$96.00	$43.30	$26.60
Kuala Lipis	$96.00	$43.30	$26.60
Krai	$122.70	$55.30	$34.00
Wakaf Baru	$131.20	$59.10	$36.30
Tumpat	$132.40	$59.70	$36.70
Haadyai	$24.20	$11.20	-
Bangkok	$83.30	$38.70	-

From Singapore

	Class 1	Class 2	Class 3
Padang Besar	$113.00	$50.90	$31.30
Alor Setar	$105.70	$47.60	$29.30
Butterworth	$96.00	$43.30	$26.60
Bukit Mertajam	$94.70	$42.70	$26.30
Taiping	$83.80	$37.80	$23.20
Ipoh	$74.10	$33.40	$20.50
Tapah Road	$68.00	$30.70	$18.90
Kuala Lumpur	$48.60	$21.90	$13.50
Seremban	$40.10	$18.10	$11.10
Tampin	$34.00	$15.40	$ 9.50
Gemas	$28.00	$12.60	$ 7.80
Segamat	$24.30	$11.00	$ 6.80
Kluang	$14.00	$ 6.30	$ 3.90
Johor Baru	$ 3.40	$ 1.60	$ 1.00
Singapore	-	-	-
Kuala Lipis	$54.70	$24.70	$15.20
Krai	$81.40	$37.70	$22.60
Wakaf Baru	$89.90	$40.50	$24.90
Tumpat	$91.10	$41.10	$25.20
Haadyai	$116.50	$52.80	-
Bangkok	$175.60	$80.30	-

Sinaran Express: Fares

From Kuala Lumpur

	Class 1 AFC	Class 2 ASC	Class 2 SC	Class 3 TC
Butterworth	$54.00	$28.00	$25.00	$17.00
Bukit Mertajam	$53.00	$27.00	$24.00	$16.00
Taiping	$43.00	$23.00	$20.00	$14.00

Kuala Kangsar	$39.00	$21.00	$18.00	$13.00
Ipoh	$32.00	$18.00	$15.00	$11.00
Kampar	$27.00	$16.00	$13.00	$ 9.00
Tapah Road	$25.00	$15.00	$12.00	$ 9.00
Kuala Lumpur	-	-	-	-
Seremban	$15.00	$11.00	$ 8.00	$ 6.00
Tampin	$22.00	$13.00	$10.00	$ 8.00
Segamat	$32.00	$18.00	$15.00	$11.00
Kluang	$42.00	$22.00	$19.00	$13.00
Johor Baru	$51.00	$27.00	$24.00	$16.00
Singapore	$55.00	$28.00	$25.00	$17.00

From Butterworth

	Class 1 AFC	Class 2 ASC	Class 2 SC	Class 3 TC
Butterworth	-	-	-	-
Bukit Mertajam	$ 8.00	$ 7.00	$ 4.00	$ 4.00
Taiping	$18.00	$12.00	$ 9.00	$ 7.00
Kuala Kangsar	$22.00	$14.00	$11.00	$ 8.00
Ipoh	$29.00	$17.00	$14.00	$10.00
Kampar	$33.00	$19.00	$16.00	$11.00
Tapah Road	$36.00	$20.00	$17.00	$12.00
Kuala Lumpur	$54.00	$28.00	$25.00	$17.00
Seremban	-	$32.00	$29.00	$19.00
Tampin	-	$34.00	$31.00	$21.00
Segamat	-	$39.00	$36.00	$23.00
Kluang	-	$44.00	$41.00	$26.00
Johor Baru	-	$48.00	$45.00	$29.00
Singapore	-	$50.00	$47.00	$30.00

From Singapore

	Class 1 AFC	Class 2 ASC	Class 2 SC	Class 3 TC
Butterworth	-	$50.00	$47.00	$30.00
Bukit Mertajam	-	$49.00	$46.00	$30.00
Taiping	-	$44.00	$41.00	$27.00
Kuala Kangsar	-	$43.00	$40.00	$26.00
Ipoh	-	$40.00	$37.00	$24.00
Kampar	-	$38.00	$35.00	$23.00
Tapah Road	-	$37.00	$34.00	$22.00

Kuala Lumpur	$55.00	$28.00	$25.00	$17.00
Seremban	$47.00	$25.00	$22.00	$15.00
Tampin	$40.00	$22.00	$19.00	$13.00
Segamat	$31.00	$17.00	$14.00	$10.00
Kluang	$20.00	$13.00	$10.00	$ 7.00
Johor Baru	$10.00	$ 8.00	$ 5.00	$ 4.00
Singapore	-	-	-	-

Supplementary Charges

Singapore/Kuala Lumpur/Butterworth
Kuala Lumpur/Tumpat
Singapore/Tumpat

Berth Charges (KTM/MR)

1st class — $20.00 (airconditioned)
1st class — $10.00 (ordinary)

2nd class — $8.00 (lower)
2nd class — $6.00 (upper)

International Express Berth Charges

1st class — $19.00 (airconditioned)
1st class — $11.80 (ordinary)

2nd class — $9.10 (lower)
2nd class — $6.40 (upper)

Express Train Charges

Butterworth/Bangkok: $2.80

Notes

Children between the ages of four and 12 years are charged half the adult fare, while children under four years travel free of charge.

AFC: Fare first class airconditioned
ASC: Fare second class airconditioned
SC: Fare second class ordinary
TC: Fare third class ordinary by Ekspres Rrakyat only.

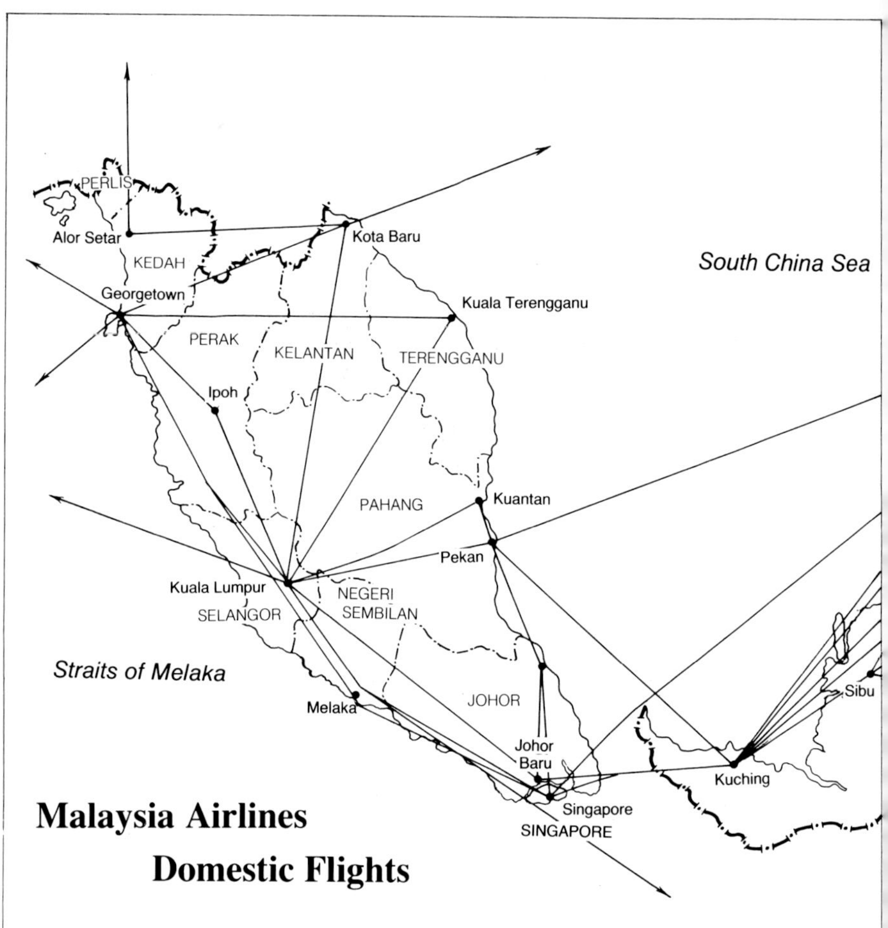

Malaysia Airlines Domestic Flights

Destination	Distance		
	Naut Mls	Km	Miles
Alor Setar-Kota Baru	116	215	134
Bintulu-Mukah	60	112	70
Johor Baru-Kota Kinabalu	811	150	93
Johor Baru-Kuching	409	757	470
Kapit-Belaga	64	118	73
Kerteh-Kuala Terengganu	54	100	62
Kota Kinabalu-Bandar Seri Begawan	91	168	104
Kota Kinabalu-Bintulu	247	457	284
Kota Kinabalu-Keningau	36	66	41
Kota Kinabalu-Kudat	76	141	88
Kota Kinabalu-Lahad Datu	147	272	170
Kota Kinabalu-Labuan	62	115	71
Kota Kinabalu-Lawas	76	104	65
Kota Kinabalu-Miri	159	294	183
Kota Kinabalu-Ranau	38	72	45
Kota Kinabalu-Sandakan	122	226	140
Kota Kinabalu-Singapore	794	1470	913
Kota Kinabalu-Tawau	151	280	174
Kuala Lumpur-Alor Setar	199	368	229
Kuala Lumpur-Kerteh	152	282	175
Kuala Lumpur-Ipoh	96	178	111
Kuala Lumpur-Johor Baru	191	354	220
Kuala Lumpur-Kota Baru	190	352	219
Kuala Lumpur-Kota Kinabalu	906	1678	1043
Kuala Lumpur-Kuala Terengganu	172	318	198
Kuala Lumpur-Kuantan	121	224	139
Kuala Lumpur-Kuching	562	1041	647
Kuala Lumpur-Penang	153	283	176
Kuala Lumpur-Pulau Tioman	186	344	214
Kuala Lumpur-Singapore	240	444	276
Kuantan-Johor Baru	141	261	162

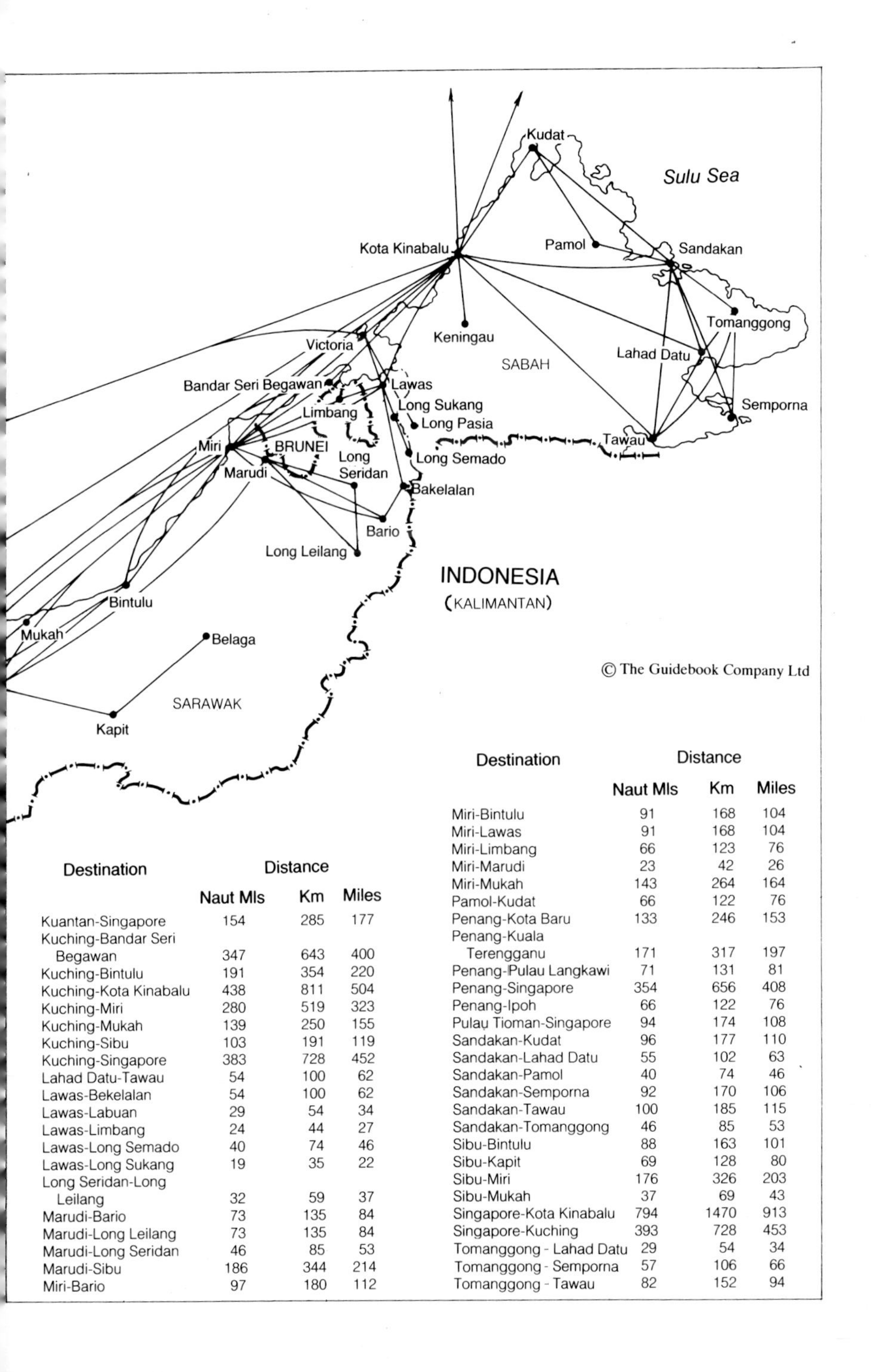

Destination	Distance		
	Naut Mls	Km	Miles
Kuantan-Singapore	154	285	177
Kuching-Bandar Seri Begawan	347	643	400
Kuching-Bintulu	191	354	220
Kuching-Kota Kinabalu	438	811	504
Kuching-Miri	280	519	323
Kuching-Mukah	139	250	155
Kuching-Sibu	103	191	119
Kuching-Singapore	383	728	452
Lahad Datu-Tawau	54	100	62
Lawas-Bekelalan	54	100	62
Lawas-Labuan	29	54	34
Lawas-Limbang	24	44	27
Lawas-Long Semado	40	74	46
Lawas-Long Sukang	19	35	22
Long Seridan-Long Leilang	32	59	37
Marudi-Bario	73	135	84
Marudi-Long Leilang	73	135	84
Marudi-Long Seridan	46	85	53
Marudi-Sibu	186	344	214
Miri-Bario	97	180	112

Destination	Distance		
	Naut Mls	Km	Miles
Miri-Bintulu	91	168	104
Miri-Lawas	91	168	104
Miri-Limbang	66	123	76
Miri-Marudi	23	42	26
Miri-Mukah	143	264	164
Pamol-Kudat	66	122	76
Penang-Kota Baru	133	246	153
Penang-Kuala Terengganu	171	317	197
Penang-Pulau Langkawi	71	131	81
Penang-Singapore	354	656	408
Penang-Ipoh	66	122	76
Pulau Tioman-Singapore	94	174	108
Sandakan-Kudat	96	177	110
Sandakan-Lahad Datu	55	102	63
Sandakan-Pamol	40	74	46
Sandakan-Semporna	92	170	106
Sandakan-Tawau	100	185	115
Sandakan-Tomanggong	46	85	53
Sibu-Bintulu	88	163	101
Sibu-Kapit	69	128	80
Sibu-Miri	176	326	203
Sibu-Mukah	37	69	43
Singapore-Kota Kinabalu	794	1470	913
Singapore-Kuching	393	728	453
Tomanggong - Lahad Datu	29	54	34
Tomanggong - Semporna	57	106	66
Tomanggong - Tawau	82	152	94

Recommended Reading

History

Brown, C.C. (Translator) *Sejarah Melayu* (or *Malay Annals*) (Kuala Lumpur: Oxford University Press, revised edition 1970. First published in 1953 in the Journal of the Malayan Branch of the Royal Asiatic Society). The classic 15th- and 16th-century court history of the Malaccan Sultanate.

Crisswell, Colin N. *Rajah Charles Brooke: Monarch of All He Surveyed* (Kuala Lumpur: Oxford University Press, reprint 1984. First published in 1978). An in-depth study of the second 'White Raja' of Borneo.

Pringle, Robert. *Rajahs and Rebels: The Ibans of Sarawak under Brooke Rule, 1841–1941* (Ithaca, New York: Cornell University Press, 1970). Best book on 19th-century Sarawak, focusing on Iban society.

Watson Andaya, Barbara and Andaya, Leonard Y. *A History of Malaysia* (London: Macmillan Education Ltd., 1982). The best and most up-to-date look at Malaysian history from the local, rather than the colonial, viewpoint.

Windstedt, R.O. *A History of Malaya* (Kuala Lumpur: Marican and Sons (Malaysia) Sdn. Bhd., 1982. First published in 1935). A slightly out-of-date conqueror's view of Malaysia, but with interesting historical details.

Historical Reminiscences

A.L. Hill (Translator). *The Hikayat Abdullah: The Autobiography of Abdullah bin Kadir (1797-1854)* (Kuala Lumpur: Oxford University Press, 1969). A Malay narrative of life in Malacca at the beginning of the 19th century.

Balfour, Patrick. *Grand Tour — Diary of an Eastward Journey* (New York: Harcourt Brace & Co., 1935). A dated but most amusing account of an early traveller's sojourn in the East. Two chapters are on Malaysia.

Bird, Isabella L. *The Golden Chersonese — Travels in Malaya in 1879* (Kuala Lumpur: Oxford University Press, 1967, reprint 1985. First published by John Murray, London, 1883). The best and most perceptive Victorian traveller's tale of Malaysia when it was a virtual *terra incognita.*

Chapman, F. Spencer. *The Jungle is Neutral* (London: Triad/Panther Books, reprint 1983. First published by Chatto and Windus Ltd., 1949). The author's true and gripping tale of three-and-a-half years of guerilla life in Malaysia's jungles during the Japanese Occupation.

Harrison, Tom. *World Within — A Borneo Story* (Singapore: Oxford University Press, reprint 1986. Originally published by The Cresset Press, 1959). A fascinating account of life with the Kelabit people of Borneo during the Second World War.

St John, Spenser. *Life in the Forests of the Far East* (Kuala Lumpur: Oxford University Press, 1974, in two volumes and in one volume in Singapore 1986. First published in two volumes by Smith, Elder and Co., London, 1862). A 19th-century account of travels in the Borneo rain forests.

Art and Culture

Chia, Felix. *The Babas* (Singapore: Times Books International, 1980). A *Baba*'s reminiscences of an intriguing cultural minority.

Lim Jee Yuan. *The Malay House* (Penang: Institut Masyarakat, 1987). An in-depth survey of Malaysia's indigenous shelters with photos, illustrations and an interesting text on the demise of traditional architecture.

Sheppard, Mubin. *Malay Courtesy: A Narrative Account of Malay Manners and Customs in Everyday Use* (Singapore: Eastern Universities Press, 1959). Good background on traditional Malay customs, many of which still apply.

Sheppard, Mubin. *Taman Indera: Malay Decorative Arts and Pastimes* (Kuala Lumpur: Oxford University Press, 1972; reissued as *A Royal Pleasure Ground: Malay Decorative Arts and Pastimes* by Oxford University Press, Singapore, 1986). An in-depth account by the nation's leading authority.

Winstedt, Richard O. *The Malay Magician* (Kuala Lumpur: Oxford University Press, reprint 1985. First published by Constable, London, 1925; revised edition by Routledge and Kegan Paul, London, 1951). A historical survey of Malay magic by an ex-colonial servant.

Flora and Fauna

Glenister, A.G. *The Birds of the Malay Peninsula, Singapore and Penang* (Kuala Lumpur: Oxford University Press, 1971, reprint 1984). An old but excellent study of the region's diverse birdlife.

Shuttleworth, Charles. *Malaysia's Green and Timeless World* (Kuala Lumpur: Heinemann Educational Books Asia, 1981). A probing look at the nation's great green heartland and its diverse fauna and flora.

Tweedie, M.W.F. and Harrison, J.L. *Malayan Animal Life* (Kuala Lumpur: Longman Malaysia, 1981). The most informative and best-illustrated book on the incredible variety of animal life on the peninsula.

Whitmore, T.L. *Palms of Malaya* (Singapore: Oxford University Press, 1985). Hardbound, well-illustrated and informative text on a little-known study.

Miscellaneous

Fauconnier, Henri. *The Soul of Malaya* (English translation first published by Elkin, Mathew and Marrot, London, 1931; reissued by Oxford University

Press, Kuala Lumpur, 1965 and Oxford University Press, Singapore, 1985). A most sensitive, evocative portrayal of Malays and their country, written by an ex-rubber planter.

Lat. *Kampung Boy, Town Boy, Best of Lat, It's a Lat Lat Lat Lat World* and others (Singapore: Straits Times Publishing). Malaysia's best-known cartoonist gives his hilarious view of life and politics. These books are constantly in print and new editions arrive yearly.

Lloyd, R. Ian and Moore, Wendy. *To Know Malaysia* (Singapore: R. Ian Lloyd Productions, 1987). The best large format photographic and text book available on Malaysia.

Lloyd, R. Ian and Moore, Wendy. *Malacca* (Singapore: Times Travel Library, Times Editions, 1986). In-depth Malacca in words and pictures.

Maugham, W. Somerset. *Collected Short Stories* (vol. 4) (Pan Books, 1976). A brilliant collection of short stories on colonial intrigues and antics in British Malaya.

Mahathir bin Mohamad. *The Malay Dilemma* (Kuala Lumpur: Federal Publications, 1970). Controversial but interesting views on Malaysia's racial problems by the current Prime Minister.

Theroux, Paul. *The Consul's File* (Penguin, 1977). Amusing short stories of small-town colonial life in Malaysia.

Index of Places